Critical Muslim 51

Desire

Critical Muslim is published quarterly by C. Hurst & Co. (Publishers) Ltd. on behalf of and in conjunction with Critical Muslim Ltd. and the Muslim Institute, London.

All editorial correspondence to Muslim Institute, Canopi, 7-14 Great Dover Street, London, SE1 4YR
E-mail: editorial@criticalmuslim.com

The editors do not necessarily agree with the opinions expressed by the contributors. We reserve the right to make such editorial changes as may be necessary to make submissions to *Critical Muslim* suitable for publication.

C. Hurst & Co (Publishers) Ltd., New Wing, Somerset House, Strand, London, WC2R 1LA

ISBN:9781911723844 ISSN: 2048-8475

To subscribe or place an order by credit/debit card or cheque (pounds sterling only) please contact Kathleen May at the Hurst address above or e-mail kathleen@hurstpub.co.uk

A one-year subscription, inclusive of postage (four issues), costs £60 (UK), £90 (Europe) and £100 (rest of the world), this includes full access to the *Critical Muslim* series and archive online. Digital only subscription is £3.30 per month.

Critical Muslim

Subscribe to Critical Muslim

Now in its thirteenth year in print, *Critical Muslim* is also available online. Users can access the site for just £3.30 per month – or for those with a print subscription it is included as part of the package. In return, you'll get access to everything in the series (including our entire archive), and a clean, accessible reading experience for desktop computers and handheld devices — entirely free of advertising.

Full subscription

The print edition of *Critical Muslim* is published quarterly in January, April, July and October. As a subscriber to the print edition, you'll receive new issues directly to your door, as well as full access to our digital archive.

United Kingdom £60/year
Europe £90/year
Rest of the World £100/year

Digital Only

Immediate online access to *Critical Muslim*

Browse the full *Critical Muslim* archive

Cancel any time

£3.30 per month

www.criticalmuslim.io

CM51

SUMMER 2024

CONTENTS

DESIRE

Photo: Rooful Ali

DESIRE

INTRODUCTION:
ORBITS OF DESIRE

Ziauddin Sardar

Let's begin with the great man himself. The Grand Sheikh. The illustrious portrayer of desires. The anthology of celebrated poems by Muhyiddin Ibn Arabi (1165–1240), *Tarjuman al-ashwaq*, is often translated as 'The Interpreter of Desire'. But anyone who, like me, speaks Urdu and has a bit of Arabic, knows that *tarjuma* simply means translation. So, Michael Sells's recent rendering as *The Translator of Desire* is closer to the original. *Shawq* is desire but of a particular kind. It is a bit like the classic Greek *eros*, the primary force of creative life, art, and thought. As Sells points out, 'in relationship to finite human subject, *shawq* is infinite; and the poet-lover within the poems is presented at once as the subject, victim, champion, and voice of *shawq*'. In much of Arabic – and one might add Urdu and Persian – poetry, the lovers never make it; and even when they do their pining increases rather than decreases!

The poems in *Translator*, ibn Arabi tells us in the preface to the book, is inspired by a young woman called Nizam, daughter of a Persian scholar. Not surprising. Great artists have muses; poets have an attractive woman or two, whom they desire, from a distant and sometimes close-up. During ibn Arabi's time, it was not unusual for young man like him to hang around the Sacred Mosque in Mecca, looking for potential what we may call in contemporary parlour – 'dates'. Once a desirable subject was spotted, she would be pursued.

The most well-known accounts of such unholy behaviour in the Sacred Mosque comes from Umar ibn Abi Rabiah (d. 712), whose ghazals are less interested in loss and sorrow and more focussed on conquests – many and frequent!

> I spotted her at night walking with her women
> between the shrine and the (Kabba's Black) stone

'Well then', she said to a companion, 'for Umar's sake
let us spoil this circumambulation
Go after him so he may spot us, then,
sweet sister, give him a coy wink'.
'But I already did', she said, 'and he turned away'.
Whereupon she came rushing after me.

It is perfectly possible that ibn Arabi met, during his younger days, Nizam
– the 'Persian Girl'

who kills with a glance
        then revives with a word
tempering fierce beauty
        with compassion.

in such circumstances. He got to know her well and fell in love with her.
She probably rejected him, as according to his own account, did most
women he seemed to have met. Anyway, he was truly inspired by her and
penned *Translator* as a homage. However, when *The Translator of Desire* was
published it caused an outrage. The ulama – religious scholars –were
scandalised. It was mercilessly attacked by the shariah-complaint brigade.

Yet, there was no lack of such works in Mecca and the Arab world during
ibn Arabi's time. The pre-Islamic romantic verse, the Udhri love poems,
was in abundance. The most famous poem from this tradition was penned
by the seventh century poet Qays ibn al-Mulawwah: the tragic story of
'Laila and Majnun'. The poet himself – Qays – falls in love with Layla binti
Mahdi (d. 688), his childhood friend. But Layla's parents object to their
marriage. She is hidden from Qays; and then forced to marry someone
else. Unable to console himself, Qays retreats to the desert and wonders
naked. His tribe give him the epithet of *majnun* – crazy, possessed by love.
Qays dies in despair, followed soon by Layla. In such stories – including the
Persian *Khosrow and Shrin* (in Urdu version, *Shirin Farhad*), the Panjabi *Heera
Ranjha* and *Sohni Mahiwal* by the great Waris Shah (1722-1798), and the
more recent *Ali and Nino* by 'Kurban Said', explored so brilliantly by Boyd
Tonkin in this issue of *Critical Muslim* – 'desire endures, but union does
not'. The Udhri tradition served as a background for the emergence of the

ghazal, the unsurpassed poetry of desire. The ghazal tradition was well established by the time *Translator* was published. Later, it would be embraced by Urdu, Panjabi, Persian, Turkish, Hausa, and Fulani languages.

There was also a great deal in the popular culture of the time to fume about. A few centuries before the arrival of *Translator*, Abu al-Faraj al-Isfahani (897–967) published *The Book of Songs*. Al-Isfahani was a writer, historian, poet, and a pioneer musicologist. He was also, in contrast to the pious ibn Arabi, a *debouche par excellence*. He observed no social etiquette and is described by his contemporaries as unclean and gluttonous. *The Book of Songs* is full of stories, anecdotes, songs, ghazals, biographies, and musical numbers about all variety of sexual desires – including some which should be left to the imagination of the individuals who have them! Much of it is basically abuse and attack of one poet to another. A rather mild sample anecdote: 'in her advanced age, the songstress was asked about her sexual prowess. She said: "the sexual desire is there but the tool is exhausted and it not unsalable anymore"'. It only gets worse from here with poems devoted to large penises and how vaginas are like pomegranates, as well as homosexual encounters and practices. Yet, it was widely read and quoted in Mecca as well as in other metropolitan cities of the Arab world. Indeed, tunes from *The Book of Songs* were played and sung in Mecca, both by resident and visiting musicians and singers. The ulama, it seemed, were not outraged.

So why the uproar about *Translator*? Largely because by now ibn Arabi was regarded as a Sufi sage with a growing reputation. How can a man, who describes himself as the 'seal of saints', known far and wide, write such erotic verse? Is he the same person who wrote such masterpieces of spirituality and mysticism as the thirty-seven volumes of *Meccan Illuminations*? Why is he hiding the true nature of the poems in some metaphoric shroud? Some even suggested he was giving a nod of approval to 'fornication'. Soon, the great and the good – scholars, jurists, writers, poets – gathered to decide on the matter. Ibn Arabi was brought before them to present his defence. It must have been quite a meeting. But we know little about it except that – somehow – ibn Arabi convinced the gathering that *The Translator of Desire* was an expression of Sufi love for God

Bollocks. There is little that can truly be described as allegorical in *Translator*. There is nothing allegorical about the girl with henna hand,

honey'd tongue, who is 'dissolved in desire'; of the poem 'In the Ruins of
My Body'; or the lady 'with the flashing smile', who needs to be covered
and hidden, of 'Your wish'; or the women of beauty 'far beyond compare',
who the poet rides at moonlit nights, and 'whispers love' to! These are
unashamedly love poems, pure and pleasurable. And I love them.
'Bewildered' is a typical poem from the collection, which reads, in Sells's
translation:

> I wish I knew if they knew
>> Whose heart they've taken
> Or my heart knew which
>> High-ridge track they follow
> Do you see them safe
>> Or perishing
> The lords of love are in love
>> ensnared, bewildered

After the mock trial, Ibn Arabi sets about to justify the allegorical nature
of the poems. The new preface to the book, transports Nizam, the 'Persian
Girl', to Anatolia, and transforms her into a mystical critic. While reciting
his poems near the Haram (Sacred Mosque), the celebrated sage tells us,
'a hand softer than undyed silk' touched his shoulder. It was yet another
maiden, who proceeds to 'fiercely criticises each of the four verses,
refuting each part of them'; and rebukes the Sheikh al-Akbar for penning
verses beneath his stature. Ibn Arabi asks her name and she answers Qurrat
al-Ayn, a nickname meaning 'comfort for the eye'. In his commentary on
Translator, ibn Arabi goes to some length to argue that the poems are not
erotic but allegorical and use ordinary words to convey mystical ideas. So,
bosoms and killer glances, shining teeth and fragrant breath, scents of
flowers and the dance of peacocks, now acquire higher spiritual value.
Even though much of it is justified with illusions to the Qur'an, it is hardly
convincing. When 'she longs for her one and only', I am afraid, she longs
for her man and not for union with God. In one way, by turning lovely love
poems into some entangled mystical chatter, ibn Arabi undermines his very
own human desire; and thus, one could argue, his humanity.

Sometimes it is much better to see things as they are. Desire is not one dimensional. It is perfectly natural for one person to desire erotic love as well as love of God. As an ordinary mortal ibn Arabi simultaneously desired amorous love and dissolution in the love of God. Or perhaps, given the opaque nature of his thought, he was telling us that we need the first to get to the second. Ibn Arabi, as Jeremy Henzell-Thomas notes in his contribution to this issue, asked his Lord to nourish him not with love, but with 'the desire for love'.

'Desire has no boundaries', notes Henzell-Thomas. And that's where the problem arises. The great al-Ghazali (1058–1111), whole-time theologian and part-time philosopher, sought to confine desire within reasonable limits. In his principal work, *Ihya ulum al-din - The Revival of Religious Sciences* – al-Gazali argues that two main desires lead us towards destruction: the desire for food and the desire for sex. 'The ego is constantly fed with both', writes Luke Wilkinson, 'but never fully satisfied. It is like a swelling tapeworm within us that, if not fed, feels like it will consume our insides'. The end result is an 'imbalance in ever-widening levels of space, from the locus of character all the way to the whole of society'. To restrain these desires, and maintain a balanced life, al-Ghazali 'recommends a simple practice: listen to the ego, feel what it desires, and then set an intention to enact with our bodies the opposite of what the ego seeks'.

Allama Mohammad Iqbal (1877–1938), undoubtedly the greatest poet-philosopher of the twentieth century, would have doubts about al-Ghazali's prescription. Not all ego, he argued, can or should be suppressed. Even though many consider him to be a Sufi, he didn't think much of Sufism, and even less of ibn Arabi. He would have agreed with Henzell-Thomas that if you cease all desire for the world, 'then you have not ceased all desire'; rather, replaced a single all-consuming desire with all others, 'one species of desire by another'. He found the Sufis to be self-contented. An expert on Persian Sufism, Iqbal declared that Sufism was not totally useless. It serves as 'opiates, narcotics' that a community needs to recover from trauma, or after a great period of activity. He was not in favour of traditionalists like al-Ghazali either, and rejected their outdated theology. As Peter Mathews Wright notes in his contribution to this issue, Iqbal challenged 'inherited metaphysical assumptions about the nature of the self'. Wright quotes Iqbal:

Nor can the concepts of theological systems, draped in the terminology of a practically dead metaphysics, be of any help to those who happen to possess a different intellectual background. The task before the modern Muslim is, therefore, immense. He has to rethink the whole system of Islam without completely breaking with the past...The only course open to us is to approach modern knowledge with a respectful but independent attitude and to appreciate the teachings of Islam in the light of that knowledge, even though we may be led to differ from those who have gone before us.

'Doctors of Divinity' with their traditional theology, Iqbal declared, can do nothing more than make 'flowery' pronouncements. One could argue that it was conventional theology of dead metaphysics, however perverted, that produced the likes of ISIS. As Anonymous tells us in their article on the ISIS Prisons Museums, 'the simplest of desires can lead to the most terrible of fates'. That's what happened to Zahida al-Ahmad, a hospital cleaner in Raqqa, Syria, who went out for a smoke after finishing her night shift. She was abducted by ISIS thugs, beaten and tortured, for not being Islamic enough. 'Her greatest desire had been to have a child. Well, God had finally answered her prayer – and ISIS had murdered the answer'. ISIS, of course, had the murderous desire to force everyone to adopt their myopic version of Islam. So, every other Muslim was fair game for rape, torture, and execution, including the Sufis who were declared 'grave-worshippers'. The ISIS type myopic desire is now exhibited in the rise of the far right in US and Europe. The goal is the same: to assimilate all difference, to eradicate the Other.

There is one mystic that Iqbal admired: Jalal al-Din Rumi (1207-1273). Mainly because Rumi declared: 'reason is the light and the guide, but not the goal'. Iqbal concurred. Pure intuition without reason was not of much use in building a civilisation. The goal, Iqbal's ultimate desire, was to free the ummah from the shackles of the West, which he thought was literally destroying the world:

> The West's tyrannies have laid all the world a desolate waste
> O Haram's architect rise to retrieve the world from this waste

Iqbal argued that the Western ideals of untruth – and we may add post-truth – are everywhere. They reappear freshly disguised in every age, in fresher and newer forms. Now in the form of imperialism, capitalism, and nationalism. Now as power and territory. Now as glamour and fame. Now in the shape of modernity. We could bring Iqbal's list of isms up to date with the additions of postmodernism and populism. Indeed, untruth now feeds an insatiable smorgasbord of unsavoury desires: from naked nationalism, racism, and xenophobia to AI generated fake news and deep fake, to landscapes saturated with neon lit advertisements, most of which are lies, and all of which are designed to induce one or other type of desire. Indeed, in the age of surveillance capitalism, desire is the main commodity and principal product of consumption. One illustration of this is the plethora of third grade novels available in airports, online, and what's left of bookshops. In an age when everyone thinks they can write and everyone is his or her own publisher, there is no shortage of self-published tomes. There is now a huge production line of self-published Islamophobic popular fiction. But here is the burb for one simply called *Desires*, which for some reason, Amazon's algorithms chose to send my way:

> *Desires*—a place where fantasies are made flesh and dreams become real. From BDSM to being a dog, Desires can provide it with bells on, if that's your kink. Stacie Clifford's only desire is to regain her sexual confidence after her recent escape from an abusive marriage. She joins Desires looking for re-education in the joys of her body. There is only one condition; her contract states emotional attraction between tutor and student is forbidden. Stacie is fine with that; her heart is so battered she has no desire to give it to anyone else. Then she meets her instructor, Dan. Instantly attracted, at first Stacie thinks it will help to make her sexually comfortable with him. But when she realises she is falling in love, she can't tear herself away, contract or no. Stacie knows that, no matter how kind and caring Dan appears, he's just doing his job. Can Stacie overcome her own Desires and walk away?

No way! She hasn't read al-Ghazali!

Even if you ignore all this and can dodge adverts hitting your eyesight from every corner, and turn off social media, you cannot escape desires altogether – for they lurk in other not so obvious spaces. In his journey to Europe from his Australian homeland, Liam Mayo experiences desire in multiple forms: as yearning for the family he is leaving behind and his craving to shrink the space between them, lack of time in trying to catch his flight, power and repression when he unquestionably follows the commands of the ground and flight crew, and in *heterotopia* - all 'other spaces' that deviate from the societal norm. Fortunately, Mayo manages to control his desires; and hence his autonomy. But there are circumstances in which one desire is controlled by another which one does not wish to have, a situation that can lead to loss of autonomy. Much like Stacie's undesirable love for Dan! Or, the simultaneous desire to lose weight and eat rich, sugar saturated cakes. Or a drug addict who wants to kick his habit but ardently desires another fix. Desires clash; the stronger one wins. Not all desires undermine autonomy, though. I love a good *biryani*; and it has never affected my autonomy.

There are other things in life than *biryani* and sex. As Mayo suggests, 'we can get the same satisfaction that we get from sex from any number of activities, like talking, writing, or painting'. There is 'a short circuit between the ontological (how we exist in the world) and epistemology (how we know the world), meaning that sexuality and knowledge are symbiotic, interconnected in complex ways'. Thus, 'desire (as a component of sexuality) is not just a biological or personal feeling, but something that interacts with our understanding of existence (ontology) and our acquisition of knowledge (epistemology). It also suggests that our desires can influence, and be influenced by, our understanding of the world and ourselves'.

Indeed, the world around us is enveloped in epistemologies of desire. Virtually all disciplines as they exist today promote one or other kind of perpetual desire. Economics is based on the desire for everlasting growth, even though it will take us the resources of several planets to continue in our present trajectory. The economy itself is detached from all moral and ethical concerns and devours all aspects of society. There is now a 'market of desire' in which 'the sexual and emotional relationships we build today', writes Tamara Tenenbaum in *The End of Love*, 'responds to the logic of the market, of decentralisation and disorganisation'. Thus our 'erotic encounters' become 'trade transaction'. Management promotes corporate desire for more and more profit even at the expense of the planet itself. Science, seen by many as omnipotent, encourages the desire of some scientists to acquire God-like power. Technology innovates unendingly whether we actually need the new gadgets or not; and seeks freedom from reality based on an unsatiable desire for escaping our own nature, for individual immortality, and for technological omniscience. Medicine treats old age as a disease, rather than a natural process of biological change, to be cured. Death is seen by some not as a natural conclusion of life but something to be conquered. You can clone your pet so you have the same (genetic?) pet for the entire span of your life. Soon humans will be cloned too! But it is not good enough to be human anymore (not even in cloned form!); we must become transhumanist, fuse our biology with technology to enhance physical abilities, longevity and cognition. Higher education, where knowledge is for sale, tends to inculcate desire. Our dominant paradigms of knowing, our social and virtual ways of being, our basic ways of doing anything, however trivial, are enslaved to unethical desires. This is the gift of modernity and postmodernism, the bedrock of conceptual epistemological and ontological categories that have shaped our world.

This makes desire complex. As Scott Jordan suggests, in contemporary times, 'it is perhaps the first brush we humans experience with the truly complex. Desire breaks the mould, taking us beyond our more infantile feelings of hunger, pain, fear, comfort, or joy. Desire is complex as it is not only subject to change but also competing against other desires, both to the self and in relation to the desires of others'. We are confronted with a veritable tsunami, endless temptations, of enumerable desires, the likes of which we have never faced in history, and which cannot be resolved with binaries. They require simultaneous efforts against vengeful capitalism and its thirst for consuming everything on the planet, replacing zombie disciplines based on lethal epistemology with more appropriate and sustainable ones, and creating a more humane and equal societies. And, then, Jordan points out: 'of course there is the colonising nature of desire'.

This colonising desire is best expressed by Hank MacLean, the father of the protagonist, Lucy, in the Amazon Prime series *Fallout*. Hank justifies nuclear holocaust and genocide because, he desires, he says, to 'make the world us. Only ours to shape'. The mechanism through which this goal is obtained is quite simple. We learn this from a native American female lawyer in the Paramount series *Yellowstone*. She tells Chief Thomas Rainwater, whose community much like Indians before him, faces decimation:

> They make their rules to be broken. The United States has broken every rule it has ever made — from its first treaty with France to every treaty with us to their last treaty with Iran. The only hold others to their rules. They make war

when they want, where they want, they take what they want. Then they make rules to keep you from taking it back. They make rules for slaves and they make rules for masters.

We can see echoes of this in the current behaviour of the US and Europe, particularly in regard to Palestine. Iqbal too saw this in his time. During his adolescence, he learned about the 1957 Mutiny and the absurd trial of Bahadur Shah Zafar, the last Mughal Emperor, his forced exile to Burma and death in destitution. Zafar was himself an admired and accomplished poet. Iqbal was most assuredly aware of his most famous poem:

> My heart is not happy in these ruined land
> I find no pleasure in this transient world
> .....
> I had requested for a long life but received only four days
> Two passed by desire and two in waiting.
> The days of life are over, it's the night of death
> Now I can sleep without any stress forever in my tomb
> How unfortunate you are Zafar! You could not have
> For burial, a plot of two yards in your beloved land.

This must have stirred his soul, just as it does mine. No doubt, Iqbal witnessed the Jallianwala Bagh massacre of April 1919, where British troops killed 1,500 people who were protesting against the arrest of pro-independence activists. He saw modernity as ravenous, mutating like a virus, changing and adjusting itself so it can continue to conquer and devour other cultures. He witnessed the alienation of technological culture with nature, which he saw as a source of serious reflection and a springboard for full realisation of our human potential. (In some of his poems, mountains tell the story of time, the sun is a metaphor for the light of truth and sustainability, and the moon feels the pain and sorrow of loneliness). He was aware that the major achievement of western civilisation was presenting never-satisfied and never-ending desire as normal and hence universal. The world made in the image of the West was not for him for it is based on insatiable desire to colonise and assimilate. In his famous poem, 'Pathos of Love', the separation of lover is not just romantic love, but the West's alienation with nature, estrangement with Others, and distance from God:

'O Pathos of love! You are a glossy pearl
Beware: you should not appear among strangers

The theatre of your display is concealed under the veil
The modern audience's eye accepts only the visible display

Now breeze has arrived in the Existences' Garden
O Pathos of love! Now there is no pleasure in display
....
This is not the garden whose spring you maybe
This is not the audience worthy of your appearance

Veracity, sincerity and purity have disappeared
That goblet is broken, and the cup bearer has disappeared

Within this desolate panorama, the Muslim themselves are in a state of slumber:

I am the spectator of the spectacle of disappointments
I am the associate of those sleeping in solitude's corner.

'Disappointments' because Muslims solicit rather than create or innovate. Whereas love – *ishq* – fortifies the ego, asking deteriorates it. The son of a rich man who inherits the wealth of his father is an asker. So are all those who rely on the thoughts of others, or worse, think the thoughts of others. Muslims excel at imitation, what Rene Girard, French American literary critic and philosopher of social science, calls 'mimetic desires', the major tool of contemporary enslavement. 'Mimetic desire', writes Girard, 'makes us believe we are always on the verge of becoming self-sufficient through our own transformation into someone else. Our would-be transformation into a god, as Shakespeare says, turns us into an ass'.

This is a result, says Iqbal, of the loss of 'Self'. By losing their Self, Muslims have not only lost their ability to produce new thought but also their ethical and moral bearing. Enough of obscurantist theology, dopy mysticism, and imitations – of our own imagined past or of the present and future of the West. It's time to walk on fire:

For a long time you have turned about on a bed of silk
Now accustom yourself to rough cotton

For generations you have danced on tulips
And bathed your cheeks in dew, like the rose
Now throw yourself on the burning sand.

The term that Iqbal uses for Self, which will lead to the awaking of the ummah, is *khudi*. It is usually translated as 'ego' or Self, and it is also used as a technical term for *tasawwuf* — mysticism. But Iqbal uses *khudi* as an amalgam of selfhood, individuality, and personality. Khudi is bound by *ishq*, usually translated as love but used by Iqbal as desire for (self)control. When *khudi* and *ishq* come together, spirituality fuses with ethics, intellect with love, and the lover realises that the struggle between good and evil is constant. Both *khudi* and *ishq* cannot be acquired by belief alone, which by itself is not enough. Nor can they be acquired by pursuing good with unethical means. Or by intellect or institution alone. All must be combined: belief, intellect, and intuition together must be used in the pursuit of ethical goals with ethical means.

The ideal Muslim is one who embodies this wholistic Self, which is like steel. But Iqbal's ideal Muslim is not to be confused with Nietzsche's 'superman' as some have suggested. Rather, the *momin*, one who submits to God, is a person who personifies truth and integrity:

O Awaited truth! Take a human form soon.
I am impatient to welcome you
To offer a thousand prostrations to you.

Iqbal, much like ibn Arabi, wrote masterpiece after masterpiece. But most of his philosophy can be found in two volumes: *Asrar-i-Khudi*, a Persian philosophical epic, translated as *The Secrets of the Self*, and the follow-up volume, *Rumaz-i-Bakhudi*, rendered as *The Mysteries of Selflessness*. The first deals with the individual in society. Iqbal argues, contrary to Sufi thought, that the religious and moral desires of humans is not self-negation — losing oneself in God — but self-affirmation. We all are individuals, want to be individuals, and recognised as individuals. We desire to become more and more individual, more and more unique. Indeed, this is an innate desire. God Himself is the ultimate individual. We enhance our individuality by achieving complete self-affirmation; and by submitting to the Supreme Individual.

If you read *The Secrets of the Self* on its own you may be led to believe that Iqbal is advocating unbridled egoism and 'self-actualisation', reminiscent of the hippies and the zeitgeist of the 1960s. Or he is perhaps advocating a cult of oneself or some libertarian cause. That would be a mistake! To get the complete picture, you must read it together with *The Mysteries of Selflessness*. There we learn that Iqbal is not really interested in individualism for its own sake, or for the sake of self-realisation. He is simply acknowledging that we desire to define who we are. He is much more concerned with the evolution of a community. The individual must be selfless and committed to community, understand its traditions, and be concerned about its future. The community, in turn, must allow the individual to be a self-affirmative individual. As the distinguished British scholar, A J Arberry notes in his translation of *Rumaz-i-Bakhudi*,

> it is only as a member of this community that the individual, by the twin principles of conflict and concord, is able to express himself fully and ideally; it is also as an association of self-affirming individuals that the community can come into being and perfect itself. Iqbal thus escaped from libertarianism by limiting individual's freedom, making him a member of a community, and from totalitarianism by limiting the community's authority, making it a challenge and not an insurmountable obstacle to the individual's self-realisation.

The true individual, Iqbal asserts, cannot be lost to the world. Rather, it is the world that should be lost in the individual: 'in his will that which God wills become lost'. Or, as R A Nicolson, another British scholar, notes in his translation of *Asrar-i-Khudi*, 'the ego attains freedom by the removal of all obstructions in its way. It is partly free, partly determined, and reaches fuller freedom by approaching the individual who is most free – God. In other words, life is an endeavour for freedom'.

We do not attain freedom from desire. Indeed, we cannot liberate ourselves from desire as life itself is an outcome of competing desires. To fulfil our desires, we need to start thinking our own thoughts, move ourselves into action, to fortify our Self, and wrap our desires with love. Iqbal is emphatic: all ideologies that claim to be exclusive, the only solution and only answer, the only way of knowing and doing, lead to decay and death. All isms – nationalism, imperialism, sectarianism, authoritarianism,

Islamism, and even mysticism – distract us from building humane and sustainable communities, and 'rob us of paradise'.

What I love most about Iqbal is his appreciation of the complex nature of desires, his emphasis on individual agency and integrative action, and his insistence that we must 'reconstruct' much of what we have taken as conventional, normal religious thought.

There is a space between tradition and modernity, fanatism and relativism, between total denial of the world and its unabashed embrace, where ideal desires flourish and where humane societies evolve. It is not where contemporary modernity is to be found for which Iqbal did little respect. As he tells us himself:

I have no need of the ear of today.
I am the voice of the poet of tomorrow.

He taught us that the ultimate human desire is for Life – glorious, exuberant, compassionate, innovative, and joyful, based on love and mutual respect, passion for nature, and trust in each other. It is through love of and obedience to God that a person 'of no worth is made worthy'.

This is how we gain freedom.

What else is there to desire?

A STICK WITH TWO ENDS

Jeremy Henzell-Thomas

Desire is one of those human propensities which is clearly a long stick with two ends, a continuum that can encompass both vice and virtue, with various intermediate stages. This is evident from its varied negative, neutral, and positive connotations ranging from base craving through hankering, urge, ambition, wish, passion, and yearning to lofty aspiration and the heart's desire.

Within religion, desire is often associated with a disposition towards sin or separation from God. In Roman Catholic theology, for example, the seven cardinal or deadly sins, first enumerated by Pope Gregory I in the sixth century and elaborated by St Thomas Aquinas in the thirteenth century, include greed or covetousness, lust or inordinate sexual desire, and gluttony. According to Al-Ghazali, 'desires make slaves out of kings.' In Book XXIII of his *Ihya 'ulum al-din* (*Revival of the Religious Sciences*) – the *Kitab Kasr al-shahwatayn,* 'On Breaking the Two Desires' – he stigmatises lust and gluttony as the 'greatest of mortal vices', and in condemning 'satiety' he affirms the need to subjugate the greed of the belly and control sexual desire through the restoration of a state of equilibrium. He equated this with the centrality of the Middle Way in Islamic ethics, the ideal of the golden mean between excess and defect, although this necessarily entails the disciplining of the *nafs al-ammara*, the commanding or compulsive self, also known as the carnal or animal self, entirely governed by its desires, passions, and instincts. The Second Noble Truth of Buddhism identifies the cause of *dukkha* (suffering) as attachment to deep-rooted craving for sense pleasures (*kama-tanha*), including greed and sensual desire as well as desire for material gain and achievement. It is this deep-rooted craving that results in our continued existence in the cycle of birth, death, and re-birth (*samsara*). Buddhists and Taoists alike often speak of the sage as one who has no desires, although such a state can only come about through reflection and enlightenment, never through belief, whether inherited or acquired. In Vedanta, the *jivanmukta*, or liberated human being, is also totally free of all desires.

In writing about 'What the Bible says about Desire', John Ritenbaugh acknowledges the destructiveness of 'lusts', those 'cravings for satisfaction of the physical appetites', as well as those less obviously 'animalistic and base' worldly desires such as 'academic acclaim' and 'social status', but he emphasises that scripture speaks of both the good and evil sense of desire, attesting to the exhortation of St Paul in his First Epistle to the Corinthians to 'earnestly desire the greater gifts' and the affirmation of David in Psalm 51 that God Himself desires 'truth in the inward parts of men' (that is, a sincere heart). Rabbi Avi Weinstein, the Director of Hillel's Joseph Meyerhoff Center for Jewish Learning, refers to the statement by the Sephardic Jewish philosopher Maimonides that if a person resolves to separate himself to the extreme from desire to the extent of denying himself every material comfort and pleasure, resorting austerely to sackcloth and ashes, 'this too is a bad way to be' and 'it is forbidden to walk on this path.' The Noble Eightfold Path of Buddhism, also known as the Middle Path, likewise avoids the two extremes, either the search for happiness through the pleasures of the senses or the search for salvation through self-mortification, which was a common ascetic practice during the time of the Buddha. And while the absence of desire is often cited as a principle of Taoism, it can legitimately be asked if it is possible not to desire, since trying to get rid of desire entails desiring not to desire, and any project to suppress desire would therefore be contrary to the spirit of the Tao and its guiding principle of *wu-wei* which is to flow naturally like water with experiences and feelings as they come and go. As David Webster writes in discussing the 'paradox of desire' in *The Philosophy of Desire in the Buddhist Pali Canon*, 'if I desire to cease desiring then I have not ceased all desire after all; I have merely replaced one species of desiring by another.'

Now, at this point, I don't want to wrap up or prematurely resolve the paradox of desire by holding tenaciously to the middle point of the stick, no matter how logically satisfying the Aristotelian golden mean may appear to be. I always recall my beloved late grandmother, born in 1896 towards the end of the Victorian era, and very much aware of the ardent way in which I often pursued my interests and activities, repeatedly intoning the maxim, 'moderation in all things' which she believed to be the essence of

'Englishness' and to which, she advised, I needed to pay heed. Astronomy had been one of my youthful passions, and I recalled how, on a visit to the Planetarium in London, I was absolutely transfixed in wonder at the projection of the cosmos onto the dome overhead. I remember giving my seventy-year-old grandmother a stiff neck when one evening I insisted that she look up at the night sky with me while I meticulously identified all the constellations in view, even pointing to the position of double stars and nebulae which were barely visible. There was little of 'moderation' in my desire to reach into the cosmos, and I spent a good part of my time as a boy of twelve mapping the night sky with a telescope I had borrowed from the public library.

The words of Deepak Chopra in *The Way of the Wizard* come to mind: 'honour each and every desire you have. Cherish those desires in your heart.' The seventeenth century English metaphysical poet George Herbert went so far as to say that 'he begins to die that quits his desires.' And as the Victorian novelist and poet, Mary Ann Evans (known by her pen name George Eliot) wrote: 'it seems to me we can never give up longing and wishing while we are thoroughly alive. There are certain things we feel to be beautiful and good, and we must hunger after them.' Another celebrated female novelist, Virginia Woolf, who rated Eliot's psychologically insightful novel *Middlemarch* as 'one of the few English novels written for grown-up people', confessed to having 'a deeply hidden and inarticulate desire for something beyond the daily life.'

Ana Waller quotes this pertinent extract from the writings of the philosopher Bertrand Russell: 'all human activity is prompted by desire. There is a wholly fallacious theory advanced by some earnest moralists to the effect that it is possible to resist desire in the interests of duty and moral principle.' Russell dismisses this as fallacious, not because a sense of duty never influences our acts, but because duty has no hold on us unless we desire to be dutiful. Russell argues that there is a 'whole system of desires' with 'relative strengths' within us, and this mirrors, if you like, the image of the long stick with two ends and intermediate stages with which I opened this essay. Waller also cites Eknath Easwaran, one of the leading twentieth century Indian interpreters of the teachings of the Indian mystic poet Kabir, in explaining how Kabir viewed the various stages of desire, and this is encapsulated in the title of Waller's essay: 'The Four Stages of

Desire: From Everything to One Thing'. While most of us, he explains, have 'numerous desires focused on the superficial aspects of life' such as appearance, material possessions, status, reputation and wealth, some have a lighter burden of desires, enabling them to focus on 'judicial goals' which they successfully achieve. A smaller cohort have even fewer desires and Waller identifies them as 'geniuses who left a significant mark on this world', citing Mother Teresa, Marie Curie, and Albert Einstein as well as 'some great musicians, poets, humanitarians, and political leaders.' Finally, he asserts, a rare few who are typically mystics are born with only one 'profoundly impactful' desire, the 'ultimate search for truth.'

Mevlana Jalaluddin Rumi avers in his *Mathnawi* that 'to follow one's own desires is to flee from God' and that 'this world is a trap, and desire is its bait' and he also advises in his *Divan-I Kebir* that 'if you would get rid of something, get rid of your desires. All the suffering and pain we go through comes from our desires', yet elsewhere in the *Mathnawi* he extols 'the desire in man and woman' instilled in them by God since 'from their union, creation results'. He acknowledges too that 'each of us has been made for some particular work, and the desire for that work has been placed in our hearts. How should hand and foot be set in motion without desire?' What's more, so much of Rumi's sublime poetry is suffused with a single, incandescent, passionate desire and longing for union with the Beloved. 'If you see your desire leading towards heaven,' he says, 'unfold your wings to claim it; but if you see your desire bends to the earth, keep lamenting.' And in affirming that 'love alone is my religion', Ibn Arabi asks his Lord to nourish him not with love, but with 'the desire for love.' Carl Jung asserted in his *Red Book* that the soul could be found in desire itself, but not in the objects of desire. 'If he possessed his desire, and his desire did not possess him, he would lay a hand on his soul, since his desire is the image and expression of his soul.'

In 2000, my last year as Director of Studies at Millfield Prep School in Glastonbury, England, I had a memorable encounter which serves as a fine example of the positive sense of desire as passion or the 'heart's desire'. One day, a man on a bicycle turned up at the school. He was Everett Briggs, an American who was undertaking what he called the 'New Millennium Ride', cycling solo from Seoul to Lisbon through twenty-two countries. His avowed aim was to link up those along the route, as well as everyone who read about the trip in newspapers, magazines, journals, or the net. This was to include at least twenty-five schools during the ride, with the students in those schools in touch with the full course of the expedition. His mission was based on his conviction that 'there is no substitute for direct cross-cultural connections and experiences when it comes to understanding, embracing, and celebrating diversity and individualism while, reducing ethnocentrism. We cannot begin to address the problems and obstacles to peaceful co-existence until we share in the common culture of all humanity.' Having cycled through South Korea, China, Mongolia, Russia, Finland, Estonia, Latvia, Italy, Slovenia, Austria, Slovakia, Poland, Lithuania, Sweden, Norway, Scotland, and Wales, he was approaching the last stage of his remarkable journey which was due to continue through France, Andorra, and Spain to end in Portugal. He said that he had always encouraged those he met and worked with 'to visualise a reality on the far side of reason, to chase their dreams.'

Impressed beyond measure with Everett's passionate vision and mission, and keen to impart its educational merit, I asked him to stay with us and speak to the pupils in the next full school assembly the following morning. He did so, earnestly advising the children to 'follow their heart's desire' and not to believe any teacher who told them that there was something they could not do. He had been a medical doctor, he said, because that was a typical profession on the conventional path to success, like law or engineering, but he confessed that he had always yearned to be a wood sculptor. After the assembly, I arranged for Everett to spend time working in the school's art department with the children to create a beautiful sculpture in wood of a ring of children in a circle holding hands, and to this day it has pride of place outside in the school grounds.

The word 'yearning' with its sense of aching longing and, in Everett's words, 'chasing dreams on the far side of reason', perhaps expresses most strongly the cosmic dimension that I associate with the deepest desires of the heart. The word *desire,* 'to wish, or long for' comes from Old French *desirrer* from Latin *desiderare*. John Ayto points out that the underlying etymology is 'something of a mystery' but may come ultimately from a base related to Latin *sidus,* 'heavenly body, star', perhaps as suggested by the *Online Etymological Dictionary*, *de sidere*, 'from the stars', indicating that the original sense of *desire* may have been to 'await what the stars will bring'. I prefer, however, to see the connection with the 'stars' as the way in which desire is kindled and fuelled by cosmic energy from the Source itself. As Darcy Lyon avers in *The Wisdom of Desire*, 'desire knows no boundary. It is simply the very nature of the universe itself. Desire is the very root of the universe.'

Of relevance here is the 'acorn theory' of James Hillman, the founder of the archetypal psychology movement, his extension of the Jungian psychology tradition. Hillman believed that we are not essentially the product of either genetics, upbringing, or environment, but we are endowed from birth with an individual daemon, genius, character, or calling, an image that is the essence of life and calls it to a destiny, just as the mighty oak's destiny is written in the tiny acorn. In confirmation of this, we have already noted Rumi's contention that 'each of us has been made for some particular work'.

The idea that human 'character' is what is already 'stamped' or 'etched' upon us is indicated by the derivation of the word *character* itself. It comes from Greek *kharakter,* a derivative of the verb *kharassein,* to 'sharpen, engrave, cut', and hence was applied metaphorically to the particular impress or stamp which marked one thing as different from another – its 'character'. The urge or innate desire to grow and fulfil its destiny is imprinted in the acorn, just as our own heart's desire burns within us as a unique manifestation of the cosmic energy from the ultimate Source of life and love. Gary Comer is surely right when he writes in *Soul Whisperer,* 'somewhere in the journey to faith is the heart's desire.'

The apotheosis of yearning was captured by the genius of Richard Wagner in his opera *Tristan and Isolde,* based largely on the twelfth century romance *Tristan and Iseult* by Gottfried von Strassburg. The legend tells us that it was the mission of the Cornish Knight Tristan to escort the Irish princess Iseult from Ireland to marry his uncle, King Mark of Cornwall. On the journey, Tristan and Iseult ingest a love potion, instigating a forbidden love affair between them which Wagner expresses with unparalleled intensity by creating an innovative musical language of searing desire and unending longing. He did so by moving away from traditional tonal harmony with its established cadences, making unprecedented use of chromaticism and tonal ambiguity, as epitomised in the very first chord of the piece, the famous 'Tristan chord', a dissonant chord which resolves not as might be expected to a concord but to another dissonant chord. The aching sense of unconsummated desire this provokes is also expressed in Wagner's use of harmonic suspension exposing the listener to a series of prolonged unfinished cadences which inspire a desire on the part of the listener for musical resolution. Susan Sontag relates how in the early years of performances of the opera (after its first performance in 1865) occasionally someone had to be evacuated from the theatre, having fainted in the course of the performance.

In one of the dreams of my life I saw myself as Tristan ardently setting off into the ocean in a flimsy canoe in search of his beloved Isolde. There was a pilot in the prow of the canoe, but I could not see his face as his back was turned towards me. I had not gone very far when the whole ocean seemed to rise up from the depths in an immeasurably vast and scintillating golden wave which towered above me, but I awoke before I was engulfed by it. I have always interpreted the dream as an imaginal representation of the *hadith qudsi* (extra-Qur'anic Word of God), 'if you come to Me walking, I will come to you running'.

The Beloved is always aware of any sincere desire to come closer to Him/Her. Imagining the Beloved as Isolde and seeing her vastly amplified, overwhelmingly loving response to my ardent seeking of her might be expected of one, like myself, who has immersed himself in the legend of Tristan and Isolde and its dramatisation in the music of Wagner. What is perhaps not widely known, though well attested in historical research, is that the medieval courtly love tradition, which gave birth to the legends of King Arthur and the Knights of the Round Table, and its associated tale of Tristan and Isolde, as well as other tales of illicit or unattainable love like that of Lancelot and Guinevere (the wife of King Arthur, to whom Lancelot was chief Knight and trusted friend), was very likely transmitted to the West through Crusader contact with Islamic mysticism and its adoration of the Divine Beloved. Yearning for union with the Beloved became symbolised in the longing for union with an unattainable earthly beloved such as Isolde or Guinevere. In such a way the paradox of the Divine Beloved as both 'utterly remote in His limitless glory' (Qur'an 59:23) and yet 'closer to you than your jugular vein' (Qur'an 16:26) is conveyed to us through the concrete imagery of romantic legends. The apparent opposites of transcendence and immanence thus resonate in a passionate longing for union.

The imagery of the ocean in relation to love of God does of course pervade much mystical poetry in the Sufi tradition. The drop entering the ocean is a common metaphor for the human soul returning to its Source, as in the poetry of Rumi and the lyric poems / songs of Yunus Emre, the unlettered fourteenth century Turkish shepherd, often called the 'greatest folk poet in Islam' whose songs are still popular today. He invites the dervish to 'dive into the ocean', for 'a spark of Love's fire can make the seas boil'. 'Beloved', he sings, 'the fire of Your love set the ocean of my heart aflame.' He compares 'Reality' to an ocean and the 'Law' to a ship, adding that 'many have never left the ship, never jumped into the sea…they stopped at rituals, they never knew or entered the Inside.'

In his book *The Marriage of Heaven and Hell,* composed between 1790 and 1793, the visionary poet and artist William Blake stated, 'those who restrain desire do so because theirs is weak enough to be restrained.' He implicates formal religion as one agent of the suppression of joy and desire: 'I went to the Garden of Love,' he writes 'And saw what I never had seen: A Chapel was built in the midst, Where I used to play on the green. And the gates of this Chapel were shut, And "Thou shalt not" writ over the door; So I turn'd to the Garden of Love, That so many sweet flowers bore. And I saw it was filled with graves, And tomb-stones where flowers should be: And Priests in black gowns, were walking their rounds, And binding with briars, my joys and desires.'

More famously, in his 1804 poem *Jerusalem*, set to music by Hubert Parry, majestically orchestrated by Elgar, and sung with patriotic fervour every year at the Last Night of the Proms by the capacity audience, Blake calls for his 'bow of burning gold,' his 'arrows of desire', his 'spears' and his 'chariots of fire' to be brought to him in the realisation of his passion to build Jerusalem in 'England's green and pleasant land'. It is hardly necessary to point out here that the association of the 'arrows of desire' with the building of Jerusalem, the heavenly city, reveals that Blake was not of course a mere hedonist, but one who believed that human desire within the material realm was integral to the divine order. In one sense his conception of desire reflects that of *libido,* a Latin word meaning 'desire, lust' originally derived from the Proto Indo-European root *leubh-,* 'to desire, love', the source of Gothic *liufs*, 'dear', 'beloved', Old English *lufu*, 'love, passion' and many other related words in Indo-European languages (for example, German *liebe*, Russian *ljubov'*). Although the word *libidinous*, 'lustful', from Old French *libidineus*, 'sinful, lusty' entered English usage in the mid-fifteenth century, the word 'libido' was first borrowed by Freud to denote in psychoanalytic theory the energy of the sexual drive, unchecked by any kind of authority, moral or otherwise. Jung, however, rejected Freud's constricting reduction of the libido solely to sexual desire, and preferred to frame 'the essence of libido' in a more expansive sense as a 'manifestation of instinctive psychic energy' or an 'appetite in its natural state' which included not only sexual energy but also 'bodily needs like hunger, thirst, and sleep', as well as 'emotional states or affects.'

And what of God? Does God have desires? We have already quoted a verse from Psalm 51 that God Himself desires 'truth in the inward parts of men' and Rumi also refers to God's desire for the best in man in his verse in the *Mathnawi* admitting that 'although your desire tastes sweet, doesn't the Beloved desire you to be desireless?' According to a *hadith qudsi*, one often related in major Sufi texts from the twelfth century and particularly cherished by Ibn Arabi and Rumi, 'I was a hidden treasure and loved (*ahbabtu*) to be known, so I created the creation to be known'. There are various other translations of the word *ahbabtu* (a derivative of *hubb*, 'love') as used in the hadith, including 'wanted', 'wished', 'liked', and 'desired.' I am aware that there are various scholars who consider this narration to be weak (*da'if*) or fabricated, but I prefer to follow Ibn Arabi, who was himself an authority on hadith.

In the same way as God 'wished' or 'desired' to be known, Ibn Arabi writes in the opening words of the first chapter ('Of the Divine Wisdom in the Word of Adam') of his *Fusus al-Hikam (Wisdom of the Prophets)*, that 'Allah wanted to see His own Essence (*'ayn)* in one global object (*kawn*) which having been blessed with existence (*al-wujud*) summarised the Divine Order (*al-amr*) so that there He could manifest His mystery (*sirr)* to Himself.' So, once again God is envisaged here as wishing or desiring to see Himself reflected in the mirror of creation. In his comprehensive discussion of the 'hidden treasure' hadith in his dissertation 'Unravelling the Mystery of the Hidden Treasure', Moeen Afnani explains that the Divine Essence wished to behold His own beauty in something other than Himself or his attributes, so creation as the mirror for reflecting the Divine beauty was brought into existence. In the succinct words of the Indian poet Ghalib (d.1869), 'in the desire of the One to know its own beauty, we exist.'

Immersion in Divine beauty pervades Ibn Arabi's *Tarjuman al-Ashwaq* (*Interpreter* or *Translator of Desires*), a cycle of sixty-one poems often assumed to be dedicated to a young woman, Nizam, from Isfahan, whom he met at the house of two eminent scholars of hadith. It has been commonly assumed by many modern scholars that it was Nizam whom Ibn Arabi encountered while circumambulating the Ka'ba and reciting a love poem, thinking he was alone. In his translation of the poems, Michael Sells added a preface as the book was going to press relating that when he was in Damascus in 2001, he came across new information concerning the identity of the young woman whom Ibn Arabi encountered at the Ka'ba. 'She touched him softly on the back' and in reacting to the final verse on bewilderment, 'protested that love is all-consuming; a true lover would have no self left to be bewildered' — a challenge that inspired him to compose the rest of the sixty poems of the *Tarjuman*. In his own preface, Ibn Arabi states that she identified herself as *Qurrat al-'Ayn* (cooling of the eye), 'an expression that refers to one of beauty's effects, namely, a moistening or softening of vision.' As Sells concludes, 'the woman at the Ka'ba may or may not have been identical to the historical Nizam. In Ibn Arabi's philosophy of love, all names for beloveds ultimately refer back to one infinite object of longing.'

Jane Clark, Senior Research Fellow of the Muhyiddin Ibn Arabi Society, agrees. In her illuminating discussion of the *Tarjuman*, she affirms that 'the love and passion which was awakened in him was not at all like the yearning of an undeveloped man for a beautiful woman; it was the love of a realised mystic for his God, and for a Divine reality which was known and witnessed as appearing in every created form, both physical and imaginal'.

Clark adds that as far as she knew Ibn Arabi did not specify at any point whether she was a flesh and blood woman, or whether, like the mysterious youth (*fata*) who inspired the *Futuhat* after accosting him as he circumambulated the Ka'ba on a previous occasion, she was perceived in the imaginal realm. 'It does not matter,' she says. 'What matters is that she was a means by which the Divine reality revealed Itself to Ibn Arabi in a way which made a forceful impact upon him.' This is clearly recognised by Nicholson in referring to the poems as 'mystical odes' in the subtitle of his translation of the *Tarjuman*. That of course honours Ibn Arabi's own intention in writing his own commentary which stressed the allegorical meanings of the poems and which was necessitated by the harsh criticism he received for supposedly writing poetry using explicit erotic imagery unworthy of a Sufi shaykh.

And so, if 'all names for beloveds ultimately refer back to one infinite object of longing' I am impelled to ask myself who was the beloved 'Isolde' Tristan was seeking in my dream when the depths of the ocean rose up in a vast golden wave in response to his fervent longing? In answer to this, I give Ibn Arabi the last word: 'it is He who is revealed in every face, sought in every sign, gazed upon by every eye, worshipped in every object of worship, and pursued in the unseen and the visible'.

BALANCING THE DESIRES

Luke Wilkinson

Take a moment to read these two words and pay attention to the range of emotions they make you feel. Focus on them briefly; maybe say them out loud: Sin, Desire.

Sin. It is a word that to a Western mind often brings immediate dread, panic, and fear—experienced as a crushing pressure upon the heart and spiralling thoughts in the brain.

Desire. This may bring a feeling in the groin area combined with a stab of guilt, located principally in the stomach area.

Sin and desire are terms rarely treated with respect among progressives. This is understandable given that the LGBTQ+ community has been rendered categorically sinful by most mainstream religions. There is much need for repair here. Putting the subsequent misuses of these words aside, we might better understand the crises of modernity by returning to their much earlier meaning. Sin, in both ancient Hebrew and Greek (*chatá* and *hamartia*, respectively) meant 'missing the mark'—to fire an arrow towards an intended target and to fall short. Sin always involves human intention: we pursue a goal but sometimes when we strike the bull's-eye, we feel an internal pang, as if the target wasn't the right one.

To understand the nature of sin and desire, we first need to briefly outline Sufi psychology in the *magnum opus* of the Persian mystic and scholar Imam al-Ghazali (d. 1111), *Ihyā 'ulūm al-dīn* (*The Revival of the Religious Sciences*). He outlines four basic elements that constitute the psychology of the human being: the ego (*nafs*), the heart (*qalb*), the intellect (*'aql*), and the spirit (*rūh*). We will focus principally on the first two here—the most important vis-à-vis desire. For al-Ghazali, aside from the physical heart, there is a more important meaning of *qalb*: the 'subtle tenuous substance' that can perceive and have knowledge of its Creator. This can see the wholeness of reality, its divinity, and longs to be at one with it. The *nafs* is the human ego, the collective sum of our experiences that makes us totally unique. If we attach too much importance to our individual ego, we draw a circle around ourselves separating us from the rest of the world; we believe that we are the only true reality.

Sufis see the *nafs* as what is called more technically *al-nafs al-ammāra bi'l-sū'*, the ego that commands. Conceiving of itself as totally separate from the rest of the world, and thus entirely alone, the *nafs* craves attachment. But because it perceives itself as wholly unique, it can only achieve this through acquiring mastery over distinct 'things' outside itself—a sense of attachment that lacks reciprocity and therefore never produces complete satisfaction. To prevent complete loneliness, the ego, then, having attached to a thing-in-the-world, already plans the pursuit of a new thing-in-the-future.

We can see the working of the *qalb* and *nafs*, and the role of desires, in the philosophical story of humanity's origin. At a particular moment after the Big Bang, the divine command to 'Be!', each part of life lived in harmonious reciprocity with the others. Then Adam and Eve (in the Islamic tradition, the blame is equally shared) set their sights on the forbidden fruit, making an intention to grasp it, rendering the fruit into a 'thing' to be owned and eaten for human gratification. It is the constant yearning to turn life into 'things' that causes us to pursue ends other than our true purpose. These states of yearning are what the Greeks and Islamic scholars like al-Ghazali understood as desires. They stem from the *nafs* and, if uncontrolled, compel the human to betray their potential by setting their sight upon a nearer, larger target for the arrow of their intention.

In book twenty-three of *Ihyā 'ulūm al-dīn*, al-Ghazali writes that the two main desires that stem from the *nafs* are the desire of the stomach and sexual desire. Desire of the stomach is the 'wellspring of desires' for it encourages an attachment to the physical world for its own sake. The desire of the stomach turns life in the world around us into 'things'. Al-Ghazali then states that, emboldened by satiety, the human, after a period of digestion, increases in their desire for sex. From here, al-Ghazali traces the widening influence of the desires of the ego. If unrestrained, one attempts to satisfy hunger and lust through fame and wealth, which makes a person arrogant. This then leads to envy, enmity, and hate between people. After that follows iniquity, injustice, and corruption. So, the two desires begin as internal forces, but if set free, come to define a human's behaviour. This then negatively affects an individual's inter-personal relationships, which in turn succeeds in poisoning relations between whole groups in society.

Desire for sex is pervasive in Western society, and due to social media, much of the globe. No one is more aware of this than the contemporary teenage boy, who is the main target for the barrage of sexual content online. He first encounters the sexual on Instagram or TikTok, perhaps from as young as five or six, where 'twerking' videos occupy a grey area in safety guidelines. At the early age of twelve, he may start to self-pleasure to such videos. This soon transitions to him exploring easily accessible porn sites, where curiosity often turns into reliance—a trustworthy source of pleasure during the uncertain years of adolescence. The ego, or *nafs*, has sought out sexual pleasure by turning the women on screen into 'things' to look at for self-gratification. But the ego is never satisfied and, owing to the de-humanisation of the women in the videos, soon loses interest. Now dependent, the teen attains climax by seeking out increasingly more extreme videos depicting socially unacceptable situations. Last year, a report by the Children's Commissioner for England found that one in three children (boys and girls) by the age of eighteen have actively sought out porn involving sexual violence. As the Oxford philosopher Amia Srinivasan warns, porn makes deep grooves upon the developing teenage brain and its understanding of intimacy, gender, love, family, and race. When our porn-viewing generation have their own sexual experiences, their ego is in control. They are using their sexual partners to pursue the climactic moment of self-gratification rather than savouring genuine intimacy.

Another form of missing the mark – the over-consumption of food – defines the modern. Protected by a magical, man-made film, it is made available from all corners of the globe. The ego rejoices – strolling through the supermarket, it is overwhelmed by all the 'things' to eat. We no longer even need to exit our homes but can peruse endless 'things' to eat while sitting on a sofa, which we will then receive, silently, from a stranger. This is the radicalisation of Adam and Eve grasping the forbidden fruit—we see a fellow being as an object to consume, with no thought of its alive-ness. Falling into thingness, our ego is constantly fed but never satisfied: having acquired the 'thing' to eat, we cannot even focus on the pleasure of consuming it but crave distraction from screen-based illusions. In other words, just as with sexual desire, the ego, when ascendant, constantly pursues these desires but can never fully enjoy them. Rather, it is always focused on the next 'thing'. Our bodies and minds follow, exhausted, bloated, stressed. This is reflected in the extreme interactions with food commonly found in modern society, such as widespread obesity, and a variety of eating disorders. During my teens, I objectified food to the point that I reduced it purely to its nutritional value in numerical terms (its 'macros') that served my pursuit of an ideal physical form—a mindset that I still struggle to escape today.

Modern society, then, has submitted to what al-Ghazali called the 'two desires': the desire for food and the desire for sex. The ego is constantly fed with both, but never fully satisfied. It is like a swelling tapeworm within us that, if not fed, feels like it will consume our insides. What, if any, is the remedy? The answer, I believe, lies in the ethical domain— which, in Islam, is tied to psychology, the science of the self. As we will shortly see, al-Ghazali suggests several psychological methods by which an individual may break free from the attachment of the *nafs* to the two desires. In our analyses of contemporary crises, living under the shadow of Hobbes, we eschew the ethical dimension of politics. Given 'the personal is political', as stickers attached to laptops and lampposts now proclaim, it seems even more necessary that ethics, the behaviour of the self, is brought back into serious political analysis.

The French philosopher, Michel Foucault, a man who devoted his career to unpicking the nature of power in modern society, was convinced near the end of his life that there was in fact one solution to the Gordian knot of the modern. The answer lay in the space of the self, what the Greeks had called *askesis* (self-discipline), where the potential for freedom lingered. Foucault located *askesis* in Islamic revolution: visiting Iran in late 1978, he was convinced that this way of governing the self was visible in the mass demonstrations. We now know that, once settled, the successful clerics of 1979 betrayed Foucault's vision. They ended up deploying the political (the state) to discipline the ethical (the self), rather than the inverse. Although Foucault wouldn't have had the 'two desires' in mind when analysing the modern, his focus upon the level of the self should encourage us to revisit the ethical as the mode of reshaping the political. I think we neglect the ethical because we wrongly believe that it takes too long: we think we must start at the level of the self and then, chronologically, work outwards from there. So what must we do ethically, and therefore psychologically, to tackle the overwhelming power of desires around us?

Return your attention to al-Ghazali's description of the desires. They produce imbalance in ever-widening levels of space, from the locus of character all the way to the whole of society. The meaning of this comes into view when we see that al-Ghazali had a two-fold understanding of action. In his introduction to the *Ihyā 'ulūm al-dīn*, he underlined that there were two forms of action: (a) external – at the level of the body: the more familiar sense to us, our physical actions; and (b) internal – competing drives within the realm of the soul.

For Islam, the path to re-balancing the desires within the human being begins at the outer level, with the body. It is the external, observable realm that our desires want us to exclusively focus upon; it makes sense to begin breaking their grip here. As some Westerners now understand, ultimately thanks to an oft-neglected British Orientalist called Thomas Walker Arnold (d. 1930), Islam literally means 'submission' – to submit ourselves to divine Oneness. It is realistic: as our ego makes us conceive of the world exclusively as 'things', one is not expected to completely believe in the unseeable before surrendering. Kierkegaard viewed religion as a 'leap of faith'. You must commit the body before the soul is certain, the external before the internal. Although the 'leap' is in fact very small; simply the act of beginning—doing one small thing differently with the intention of weakening the ego—it feels bewildering. With the ego still dominant, one feels uncomfortable submitting to something else; the ego can only see No-thing as some 'thing'. One will have to take steps to break the desires, weaken the ego, and then align with deeper reality. This is the importance of revealed law, *sharī'ah*, for the Andalusian mystic ibn Arabi (d.1240). He highlights that, after the servant starts to submit his body to revealed prescriptions, rather than to the ego, they realise that their bodily actions stem from the loving Oneness that holds every falling raindrop, not from their individual capabilities.

> *You did not throw when you threw but Allah threw...*
> Qur'an 8:17

To set out on this journey of re-harmonising our soul, al-Ghazali recommends a simple practice: listen to the ego, feel what it desires, and then set an intention to enact with our bodies the opposite of what the ego seeks.

Take the desire for food. You are walking through a supermarket and see an unrecyclable, American snack. Take a moment. You can hear your ego saying 'take it, you deserve it, you've had a hard day. What difference are you going to make? Global warming is unstoppable.' But, instead, set a little intention to yourself to not let your body follow your ego this time, to not pick up the brightly-coloured product. If you do this right, you might walk away with a feeling of lightness, a brief quietness. Then your *nafs*, annoyed that it has been denied this time, will likely respond with, 'look at me, I am such a self-disciplined person unlike all these hopeless sheep around me'. You have won a battle, but not the war. Although it is not considered completely reliable, a hadith famously narrates the Prophet leaving the battlefield (where he defended the oppressed), saying to a companion: 'we have returned from the lesser jihad to the greater jihad.' 'What is the greater a?', the companion asked. 'The struggle with one's own *nafs*.'

There must be a pure intention when one tries to challenge the desire of the stomach. As al-Ghazali says, some people fast but with the intention to show off their discipline to everyone else; in which case, they have used an ego-weakening practice for the reverse effect. For these kinds of people, the ego is more complex; it encourages self-discipline to increase the power of the self: 'resist that unhealthy food, run at 5am, then I can feel good about my*self*'. Again, al-Ghazali's advice for these types is to listen to one's ego, and then do with one's body the opposite of what the ego wants. This may mean for the self-disciplining person that they occasionally should eat something a bit sweet, or sleep in a bit more. By making small steps to use our bodies to do the opposite of what the ego wants, we may eventually find a harmonious relationship with our desires, where they in themselves, or the suppression of them, no longer control us.

The same method of weakening the ego applies to the desire for sex, the other main desire for al-Ghazali, which dominates contemporary society so intensely. Here, as a straight man, I will speak to that perspective. You are walking down the street. It's the evening and you have put on your best clothes. You are looking around and you see an attractive woman approaching you in the street. You look away. You feel a rush of excitement, and have a strong desire to look again when she comes closer, and maybe even to establish eye contact (or if you are particularly aroused, to scan other parts of her body). You look again and you wish you were with her, or more specifically, could 'have' her. If you are in a relationship, you may feel restricted by your current partner and may briefly want to be 'rid' of her. If you aren't in a relationship, you may wish you had the confidence to talk to the woman; or maybe you possess such confidence and do indeed strike up a conversation. In all three instances, perhaps excepting the third one, which may eventually lead back to the human, you have turned another human being into an object of sexual desire, robbing them of their equality.

Here al-Ghazali reminds us of the example of the Prophet and the Islamic way of life. The first 'look' is unintentional, not motivated by sexual desire, and therefore is acceptable. The second 'look' is acting upon sexual desire, where one's eyes are partly fulfilling this sexual desire, and therefore is classified as a sin – you have missed the mark by objectifying other human beings for the pleasure of your ego. When speaking to his son-in-law Ali, Muhammad said: 'Ali, do not let a second look follow the first. The first look is allowed to you but not the second'.

This may seem over-the-top but is even more relevant in our pornified society. Porn is a radicalisation of 'looking' where one has endless women and men available online that remove their clothes and commit sexual acts for the onlooker's viewing pleasure. No longer does the person have to even risk the fear of being spotted staring at a woman with lust, but can look from any angle they want at the flesh on their screen. This is an extreme, one-way version of what Sigmund Freud called *Schaulust* (the pleasure of looking). Then the onlooker almost certainly goes further, fulfilling sexual desire with the hand. This receives further criticism from the Prophet. Masturbation is the complete fulfilment of sexual desire through the ego alone – for it is self-pleasure, and therefore it removes all intimacy whatsoever. And intimacy, as we will see below, is the real purpose of sexual desire. The absence of intimacy leads to feelings of emptiness after the climax.

So, if we stop after the first 'look', using our body to resist our ego's urge to look again with sexual intent, we resist objectifying women into sexual objects. We see them as fellow hearts, utterly unique, worthy of respect in this sense, rather than as objects for male pleasure, as porn encourages us to see them. Given that women operate as sexual objects for the male gaze across most of social media and, before that, in the cinema (as the feminist film theorist Laura Mulvey wrote in 1973), this is extremely difficult. Srinivasan calls for an immediate cessation to the constant flux of female (and male) flesh available online. As a man, this would obviously mean never visiting porn sites, but also probably removing oneself from social media, which is so often the gateway to porn. In contemporary society, this is a tough ask. I think al-Ghazali would counsel something like this (again, I speak from my perspective as a straight man): You are tired and bored, so your hand flicks automatically to the Instagram icon. The portal opens, and you see a few friends' faces before the body of a scantily clad woman – 'tall, tanned, young, and lovely' as Sinatra croons – hits your eyes. This is the first look. Now, stop. Listen to your ego. It wants to look again, for longer, to scan the flesh and take pleasure in it, to replay the actions you have seen on porn sites but with this body and face, to look at the lustful eyes that have been forever fixed, forever staring at you, and to imagine you are the object of this lust. But you look away from your phone, you close Instagram, or you simply scroll past. You have won a successful battle against the sexual desire of the *nafs*. You have begun. No doubt you will make missteps in the future. But every time you take that second look, seek the forgiveness of the ever-forgiving, *ar-Rahim*, and make an intention to strive again. Remember the following words from the divine, spoken through the human Muhammad [although the word 'he' is used here, it is intended equally for women]. He said, 'Allah almighty says:

> Whoever draws close to Me by the length of a hand, I will draw close to him by the length of an arm.
> Whoever steps towards Me by the distance of an arm, I draw a distance of a wingspan nearer to him.
> Whoever comes to Me walking, I will come to him running
> Whoever meets me with enough sins to fill the earth,
> not associating any partners with Me,
> I will meet him with as much forgiveness.

Islam does not, however, see sexual desire as something that should be overcome. The Companions asked the Prophet: 'O Messenger of God! When one of us fulfils his sexual desire, will he be rewarded [by God for so doing]?' And he responded, 'if he acts upon it lawfully, he will be rewarded'. In other words, the Prophet encouraged sexual exploration as worthy of divine reward if it was practiced within the confines of marriage. According to some hadith, if a man consistently failed to sexually fulfil his wife due to being engrossed in additional spiritual practices, this could even be grounds for divorce. Thus, the desire for sex, like the desire for food, has a higher purpose when brought into balance.

So far, we have been thinking through the first steps, using the body to counter the ego's desires. We have been dealing with the familiar level of the external, the observable, only referring in passing to the nature of the internal desires. The path of Islam only begins here. Consider the act of praying. Although inconvenient, it is relatively easy to place one's forehead on the floor at five moments throughout the day. But, ask yourself this: do you bow with your whole being in loving submission to the creative flow of the divine? Few achieve this five times a day. We must now journey deeper, to the internal realm.

Recall how al-Ghazali presented two forms of action, internal and external. The inner-outer distinction regarding action is also prominent in the work of Allamah Muhammad Iqbal (1877–1938), a South Asian poet-philosopher. He delivered a series of lectures that partially sought to reinterpret al-Ghazali's *Revival (Ihyā)* in reference to modern society – which he aptly called *The Reconstruction of Religious Thought in Islam*. Like al-Ghazali, by action he refers both to the level of the body and to the level of the soul, but Iqbal adds a temporal element. Actions by the body primarily occur in space; the body occupies a space in the world, and when we move our bodies, we affect the space around us which is populated by other people and life-forms. Internal actions – within the self – do not occur in space at all; there is no physical 'space' of the soul or consciousness. This is the blunder of any crude materialist: that you can carve open the human body and point to where consciousness originates. The actions of the soul occur beyond the 'where', purely within the realm of time.

So how does this relate to *nafs* and *qalb*? Drawing on his Cambridge education and the French philosopher Henri Bergson, Iqbal gives two meanings of time: serial time and real time. Serial time is the idea of time as made up of distinct moments, embodied in the modern-day tick of second hand. Real time is a deeper flow that is felt as a singular, indivisible 'Now'—most profound when engaging in an all-consuming form of exercise or when one has sat in meditation for a while. For Iqbal, two elements within the human relate to these two forms of time. The ego, or *nafs*, exists in serial time. Take a moment to reflect on a recent time that you tried to be 'in the present moment'. When trying to be present, you might immediately hear the ego complain; it is deeply unhappy in the present and always yearns for the next thing in the future or replays past events. Meanwhile, the *qalb* exists in real time, the continuous flow of 'now'. If we sit in meditation long enough, we may sink, or rise, into the *qalb*, where we suddenly no longer experience time as discrete moments but as a whole. This is time as no-thing. It cannot be divided or separated like things; we instead move with the flow of this time, like a single drop in a river. Here we may feel and surrender to the divine breath as the No-Thing that is the source of all being; the Existence that grounds all non-existence. *Ar-Rahman*. This time, this soft, perfumed breath, overlaps all spaces and all moments. 'Do not vilify time, for time is God', said the Prophet. 'Our command was but one, swift as the twinkling of an eye', states the Qur'an (58:50).

Although submission begins at the bodily level, in space, this is only the beginning of how one relates to the two desires. Through your body pursuing the opposite of the desires, the ego, incessantly fixated upon future moments or replaying past moments, takes up less physical space in your life. You find a deeper flow that is roaring with gentle creativity. Having enacted the opposite of what the ego wants, and going through great difficulty resisting it, the desires for food and for sex come into a natural balance. This is why Islam is often referred to as *al-mizan* – the balance, or the middle path (with obvious parallels with Buddhism and Aristotelian morality). *Harmonie*, the ancient Greek term for harmony, referred to Heraclitus's lyre, in which the tautness of the strings, pulling in opposite directions, produce spontaneous music. This is the aim of Islam; not to remove the ego, *nafs*, and its desires altogether, but to bring the soul into a harmonious relationship between *qalb* and *nafs*. In *harmoniē*, or *mizān*, desires become a mirror to God.

As al-Ghazali shows us, the Prophet offers the perfect example of how the ego's desires for food can, once brought into *mizan*, become transformed into a channel towards the divine. For Muhammad, a simple, humble man, food did not dominate his life. Muhammad often fasted outside Ramadan and warned against frequent indulging in extravagant food, but also worried about ascetics who had converted to Islam and brought a strong modality of self-punishment to the spiritual life. When hearing a companion of his, Uthman ibn Mazun, intended to become celibate and receive food solely through begging, spending all day fasting and all night in prayer, Muhammad repeatedly urged him to find the path of balance, *al-mizan*:

'Thou fastest every day and keepest vigil every night in prayer. Do not so, for verily thine eyes have their rights over thee, and thy body has its rights, and thy family have their rights. So pray, and sleep, and fast, and break fast.'

Feel the *harmonie* of that last sentence. The prophetic example seems jarring to most of us moderns, who either have little self-control when it comes to food or have developed a harsh form of self-discipline, where, in constantly restricting what we can and can't eat, we exert much mental energy thinking about food. Recent praiseworthy podcasts such as 'Food, We Need to Talk' use science to show how far off we are from having a healthy, normal relationship with food, and how we can change. In the Islamic way of life, the way of *al-mizan*, food is simply a source of energy allowing one to strive internally and externally. So there is no need to take the process of its consumption too seriously. But the Qur'an also tells us that food, when we truly appreciate it as the efforts of another creature, is a sign of God. So we should take the ritual of eating seriously. Turn to the part of the Qur'an called *an-Nahl* ('The Bee') and read the first eighteen lines, or let the following words reverberate in your mouth and heart:

And your Lord inspired the bees:
'Make homes in the mountains, the trees, and in what people construct, and feed from [the flower of] any fruit [you please] and follow the ways your Lord has made easy for you.'
From their bellies comes forth liquid of varying colours, in which there is healing for people.
Surely in this is a sign for those who reflect.
(16:69)

The flower opens, the bee feeds, and we savour the taste. The Qur'an reminds us to appreciate the wider natural cycle involved in every piece of food we place in our mouth. This requires feeling these verses with our *qalb*, which exists in the 'now' that overlaps distinct moments, and thus can appreciate the past, present, and future movement of life in our food. From here, we can cultivate a living relationship with what we eat, reflecting the constant flux in which both of us, the food and ourselves, exist. Whisper to yourself these words the next time you crush an apple with your teeth:

'Your seeds shall live in my body,
'And the buds of your tomorrow shall blossom in my heart,
'And your fragrance shall be my breath,
'And together we shall rejoice through all the seasons.'

Khalil Gibran

Islam also offers a similar path regarding the desire for sex. Although muzzled by early Christian ascetic influences and, much later, by colonial Victorian morality, the desire for sex was originally regarded in early Islam as entirely natural, God-given, and therefore, when brought into balance, a potential mirror to the divine. Without our ego in control, which objectifies and relentlessly seeks escape from the present, we cease to regard other women or men as 'things' to use in impatiently pursuing the goal of climax. Instead, if we truly love our partner, we feel the desire to transcend the utter singularity of the ego and remove all layers of division between ourselves and another. One can only achieve this insight if one is fully present when making love with a partner whom one fully trusts – where one has let down the guard of the ego and opened one's heart to another in total vulnerability. This is very hard to feel completely without having undergone a spoken, witnessed commitment to stay exclusively with one another for the rest of one's life. Thus, the revealed law holds that sex must only occur within the bounds of marriage.

Once enjoyed within a loving marital relationship, sex has a central cosmological purpose. Al-Ghazali highlights that sexual desire was created for two reasons: to produce children and for 'knowing its delight'. The first reason is easily understood, but what about the second? Let us recall that the human finds it easiest to believe in the world of sense-perception. As al-Ghazali states, 'what cannot be perceived through experience will never be greatly desired'. During sex, the body rejoices when one loses oneself with another. This gives a direct taste of the spiritual desire in the heart, *qalb*, to be united with the one whose loving breath holds every atom within you at every moment, *al-Wadud*, the all-loving. As Ibn Arabi tells us, love does not have an object; it pursues nonexistence. In sex, we experience that the *qalb* is the absolute opposite of the *nafs*; it seeks total union with No-Thing, the truly existent. More radical Sufis describe the desire for union with the divine using the word *ishq*, which suggests an erotic love. If the *nafs* and *qalb* are held in *al-mizan* like the taut strings of Heraclitus's lyre, the desire for sex, from the *nafs*, can lead to startling insights into our deeper spiritual longing within our *qalb*. Read the prayer of the early mystic Rabia Al-Adawiyya Al-Qaysiyya (d. 801) and hear the passion in her words:

> O my Lord,
> if I worship you
> from fear of hell, burn me in hell.
> If I worship you
> from hope of Paradise, bar me from its gates.
> But if I worship you
> for yourself alone, grant me then the beauty of your Face.

You may say, all that is well and good on an individual scale; but how do I change the hegemony of the desires for food and sex in our contemporary society? Return your attention to al-Ghazali's description of the ever-widening arenas of corruption, from the self to society. We may fairly assume that to undo the iniquities caused by the two desires in society at large will require us to navigate through the same stages chronologically—we have to start with ourselves, working to weaken our desires at the level of the *nafs*, and then, after much struggle, we can help progressively wider spaces, from the familial to the societal. The consequent idea of 'focus on yourself, and *then* help others' courses through most self-help books of today. I like the message, except for that single and troublesome word: 'then'.

As we have seen, the *qalb* exists in a deeper form of time, the continuous 'now'. Here it has the potential to directly witness the constant creative flow of the divine. This ever-expansive time overwhelms all spatial dimensions. This means that when we allow ourselves to connect to the *qalb* rather than the *nafs*, when our internal realm aligns with this creative flow, it simultaneously expands to our outer actions too. Having meditated and connected to the *qalb*, or when we exercise for the sake of moving our bodies in nature (rather than for the sake of the ego, as in the gym) – and therefore at least succeed in briefly quietening the ego – goodness becomes very easy in the moments that follow: we are patient, kind, and loving, in line with the divine spirit within us. So there is no 'and then' between weakening the ego and doing good to others, it just happens. We might simplify the self-help dictum from 'focus on yourself, and then help others' to 'focus on your heart, and help others'. Doing good for others, the bodily enactment of the heart's alignment with divine mercy, only weakens the ego further, and increases one's alignment with the heart. It is for this reason that the giving of charity was a practice underlined so heavily by the Prophet. Through internal action of overcoming desires, thereby weakening the ego, our external actions heal the dominance of desires in those around us, and, casting wider than this, in society at large. The efforts of one heart can have effects on all hearts, as we are each, and all, one: 'The creation and resurrection of you [all] is as simple [for Allah] as that of a single soul' (31:28).

The prophets and messengers of the past are the ultimate examples of how the purified heart of one person may heal entire peoples. The beloved Prophet Muhammad lived during a time in which desires raged rampant, leading to ceaseless internecine warfare, exploitation, and savagery, in which women were always the victims. He revolutionised entire societies primarily through his beautiful character. He is principally remembered by those that follow his example for his perfect character above all his other achievements (such as directly receiving the word of God – no small matter – or rapidly establishing a stable system of government in the most ecologically and politically abrasive place on earth). With an array of rigorously accurate records of his words and actions, we all have access to the prophetic example of how character can bring spontaneous ethical revolution to the world around us. All that is left to do is to take the first small step. As a common mystic expression goes:

'there are only two rules in religion: begin and continue'.

We all can take our little steps, and continue to take them, so that we may draw closer to the loving, ever-creative, breath of *ar-Raḥmān* that permeates each and every life in this universe.

READING AND REFORM

Peter Matthews Wright

'Anything from the sound of a word to the colour of a leaf to the feel of a piece of skin,' wrote the late American philosopher Richard Rorty, can 'serve to dramatise and crystallise a human being's sense of self-identity'. Indeed, 'any seemingly random constellation of such things can set the tone for a human life' and act as 'an unconditional commandment to whose service a life may be devoted'. No one else needs to comprehend why such a commandment may be deemed unconditional; it is enough that one person accepts it as such. From this realisation, Rorty continued, came Freud's great insight that every human life is 'the working out of a sophisticated idiosyncratic fantasy'. I will attempt, in what follows, to redescribe religion as Rortian 'cultural politics', and then enlist the result in a critical modernist effort to reimagine the global Muslim community, the ummah, as 'an alliance without an institution'. In all candour, it is the working out of this sophisticated idiosyncratic fantasy that has occupied my life for the better part of three decades.

When I chose to study the philosophy and classical languages of Western Europe, as an undergraduate, I had hoped to get in touch with my cultural roots. I had been taught that ancient Greece and Rome is where I would find them. What I found instead were two fascinating but, as far as I could tell, alien civilisations. One might think that the Greeks' remarkable accomplishments in moral and political philosophy, poetry, and scientific rationality would have spared them an inferiority complex; but so long as Asia cast its shadow over the eastern Mediterranean, they could not be satisfied. Eventually, a Macedonian would attempt to assert Greek cultural superiority over Asia—through military conquest—only to find in a vanquished Iran a civilisation of enviable splendour.

The Romans absorbed the Greeks and concocted a curious blend of civil order and imperial brutality. This looked familiar to me, for I grew up during the Vietnam War era: *plus ça change, plus c'est la même chose*. The more things change, the more they stay the same! And although I would like to believe that the Roman Empire's Christianisation led to its overall moral improvement—its gentling—the historical record seems quite mixed on that score.

Entering my senior year, my overall mood was one of discontent. One bright spot, however, was my election to Phi Beta Kappa—an occasion that prompted me to reread 'The American Scholar,' the nineteenth century American essayist Ralph Waldo Emerson's 1837 address to that society's Harvard chapter. Although I had lost interest in pursuing graduate study in either philosophy or classics and was confused about what direction to take after graduation, Emerson told me not to worry: the world, he argued, is but the 'shadow of the soul'. Get to know it and you will come to know yourself. Dive in! 'Take your place in the ring, to suffer and to work' and, in time, you shall 'pierce its order... dissipate its fear', 'dispose of it within the circuit of expanding life'. For Emerson, the 'true scholar' is not a bookworm but, rather, a robust active soul. Life teaches us what we need to know and, what is more, provides us with 'the raw material out of which the intellect moulds her splendid products'.

Emerson romanticised what William Blake had once disparaged as 'the same dull round over again'. Nevertheless, I embraced his argument. Armed only with his assurance that such was the road of the true scholar, I took a job with an insurance company and, after a few years, enrolled in law school—working by day and studying at night. Heck, if Wallace Stevens could do it, so could I.

Besides, nothing could prevent me from being what I had been since childhood: a devourer of books—as was Emerson himself. Books, he declared, are 'the best of things, well used'. And by 'well used' he meant as a source of inspiration and an opportunity to practice a kind of transcendentalist hermeneutics: 'when the mind is braced by labour and invention,' he said, 'the page of whatever book we read becomes luminous with manifold allusion'. And *that* is why we read. To the discerning, 'every sentence is doubly significant, and the sense of our author is as broad as the world'. But remember: only what we can use to further our own vision of the truth will repay our efforts. The rest is so much froth. Transcendentalist hermeneutics is 'creative reading,' he said. So 'be an inventor' if you wish to read well.

Fast forward to 1995. The text, which I had been studying with a group of lawyers and law professors, was Ludwig Wittgenstein's *Philosophical*

Investigations. The passage, which I had been mulling in Emersonian fashion, was as follows: 'what is your aim in philosophy? — To shew the fly the way out of the fly-bottle'. And because, for ten years prior, I had obsessed over Wittgenstein's earlier work, *The Tractatus,* the later passage called to mind this 'manifold allusion': 'that the world is *my* world, shows itself in the fact that the limits of the language...which I understand...mean the limits of *my* world'.

If I am Wittgenstein's fly, I asked myself, what is the fly-bottle whose walls, though transparent, entrap me? The answer, I decided, would have something to do with the limits of my language. For my language—which is both history and culture reduced to sounds and marks—articulates and circumscribes my world. To that point in my life—I was then thirty-five—what I would call 'my world' had been built, brick by cultural brick, of Euro-American languages, literatures, religion, politics, history, philosophy, and law. Instinctively—not unlike Alexander the Great, but with different intentions and a different method—I turned, for new light, towards the East.

But not too far to the east. Reading Wittgenstein had inspired me to try to reproduce the philosopher's own reading habits—the better to trace his 'manifold allusions'. This methodology brought me to the later Tolstoy and to a question that had occupied many Russian intellectuals since at least the time of Peter the Great: does Russia belong to Europe or to Asia? If to Europe, what is one to make of the fact that almost eighty percent of the Russian landmass is in Asia? Tolstoy was personally enmeshed in this controversy by virtue of his move, at the age of fourteen, to Kazan, his reading of Russian folktales alongside the *Arabian Nights*, and his enrolment in the faculty of Oriental Languages at Kazan University, which required its students to acquire a knowledge of Arabic and 'Turco-Tartar'. Late in life, he would pen a final masterpiece, *Hadji Murat,* a novella that offers a portrait of the Russian Empire's attempts to subjugate Chechen tribespeople, who were and remain mostly Muslim. Tolstoy's sympathies were clearly with the underdog Chechens, but his spare prose avoids Romantic overreach. In my view, the novel remains one of the best introductions to that conflict, which is still ongoing.

Concomitantly, in my legal practice, I was being introduced to yet another ongoing conflict: this one taking place all around me. As it turns out, I was not alone in noticing parallels between the books I was reading and the life I was living. Writing in 1995, the literary historian Alfred Kazin observed: 'the "Russian novel", if that still means anything, is being lived all over this country in poverty, racial conflict, homelessness, drug addiction, and the increasing numbers of so-called redundant workers thrown into the streets every week by one technological replacement after another'.

As a criminal defence lawyer, I was meeting people Kazin would compare to characters familiar from Russian novels. The poor, disproportionately people of colour, often unhoused or living in substandard housing, afflicted by a variety of addictions, abused physically, sexually, undereducated in underfunded city schools, became both clients and conversation partners. Several of them had converted to one form or another of Islam, either in prison or in their neighbourhoods of origin. And the ways in which they talked about their conversion—how religion *functioned* in their lives— whether behind bars or on the outside, struck me, and aroused my curiosity.

As a member of what was, then, the white liberal Protestant majority in America, I grew up believing that religion was a private matter. The days when Protestantism was associated with radical politics, even regicide, were long past. There had been, it is true, a resurgence in the 1960s and 1970s of political activism among liberal Christians—Protestant and Catholic, black, and white—and, as a teenager, I was thrilled to witness the late chaplain William Sloane Coffin deliver a fiery sermon from the pulpit of the church where, as an infant, I had been baptised. But the message typically preached from that pulpit emphasised God's blessings upon each of us as individuals. The gross racial and economic injustices that were then propelling the Civil Rights Movement forward, and the obscenity that was the Vietnam War, were acknowledged from time to time, and our charity was encouraged. But, to my recollection, the most tendentious argument to divide the congregation into opposing camps was over a proposal to add a wing to the church building that would house a basketball court so that the youth group need not continue to use the facilities of the local high school.

Such concerns would have struck my incarcerated Muslim interlocutors as risible. For them, no less than for the adherents of other traditions, religion offered private solace; but Islam's communal dimension offered something more. Prison is a dangerous place: to have a brotherhood available to watch your back in an environment where physical and sexual violence are routine becomes a matter of survival. Under such circumstances, the Islamic emphasis upon the right of the oppressed to defend themselves, and the obligation—of those who are able—to come to their aid, has a practical appeal that the much quoted (if infrequently observed) Christian teaching to 'turn the other cheek' manifestly lacks.

The incarcerated Muslims I met during my decade of legal practice, mostly African American, taught me other valuable lessons about religion, including the way in which it can function as a form of cultural politics. I take that term from the writings of Richard Rorty, although I deploy it somewhat differently than he did. I will expand on that issue momentarily.

In the meantime, I wish to recount a conversation I had with a jailed black Muslim sometime in the mid-1990s. I do not recall now whether he had converted to Islam in prison or earlier in his life. What I do recall—indeed, will never forget—was the reason he gave for converting. He believed that growing up black and poor in America, with an absent father and an alcoholic mother, had all but guaranteed that he would find himself, at some point in his life, behind bars. The other options open to him, he said, were the military, the madhouse, or the cemetery. He did not feel that he was cut out for the first option and was not yet ready to face either of the latter two. 'And why should I join the military anyway?' he asked. 'Why should I risk my life for a country that has never accepted me for who I am? In Africa, my people are Muslims: we are scholars and kings. I am called an "African American", but I only identify with the first part of that name'.

I will confess that, as I listened to him speak, I was having difficulty crediting his story as the narrative of a religious conversion. He made no mention of God, repentance, the afterlife, or any of the familiar tropes that someone with my religious background would naturally expect to hear. It was only later, upon further reflection, that I would enlist Wittgenstein's help in making sense of what I had heard. And here is what the Viennese thinker taught me: my interlocutor *was* in fact relating the story of his religious conversion, but the limits of the 'religious language' I had learned growing up had placed limits upon *my* world and, therefore, upon my ability to understand *his* world.

This was a revelation to me, and my reading took off in a whole new direction. I developed an insatiable desire to read about Islam. In what time I could spare and, to be honest, even when I couldn't spare it, I began to read every book I could get my hands on about Islam, its history, teachings, and the cultures it informs and thrives in. One afternoon, during my lunch break, I wandered into a bookstore near my office to see what, if anything, might be on the shelves related to my new interest. The number of titles dedicated to Islamic Studies tended then (as now) to be thin. Yet in the 'World History' section that day was a book that would alter my understanding not only of Islam but also the very category of world history itself: the first volume of Marshall G. S. Hodgson's magisterial three-volume *The Venture of Islam: Conscience and History in a World Civilization*.

With Hodgson, my informal religious education acquired not only additional breadth but also historical profundity. His *Venture of Islam* begins, not as one might expect—in the late sixth or early seventh century of the Common Era—but roughly four thousand years earlier: with the invention of agriculture, the urban revolution that it sparked, and the resulting division of labour that made ancient literature possible. Without warning, I found myself in territory that was both oddly familiar and yet undeniably strange—and this peculiar combination of the recognisable and alien drew me in. Standing in the aisle of the bookstore, and glancing through this densely written work, it occurred to me just how Eurocentric was my knowledge of the ancient world. A map entitled 'The central Mediterranean through India, c. 600 C.E'. brought this realisation home. Central Mediterranean? India? But where, I wondered, is Western Europe? The cartographer had allowed it to fall somewhere outside the margins of his map and he did so because the implacable stone of historical fact is this: around the year 600, compared to other cultures flourishing in what Hodgson named the Afro-Eurasian *oikumene*, the culture of Western Europe was, in a word, Nowheresville. Moreover, it would remain an intellectual and cultural backwater for another thousand years.

I had never heard of this Marshall Hodgson or of his 'venture' through Islamic history, but those few pointed phrases and that map designed to shift the reader's geographical perspective—and thereby invite a different perception of the past—satisfied me that here was a book I needed to read. As I strolled towards the cash register with Hodgson's volume under my arm, I had no idea that I would eventually read his entire trilogy—repeatedly—or that I would leave my law practice in the summer of 2001 to enter a Ph.D. programme in Islamic Studies. Hodgson's *Venture* no doubt contributed to that decision, but conversations like the one recounted above carried just as much weight. For those conversations combined with my reading to enable me to chip away at the glass walls of my cultural fly-bottle.

Perhaps the icing on the cake was yet another book I read while 'reorienting' my thinking on these topics: Gauri Viswanathan's *Outside the Fold: Conversion, Modernity, and Belief*. For Viswanathan, religious conversion is as much a 'knowledge-producing activity' as an event signalling a 'spiritual transformation'. She offers several case studies in which the knowledge produced through conversion forms the basis of cultural critique—most legible, she argues, when the converts choose to affiliate themselves with 'minority' or alternative traditions. She writes:

> I shall offer as the principal argument of this book that conversion ranks among the most destabilising activities in modern society, altering not only demographic patterns but also the characterisation of belief as communally sanctioned assent to religious ideology. Although it is true that...conversion is typically regarded as an assimilative act—a form of incorporation into a dominant culture of belief—conversion's role in restoring belief from the margins of secular society to a more worldly function is less readily conceded. The worldliness I have in mind relates to civil and political rights. Why, for instance, does history throw up so many instances of conversion movements accompanying the fight against racism, sexism, and colonialism? What might be the link between the struggle for basic rights and the adoption of religions typically characterised as minority religions? What limitations of secular ideologies in ensuring these rights do acts of conversion reveal? Does that act of exposure align conversion more closely with cultural criticism? And finally, what possibilities for alternative politics of identity might be offered by conversion as a gesture that crosses fixed boundaries between communities and identities?

In the history of the modern West, Protestantism has tended to reduce religion to belief which, in turn, has retreated into the private sphere. Wittgenstein and Hodgson helped to show me the way out of that modern Western fly-bottle, thus allowing me to understand the life story of an incarcerated black Muslim as he intended it to be understood, that is, as the narrative of his religious conversion. Viswanathan's book confirmed for me the correctness of that view.

Let me now return to the suggestion I made earlier concerning religion's ability to function as a form of 'cultural politics'. Recall that I owe that term to Richard Rorty who, I should mention, credited the notion to John Dewey.

For both Rorty and Dewey, cultural politics is what philosophy looks like when traditional metaphysical claims have been abandoned. Why did these philosophers argue that such claims—which many people view as the very stuff of philosophy—could be dispensed with? As Rorty put it: '...we should try to create a world in which human beings devote all their energies to increasing human happiness in this world, rather than taking time off to think about the possibility of life after death'.

Rorty assumed that philosophers would have an easier time than religious believers in abandoning such claims. But if metaphysics mattered to my incarcerated Muslim's conversion, he neglected to mention it. Perhaps his level of education might account for his silence—he never completed high school—but lack of education does not prevent unquestioned adherence to religious or metaphysical dogmas. Quite the opposite.

I wonder what Rorty would have made of Sir Muhammad Iqbal, one of the twentieth century's foremost Muslim intellectuals, had he known of him. In his book *The Reconstruction of Religious Thought in Islam*, first published around 1930, in a chapter dedicated to challenging inherited metaphysical assumptions about the nature of the self, Iqbal wrote:

> Nor can the concepts of theological systems, draped in the terminology of a practically dead metaphysics, be of any help to those who happen to possess a different intellectual background. The task before the modern Muslim is, therefore, immense. He has to rethink the whole system of Islam without completely breaking with the past...The only course open to us is to approach modern knowledge with a respectful but independent attitude and to appreciate the teachings of Islam in the light of that knowledge, even though we may be led to differ from those who have gone before us.

I think it interesting that both Iqbal and Rorty chose to take issue with the metaphysics of personal identity and that questions of personal identity lay at the heart of that black Muslim's non-metaphysical conversion narrative. Rorty knew that dispensing with traditional metaphysical claims does not make the questions prompting them disappear, but it changes the way in which people try to answer them. It also frees people up to focus their energies on other matters—like 'increasing human happiness in this world'. As both Rorty and my interlocutor understood, that would mean addressing the kinds of issues with which a young, black, high school dropout from a broken home in inner city Pittsburgh had to contend—with predictable results. What was not necessarily predictable—until Viswanathan's study made it legible—was the latter's turn to religion, rather than philosophy, as a form of cultural politics.

Let's take a closer look, then, at what that latter term entails. In the preface he wrote to the fourth volume of his philosophical papers, *Philosophy as Cultural Politics*, Rorty argued that 'the history of philosophy is best seen as a series of efforts to modify people's sense of who they are, what matters to them, what is most important'. On this account, philosophers place questions of personal identity at the forefront of their activities—not for the purpose of speculating about what human beings really and truly are, but to encourage them to think about who they might become. Rorty continued:

> Interventions in cultural politics have sometimes taken the form of proposals for new roles that men and women might play: the ascetic, the prophet, the dispassionate seeker after truth, the good citizen, the aesthete, the revolutionary. Sometimes they have been sketches of an ideal community—the perfected Greek polis, the Christian Church, the republic of letters, the cooperative commonwealth. Sometimes they have been suggestions about how to reconcile seemingly incompatible outlooks—to resolve the conflict between Greek rationalism and faith, or between natural science and the common moral consciousness. These are just a few of the ways in which philosophers, poets, and other intellectuals have made a difference to the way human beings live.

In these remarks, Rorty raised at least two issues worth lingering over. First, in the final sentence, he expanded his list of those who have successfully practiced cultural politics. While he did not include the religious faithful in this list, he did not explicitly exclude them either. His assumption that those who make this list are best described as 'intellectuals', however, strikes me as unnecessarily narrow. Pace Rorty, I don't see any reason to restrict the class of those who might practice cultural politics to that group—even if it were broadened to include those whom the twentieth century Italian philosopher and writer Antonio Gramsci deemed 'organic'. I suspect Viswanathan would reject that restriction outright.

A second aspect worth highlighting is the plasticity of personal identity he presumed. Throughout his later work, Rorty termed this human quality 'the contingency of selfhood,' and I will adopt his usage. For Rorty, an individual's 'selfhood,' her personal identity as she first comes to terms with it growing up, is contingent upon a series of accidents: when and where she was born, into what sort of family, race, religion, and socioeconomic status. Traditionally, however, such aspects of selfhood would not typically be considered mere accidents. They would instead be understood as decreed by God or inscribed, somehow, in the very nature of things. As in ancient Greek tragedy, there was no escaping fate. As Rorty tells the story, it took a scholar of classical Greek, Friedrich Nietzsche, who was also, not incidentally, the son of a Lutheran pastor, to try to make a lasting break with this philosophical and religious inheritance. It is crucial to understand, however, that Nietzsche was, in many respects, Emerson's disciple—and Emerson was, in turn, a disciple of Persian poets, Hafez chief among them.

Here is the Sage of Concord, in a much-neglected essay on Persian poetry published in *The Atlantic Monthly* in 1858, declaring the contingency of selfhood in no uncertain terms: 'we accept the religions and politics into which we fall, and it is only a few delicate spirits who are sufficient to see that the whole web of convention is the imbecility of those whom it entangles—that the mind suffers no religion and no empire but its own'. This is the radical Mr. Emerson that our history and philosophy departments have virtually ignored, and our English departments have attempted to erase from cultural memory. That they have been largely successful in suppressing Emerson's radicalism is, to someone like me, a matter of concern; but the lesson Rorty would draw from such conservatism is inspiring.

Rorty insisted that the human condition is never completely scripted. Therefore, if a few generations of educators successfully sanitise Ralph Waldo Emerson—or, for that matter, the late American Baptist minister and activist Dr. Martin Luther King, Jr.—so that students may read them without questioning the *status quo*; or, on the other hand, successfully demonise the late American Muslim minister and activist Malcolm X or the twentieth century Lithuanian-born activist Emma Goldman, so that students will not read them at all, a subsequent generation of educators can reverse that process. Rorty's authority for this claim was Nietzsche who, by defining truth as 'a mobile army of metaphors' made it impossible, in the final analysis, to pin truth down once and for all. Indeed, for Nietzsche (as for Rorty and Emerson), there is no 'final analysis' except in the sense that our mortality limits the number of analyses available to us all. The good news is that, so long as there are human beings, there will be fresh takes on the nature of things;

and each new take will either dust off old metaphors or attempt to displace them with untried new ones.

In addition to Nietzsche's perspectivism, Rorty relied on the nineteenth century German philosopher Georg W. F. Hegel's historicism to make his case. As problematic as many might find Nietzsche's definition of truth to be, it is difficult to refute Hegel's observation that truth is always articulated in time—and time, incontestably, moves on. For this reason alone, truth cannot avoid being a moving target—a mobile army of metaphors. By contrast, Plato's timeless realm of forms is 'just a fable'. Or, in Muhammad Iqbal's words, 'the terminology of a practically dead metaphysics'.

Terminology matters: it can be either friend or foe. On the one hand, it can consist of 'an entrenched vocabulary which has become a nuisance' or, on the other, 'a half-formed new vocabulary which vaguely promises great things'. This is Rorty, again, describing the method of what he will subsequently call 'cultural politics'. As he put it in his earlier book, *Contingency, Irony, and Solidarity*:

> The method is to redescribe lots and lots of things in new ways, until you have created a pattern of linguistic behaviour which will tempt the rising generation to adopt it, thereby causing them to look for appropriate new forms of non-linguistic behaviour, for example, the adoption of new scientific equipment or new social institutions. This sort of philosophy... works holistically and pragmatically. It says things like 'try thinking of it this way'—or more specifically, 'try to ignore the apparently futile traditional questions by substituting the following new and possibly interesting questions'.

I think Muhammad Iqbal would agree with Richard Rorty's method of redescription to this point. In fact, I would argue that in *The Reconstruction of Religious Thought in Islam* Iqbal practiced that method—decades before Rorty articulated it. The two thinkers would part company, however, when it came to deciding what to do with the past. Elaborating his method, Rorty wrote: 'it does not pretend to have a better candidate for doing the same old things which we did when we spoke in the same old way. Rather, it suggests that we might want to stop doing those things and do something else. But it does not argue for this suggestion [based on] antecedent criteria common to the old and the new languages games. For just insofar as the new language really is new, there will be no such criteria'. Iqbal admonished his fellow Muslims that the task before them was immense: nothing short of rethinking the entire 'system of Islam' would do. However, he included a caveat: this task had to be accomplished without, in the process, completely abandoning the rich heritage of Islamic traditions.

Therein lies a significant rub.

In his 2005 study of Abu Hamid al-Ghazali (d. 1111 C.E.), South African-American Islamic scholar Ebrahim Moosa took Iqbal's challenge to heart. After quoting the same section of *Reconstruction* that I cited above, Moosa mused:

> Not only is this a Herculean task—to rethink the Muslim tradition—but it is an equally daunting challenge. It requires the renewed Muslim subject to be different from the past due to temporal change, yet there remains a demand that subjectivity be simultaneously continuous with the past. We see glimpses of this creative tension throughout the work of Ghazali. Perhaps the twenty-first-century challenge—greater even than the challenge of the Ghazalian or post-Ghazali, intellectual project—anticipates an even more radical solution: to discover a subjectivity that is competent to will a paradigmatic transition within Islam.

In this passage Moosa, like Iqbal before him, calls upon modern Muslims to accomplish within Islam what philosopher of science Thomas Kuhn famously termed a 'paradigm shift'. He asserts that a subjectivity competent to will such a transition—to 'reconstruct' a religious thought-world or, in Wittgenstein's metaphor, 'show the fly the way out of the fly-bottle'—would have to be a remarkably imaginative one. It is important to note, however, Moosa's agreement with Iqbal that a complete break with the past would be undesirable. And so, he looked back to the flowering of Islam's classical tradition for an individual whose record of creativity—or 'poetics of imagination' as he put it—could serve as a model for anyone courageous enough to attempt this 'Herculean' task. In the figure of al-Ghazali, Moosa settled upon a worthy choice—and yet, as we saw, Emerson had already made a similar move, invoking the spirit of Hafez for the more radical claim 'that the mind suffers no religion and no empire but its own'.

Indeed, both Emerson and Rorty often implied that, absent a complete break with the past, no paradigm shift is possible. It would be difficult to find a more powerful statement of this position than the opening lines of Emerson's first book, *Nature*:

Our age is retrospective. It builds the sepulchres of the fathers. It writes biographies, histories, and criticism. The foregoing generations beheld God and nature face to face; we, through their eyes. Why should not we also enjoy an original relation to the universe? Why should not we have a poetry and philosophy of insight and not of tradition, and a religion by revelation to us, and not the history of theirs?

And Rorty echoed Emerson by praising Nietzsche's conviction that 'human life (is) triumphant just insofar as it escapes from inherited descriptions of the contingencies of its existence and finds new descriptions'. Weighing the approaches of Emerson and Rorty, on the one hand, against those of Iqbal and Moosa, on the other, I cannot help but wonder if the former's redescriptions ask too much of the rising generations they hope to tempt, while those of the latter do not ask enough.

To his credit, Ebrahim Moosa confessed himself as perplexed about this matter as anyone. But then he made an interesting move. He wrote: 'if the contours of the Ghazalian/post-Ghazali project I envisage remain difficult to discern, one can at least begin to imagine the kinds of friendships and alliances that any such rethinking will involve. With whom from the past will the coming generation of thinkers commune?' To be frank, I find Moosa's image of 'friendship' with the dead who yet live on in the metaphors they leave behind quite lovely. In and through it, I find a way forward: for despite Emerson's call for 'an original relation to the universe' he, too, made 'friendships and alliances' with figures from the past. I have already mentioned his deep affection for Hafez, but I should also mention the thirteenth century Persian poet Sa'adi and, one of Muhammad Iqbal's heroes, the beloved thirteenth century poet Jalaladdin Rumi.

'By engaging with the thinkers of the past,' Moosa continued, 'we anticipate the intellectual communities of the future'. And then, shifting his focus to the late philosopher Jacques Derrida, Moosa noted that the French thinker believed that 'when we do so', we imagine 'an alliance without an institution' in which the thinkers and philosophers of the future already exist. The reason that the thinkers of the future already exist is that we visualise them, address them here and now as a possible future hope and desire. In all these fictive acts, we are already declaring our friendship with the philosophers of the future, and in this gesture, we become their heralds and precursors'. There is a lot to unpack here—too much, in fact, for me to do complete justice to in the remaining space of this essay. Therefore, I will only offer two observations that I hope may illuminate what I see as the relevance of this passage to all that I have said so far.

At the outset, however, I feel obligated to take exception—as I did with Rorty—to the limitations Moosa imposed upon our list of future friends and allies. As I discovered in a maximum-security prison long ago, we cannot anticipate the conditions under which the walls of our fly-bottle may become visible. Nor can we predict who might be responsible for cracking the glass. Which is not to suggest that thinking can be avoided in this process—far from it. But traditional philosophic or religious thought may prove unavailing. My argument is not about religious or philosophical business-as-usual: it is about religion as cultural politics.

Back to the task at hand. The first observation I wish to make is that Moosa, in order to find the metaphors he needed, enlisted the aid of a modern French intellectual—not a fellow Muslim past or present but a Jew born in Algeria, meditating upon the future of *his* fictive 'friendship' with the nineteenth century German philosopher Karl Marx, after the collapse of the Soviet Union! My second observation follows from the first: this might seem an unlikely alliance for a Muslim intellectual to forge in his quest to induce a paradigm shift within Islam while maintaining some degree of continuity with the past. But then, could we not say the same of Emerson's call for an 'original relation to the universe' that looks, for inspiration, not only within the solitary self but also to thirteenth and fourteenth century Persian poets?

If the reader is struggling to make sense of Moosa's project, or Emerson's, or both, I would suggest that the difficulty lies in the fact that, in their prose, Moosa and Emerson were already inhabiting the future paradigm shift that Moosa, following Iqbal, and Emerson, following his poetic muses, had imagined. Let me suggest what, in my view, can make that shift a reality: trading religious affiliation for religious affinity and, in the process, shifting the religious paradigm from identity politics to cultural politics.

Let me explain. According to Merriam-Webster, to affiliate with someone or something typically involves a subordinate relation of 'membership'. An affinity, on the other hand, involves sympathy marked by a community of interest. In subtle and not-so-subtle ways we, all of us, are under continual social pressure to affiliate with one religious or racial or ethnic or political or gendered identity or another, at the cost of submerging our complex and inherently contingent selfhood in the larger identity of a group or organisation. Rather than being encouraged to cultivate sympathies in which mutual interests create voluntary and often ephemeral associations of the like-minded, 'authentic' identity is increasingly acquired by affiliating with groups that, under the auspices of the Liberal procedural or authoritarian state, are accorded official sanction. One advantage of this arrangement is that it facilitates the distribution of entitlements. A disadvantage is that it also facilitates surveillance, discipline, and even punishment. As Emerson and, not incidentally, al-Ghazali understood, our affiliations are frequently accidents of history and birth. By contrast, affinities result from conscious decisions made in pursuit of one's passions. The tethers of affined community are achieved not by accident or by coercion but rather by consensual communion.

Moosa objects to social pressures that force those to whom they are uncongenial into exile: they are 'marginalised by the tyranny of the majority'. Exiles, however, *can* form bonds of mutual solidarity through alliances without institution, 'imagined friendship' and 'community without community'. And by 'exile' he means not only physical displacement but also spiritual, political, and 'other conceivable forms of suffering and marginalisation'. But it takes courage to choose affinity over affiliation and a principled willingness to sacrifice as much as possible the inherited benefits that can accrue to in-group identification—especially if the identity in question is hegemonic. The pay-off, however, comes not only through solidarity among exiles, but in a form of friendship that 'can transform and reconcile the "self" with the "other"'.

Such courage and principle constitute the moral backbone of cultural politics.

In the fraught party and identity politics of the current moment, the reconciliation of which Moosa wrote can no longer be deemed a luxury. But the problem of contending identities is as old as the human tendency to band together with people who are 'like us,' while avoiding others—a tendency that feels perfectly natural and may even be written into our DNA. But not all tendencies that feel natural are to be encouraged. In an essay published in 1965, theologian and ethicist Reinhold Niebuhr referred to this tendency as 'tribalism,' and he called it 'the chief source of man's inhumanity to man'. For it seems that our sense of obligation to others often cannot transcend the limits imposed by group affiliation. Niebuhr wrote: 'any distinguishing mark between the "we-group", in which mutual responsibilities are acknowledged, and a "they group", who are outside the pale of humanity, may serve the tribal character of human nature. The distinguishing marks of tribalism may consist of common racial origins, or language, or religion and culture, or class'.

Some may read these words and shrug: 'but if this tendency is just "human nature", perhaps even part of our genetic inheritance, are we not powerless to resist it?' The practitioners of cultural politics will reply: 'the limits of our language need expansion. Try thinking of it this way...'

Try thinking of it like the Spanish intellectual José Ortega y Gasset—not a religious believer—who, in an essay composed around the time that Muhammad Iqbal published his *Reconstruction of Religious Thought*, declared that human beings have no nature, only history, and it is therefore meaningless to set limits to what we can become.

Try thinking of it like Rabbi Jesus, who is remembered to have told a story about a man who had the misfortune to fall among thieves, was beaten, robbed, and left for dead by the roadside. Several of his fellow Jews encountered him, but passed by, pretending not to see. Then a Samaritan—someone many Jews considered 'unclean'—found him, picked him up, and tended to his wounds.

Try thinking of it like the Prophet Muhammad, who is remembered to have said 'blessed are the strangers,' inspiring Ebrahim Moosa 'to reread the past so that the Muslim subject will be able to project the hope...of a future marked by friendship and just coexistence...among a plurality of discursive communities'.

Try thinking of it like the rising generation of Americans, nearly one-third of whom report that they are religiously unaffiliated, and yet who have put their bodies on the line because Black Lives Matter and Palestinians deserve to be free.

And be admonished by words attributed to the second century rabbi Tarfon the Sage: 'it is not your duty to finish the work, but neither are you free to desist from it'.

THE ISIS PRISONS MUSEUM

Anonymous

The simplest of desires can lead to the most terrible of fates. That's what Zahida al-Ahmad found out one night when, exhausted after work, she desired a cigarette. She worked as a cleaner in a hospital in Raqqa, Syria, and she'd just finished a long night shift. Standing alone in the street outside the hospital, she lit up, and filled her lungs. As she smoked, she could hear a vehicle approaching. This, she thought, would be the bus to carry her home.

Next she knew, she was grabbed and forced into the vehicle. It wasn't public transport, she now realised, but a van carrying a patrol of the ISIS Hisba Diwan. Zahida was handcuffed, driven across the city to the working-class Rumaila neighborhood, then pushed from the van into an impromptu prison, where the torments began in earnest. Bearded, masked men in black, Afghan-style clothes harangued and insulted her. They beat her. At one point they beat her hard on her abdomen with a glass cola bottle. Shortly afterwards, she began bleeding. When the bleeding increased, her tormentors sent her back to hospital. There she learned that the beating had caused her to miscarry the baby in her womb. She hadn't even known she was pregnant. In fact she had been praying, and failing, to become pregnant for the previous decade. Her greatest desire had been to have a child. Well, God had finally answered her prayer – and ISIS had murdered the answer.

The year was 2014, and ISIS had seized control of Raqqa and most of the surrounding areas from the coalition of Free Syrian Army and jihadi militias that had freed the city from Assad regime control a year earlier, in March 2013. Raqqa had been the first provincial capital to free itself from the regime. Though it was a questionable liberation – the fighters that chased away Assad's forces were in general not locals, and many were either Iraqis or Syrian jihadists seasoned on Iraqi battlefields – people had high hopes for the future. Civil society had been very active in the preceding months, and had big plans now. But the ISIS takeover stymied all forward movement. Following its victories in Iraq later in 2014, the organisation swept across huge swathes of eastern Syria, capturing hard-won liberated territory upon which to establish a new dictatorship. This served Assad and his foreign backers very well. The Syrian Revolution was defeated by ISIS before it was crushed by Iran and Russia.

Zahida's story, and hundreds of others, are preserved by the ISIS Prisons Museum, a virtual (online) space which documents ISIS crime scenes, puts the crimes in their social, historical, and political context, commemorates the victims, and amplifies the voices of survivors. The project brings together investigative journalism, human rights advocacy, and cutting edge technology. Visitors to the museum will be able to take virtual tours of ISIS prisons and to learn — via text, voiceover, and videoed witness testimony — what happened in each room. The dozens of mass graves that ISIS left across Syria and Iraq will receive similarly thorough treatment. And special investigations will cover topics from the genocide of the Yazidis to the massacre of the Shaitat tribe. The IPM launched in October 2024.

The virtual tours show the prisons as they were when IPM teams first entered them, very soon after they had been abandoned by ISIS. The IPM investigators were looking for colleagues who had disappeared into these prisons. They never found them, but they did find a wealth of documentary material: over 70,000 documents and over fifty laptops left behind by the fleeing fighters. There were handwritten notes, arrest and referral documents, informants' reports, audio recordings of interrogations, circulars, financial records, and other internal correspondence.

The prison buildings themselves were documents. The IPM found names scratched on the walls of what had apparently been cells, as well as lines of scripture or poetry. These were potentially vital clues for those searching for the many thousands of disappeared. But the buildings were bomb-damaged, at risk of collapse or demolition, or were being reclaimed by their owners, and restored. That meant that the evidence inherent in the buildings — the stories told by the walls — was about to dissolve. So IPM photographers used 360 degree photography to record every inch of every room in over fifty buildings used as prisons by ISIS. This photography is the basis of the IPM's 3D tours. Museum visitors see the buildings as they were then, usually sometime in 2017 or 2018, depending on the building. But they can also click on the 'animation' button to see the rooms as they were under ISIS, with detainees crammed into group cells, or closed in the dark of solitary, or being tormented by the investigators. The IPM's picture of what the prisons were like under ISIS is based not only on analysis of the buildings, but also on witness testimony. Thousands of hours of testimony have been filmed. Usually, it involves former prisoners standing or sitting in their former place of detention and describing what happened there.

Like Zahida al-Ahmad, who wanted a cigarette at the end of her shift.

Zahida was detained and beaten in what had been an ordinary home. It was owned by a Kurdish family who had fled the city on ISIS orders. (Though in some areas the organisation had welcomed Kurds into its ranks – indeed the ISIS assault on Kurdish-majority Kobani was led by a Kurd – it ordered all Kurdish civilians to leave Raqqa province once it started losing battles to the so-called Syrian Democratic Forces, whose nucleus was the Kurdish nationalist Democratic Union Party, or PYD – an offshoot of the Turkish-Kurdish PKK.) When ISIS confiscated the house, it barred or blocked the windows and installed cement and metal partitions to separate off solitary confinement cells. There was a men's section and a women's section, an investigations (or interrogation) room, and a room to house a 'sharia' judge.

Rumaila Prison belonged to the ISIS Hisba Diwan. 'Hisba' means something like 'accountability'. In early Islamic polities, the Hisba Diwan concerned itself with regulating commerce in public markets. The *muhtasib* official was responsible for checking that weights and measures were correct. In some cases, he was also charged with maintaining the roads and cemeteries. In the modern period, however, Hisba has been repurposed as a 'morality police' which monitors private behaviour, imposes dress codes and the like. Saudi Arabia's Committee to Promote Virtue and Prevent Vice – now defunct – was a particularly influential example of the phenomenon. The ISIS version, of course, was still more extreme. Its Hisba Diwan was also the mechanism by which it imposed itself on the sections of society which wanted nothing to do with politics. Hisba patrols spread fear, and Hisba informants hidden in the population undermined social cohesion. The Hisba Diwan, therefore, was the chief means by which ISIS established totalitarian rule.

The people detained in Rumaila Prison were accused of a range of 'offences', from shaving to 'sorcery', but most were charged with trading tobacco. In one room, seven men who smuggled and dealt cigarettes were chained together for months on end. This meant that when one of them needed to use the toilet, the others had to go too. In the end, community mediation won their release, in return for enormous fines paid to ISIS. (The organisation's desire for resources surely motivated its bullying of the population as much as its desire for political control. It confiscated homes, cars, gold, weapons, cash and livestock from those it declared criminals or apostates.) Because the seven tobacco traders were released, the IPM has their testimony. They lived to smoke another day – but one nearly died of diarrhea inside. And all had feared they would die.

ISIS prisons, like the streets outside, became laboratories of fear. The guards mounted screens in the group cells on which they broadcast beheadings and executions by shooting, as well as bombings and battle scenes. In some cases, prisoners were obliged to watch videos of fellow prisoners, or neighbours, being murdered in the squares of their home towns. They lived in constant apprehension of being murdered themselves.

One of the tobacco traders was told by his judge: 'I'll behead you, and crucify your corpse for three days, and make your wife and children take photographs'. Another was taken blindfolded to a desert location, was told to say the *shahada*, then felt a gun barrel against the side of his head. The witness – a big man called Talal al-Shuweimi – breaks into tears when he reaches this part of his testimony. Of course, the bullet never came. This was a mock execution – a practice ISIS fighters seemed to enjoy, and one of their gangster-movie innovations on *sharia*.

Syrians tend to be heavy smokers. ISIS banned smoking absolutely, but people kept on smoking, partly because the addiction is so powerful, and partly out of a sense of resistance. Men like Talal al-Shuweimi began dealing tobacco because they'd lost their previous jobs as a result of the revolution and war. Those who bought the cigarettes from men like him, and then sold them in small amounts to consumers, were generally women. To be more specific, they were generally widows and single mothers, or the wives of men who were disabled or who had lost their jobs. In most cases, they had no choice but to sell cigarettes. These unfortunates also found themselves in Hisba prisons, and more often than not in solitary confinement. The witness Shamsa al-Nahar recounts nearly losing her mind in a tiny, filthy, lightless cell, beating her arms against the walls and screaming. The men who'd put her in there – these supposed men of religion – shouted through the metal door that she should seek refuge in reciting the Quran.

The Hisba Diwan had a raging desire to control or frustrate the desires of others. It banned tight trousers and 'infidel' haircuts. It forbade eyebrow plucking and visits to the public baths. It detained men for eating picnics with their female relatives. It stoned women accused of fornication. It threw men accused of homosexuality from high buildings.

Part of this came from an almost colonial desire to educate and discipline the natives. Although plenty of locals joined the organisation, especially once it became the only game in town, plenty of 'muhajir' foreigners did too. The top leadership was largely Iraqi. ISIS looked down on local people, and mocked their culture. In ISIS language, those affiliated with the organisation were 'the brothers', while the rest of society was al-aam, meaning 'the generality' or 'the commoners'. So patrols of foreign young men would arrest, insult, and flog local shopkeepers and householders, while the Hisba Diwan's Women's Division – which employed women from western countries as well as north Africa and the Gulf – monitored, arrested, and often tortured local women for perceived religious shortcomings.

From the ISIS perspective, Raqqawis were either too lax in their religious practice, or the religion they practiced was wrong. Though Salafism had grown in recent decades, the dominant forms of Islam in Raqqa (and elsewhere in Syria) were greatly influenced by Sufism. The Rifaiyya, Qadiriyya, Naqshbandiyya, and Khaznawiyya orders all flourished. But ISIS called Sufis qubouriyeen, or grave-worshippers. It banned Sufi books, used bombs and bulldozers to destroy shrines as well as ordinary people's gravestones, and it detained and tortured those it accused of following Sufi practices. In December 2014, it arrested and executed the prominent Sufi Sheikh Muhammad Tawfiq Ajjan al-Hadid, who was ninety years old. Sheikh Muhammad al-Maght, known in Raqqa for his religious singing, also died in ISIS custody. It seems he died under torture.

For ISIS as for its Iraqi and Syrian Baathist predecessors, the prison system was the central tool of governance. The ubiquity of prisons and the abuses perpetrated within them struck fear throughout society, turning it all into a vast prison. The constellation of prisons housing various target groups occupied every conceivable type of building. A gymnasium was turned into a prison. So was a dam on the River Euphrates. And a traditional family home in Mosul, with domes and vaulted *iwans*. And very many churches.

The Hisba Diwan's headquarters in Raqqa was the Muawiyah School Prison. As the name suggests, the building had served as a secondary school before it was commandeered. ISIS used the bright upstairs rooms for administrative purposes. It turned the dank, airless basement into a torture and detention center. Its Wadi Street Prison was likewise a basement, this one underneath a city centre shopping mall. Hisba patrols would pick people from the crowds for wearing trousers which reached below the ankle, or perhaps for using the phrase 'Ya Muhammad!' to express surprise, then would whisk them downstairs for flogging.

There were prisons specifically for detaining Yazidi women and children. On the walls of one of these, the IPM team discovered drawings scratched by children. The pictures appear to portray the moments when armed men arrived in their villages on pick-ups to abduct them.

There were prisons which belonged to the 'Islamic Police'. This wasn't a 'morality police' like the Hisba Diwan. Instead, it dealt with the kinds of things – like theft, or assault – which police generally deal with.

And then there were the 'security prisons', in which ISIS held those it considered its political or military opposition. These categories covered those suspected of any affiliation with the Assad regime, Syrian opposition factions, the Iraqi government, the Syrian SDF or the Iraqi-Kurdish pershmerga. They included people who kept weapons at home, or who used the internet at home, or who communicated with relatives living in areas beyond ISIS control. They also included members of civil society, such as religious scholars, lawyers or academics, who refused to pledge allegiance to ISIS. And in Iraq they included men and women who were, or were thought to be, Shia Muslims.

The ISIS Prisons Museum website will launch with a focus on the two largest ISIS security prisons – the Stadium Prison, in Syria, and the al-Ahdath, or Juvenile, Prison, in Iraq. That means that each prison will be illuminated by a 3D virtual tour, witness profiles and testimonies, a catalog of relevant documents, and a special investigation into the history and workings of the institution.

The history of the stadium in Raqqa provides a sad commentary on recent Syrian history. The Assad regime designated the land for a sports facility in the 1970s, but for several decades only a perimeter wall was built. Meanwhile the land, which had been on the outskirts of the city, was absorbed by urban sprawl into the centre. Traffic fumes turned the perimeter wall black, which prompted people to call the facility the 'Black Stadium' from its inception. Work on the stadium itself, and on the rooms underneath, finally got underway in 1995. It was finished in 2006, and then a generation of Raqqawis used the place for sports classes and events. When anti-regime protests broke out across the country in 2011, it was closed. When the regime was chased away, revolutionary activists set up a media centre there, but that was almost immediately supplanted by a '*sharia* committee' belonging to Islamist and Jihadi militias. When the militias were chased away, ISIS redesigned and repurposed the rooms under the stadium as 'Point 11' – a name redolent of the Iraqi Baathist *mukhabarat*. The stadium became the largest of all ISIS prisons, and perhaps the most terrible.

The history of al-Ahdath Prison in Iraq is a story of increasing authoritarianism and then social breakdown. The building – in Mosul, near the banks of the Tigris – was built to be an orphanage. A few years afterwards, the orphanage closed and a juvenile detention centre opened instead – *ahdath* means juvenile detention. Juvenile offenders were kept here separate from adults, but in crowded and often insanitary conditions, and at risk of physical and sexual abuse by the guards. Later on, under the Anglo-American occupation and then the new Iraqi government, the juvenile detention centre became a prison for insurgents convicted of terrorism. At one stage extremists flew al-Qaeda flags and played Salafi anthems in the group cells. When ISIS seized Mosul in 2014, the jihadi types who had previously been incarcerated in the prison became the governors. They crammed the cells with retired policemen and army officers, Shia Muslims, and anyone who uttered any criticism of ISIS rule. They tortured these people terribly, and they killed a lot. A 'death squad' arrived in the prison by night to take away men who were never seen again. But ISIS occupation of the Ahdath Prison lasted only forty-two days, until warplanes of the Global Coalition struck it with missiles. Dozens of prisoners were burnt or blasted to death.

Survivors of that prison and others have told the IPM of their terror of Coalition bombing. Once they were locked in an ISIS building, they knew they were tied to a target. But terror of all forms was always all around them, by their captors' design.

At al-Ahdath Prison, if they were holding several members of a family, the 'brothers' would fire bullets nearby one blindfolded detainee, and pretend to have murdered his relatives. At the same site, they told two brothers to choose which one of them would be killed. (The brother without children volunteered, for the sake of his nephews.) At the Stadium Prison, the jailers used to enjoy throwing an orange 'execution suit' into a group cell and leaving, so the men and boys inside would each assume that they would die. On its videos for international release, ISIS used the Guantanamo-style suit to make some kind of anti-imperialist point. But there was no international audience to the execution suit theatrics in the cells, public squares, or anonymous roadsides of Syria and Iraq. Only locals.

People saw other people in orange suits having their throats cut on those screens on the walls of Hisba as well as security prisons. You could arrive in a Hisba prison without any prologue at all. You might be out shopping when suddenly you were grabbed, pushed into a cell and forced to watch beheadings, and then at very least you'd be flogged before your release, however old you were, however young. People lived in constant fear of these imminent nightmares.

The 'brothers' surrendered to, and nourished and cultivated, their raging desire to terrorise; that is, to tyrannise over the emotions of others, to dominate their consciousness to such a monstrous extent. At the Naeem roundabout and public square in Raqqa, people were whipped, shot, and crucified. Hands were amputated. Heads were hacked from bodies and stuck to metal railings for passersby to see. The corporal and capital punishment spectacles were observed by the 'brothers' themselves, but also by nearby shopkeepers and others unlucky enough to be out in the streets, who were rounded up and made to watch. ISIS needed an audience.

Famously, the organisation cared greatly about the media impact it made. It wished to impress the world with its ruthlessness and gangster defiance, both to deter its enemies and to recruit potential friends. When they filmed child executioners, or men with British accents murdering American journalists, they were giving the world media stories that they knew the media would make headline news. They progressed through ever more theatrical displays of savagery until arriving at the spectacular murder of captured Jordanian pilot Muath al-Kasasbeh in January 2015. Kasasbeh was dressed in an execution suit and placed in a cage in the desert. Then he was set alight. His immolation was shot from various angles. The footage was edited and finely produced. Then the video was released onto the internet, and reported on everywhere the next morning.

The ISIS Prisons Museum will not exhibit any ISIS propaganda. Instead it will platform victims, survivors, resistors. This fits with its grassroots origins. Its energy arises from the ferment of Iraqi and Syrian societies in the tumult of civil war and radical change, and specifically from the citizen journalism that took root in both countries. It is motivated by the desire to inform, and it works on the assumption that society, when properly informed of the problems before it, will work to solve those problems.

The simple desire to inform – against solid walls of silence – may be revolutionary in the Syrian and Iraqi contexts. But all of us everywhere need to be informed. Because it's not as if ISIS prisons just dropped from the skies. They morphed out of the prisons that already existed; they grew from a context of interlinking regional and international detention systems. Technologies of oppression travel easily. Methods of torture and surveillance slip through borders and across political lines. Moazzam Begg, a British prisoner in Guantanamo Bay, was threatened by his American captors that they would hand him over to torture by the Syrian regime. Canadian citizen Maher Arar was in fact handed by the US into Syrian custody, where he was tortured underground for over a year.

ISIS learned its methods from the Iraqi and Syrian intelligence services, and from the halls of US occupation prisons. The Iraqi and Syrian regimes learned their methods from Soviet and East German intelligence, and from the Nazis. To add to which the human truth that victims learn from their tormentors in various ways, and often become tormentors themselves.

They feel the desire to turn the tables, which means to do unto others the same as was done to them.

The Sunni identity politics and sectarian extremism of ISIS is to some extent a response to the 'secular' Alawi sectarianism of the Assad regime and the expansionist Shia sectarianism of Iran. Iranian-backed militias had begun their mass expulsion of Syrians before ISIS established its rule, and many Sunni Iraqis failed to resist ISIS when it seized Mosul as much as they might have if they weren't desperate for liberation from the sectarian Iraqi state. ISIS is only one turn in a wheeling cycle of oppression.

The mass graves that the ISIS Prisons Museum is investigating further illustrate the point. In some of them the corpses lie layer atop layer, because Iraqi or Syrian Baathists, Iranian-backed militias, and criminal gangs, as well as ISIS, have all thrown there the results of their crimes. And sometimes there are bodies there that were killed by bombing rather than execution or torture, and whose friends didn't have the time to bury them individually. Some of these bodies were fighters, some were civilians. It's difficult to disentangle the knots.

ISIS itself is a combination of technologies and cultures. A useful explanatory equation is this: Salafi-Jihadism + Baathism = ISIS. It's a formula which works both in theory and practice. Theoretically, ISIS marries the Salafi-Jihadist ideology and rhetoric of al-Qaida to Baathist statecraft. ISIS in power was as ponderously bureaucratic as the Baathist regimes. It built the same kind of mass surveillance state, and ruled, as the Baathists had, by terror, torture, and mass detention. Like the Baathists, ISIS saw opposition as heresy, and responded to any challenge with collective punishments including massacres.

In terms of actual practice, there are direct links between Baathist and ISIS operatives. Very many top-ranking ISIS executives were previously officers in Saddam Hussein's military or security services. And cooperation between Assad's intelligence services and ISIS (and its predecessor, the Islamic State of Iraq) goes back to 2003. The German journalist Christophe Reuter unearthed the documents that proved these connections. He describes, 'a strange relationship ... between Syrian generals, international jihadists and former Iraqi officers who had been loyal to Saddam – a joint venture of deadly enemies, who met repeatedly to the west of Damascus'.

Add to these totalitarian traditions a dash of apocalypticism, as well as some of the more violent elements of twenty-first century global culture, and there you have the makings of ISIS. The influence of horror and action movies and computer combat games and gangster rap, is very strong, as the high-production execution videos demonstrate.

Because the world's prisons interlock and cross-fertilise as surely as its cultures and politics, so the Prisons Museum must embrace the world widely. A section of the website, therefore, will build a library of survivors' accounts of incarceration and torture regionally and globally, so that similarities and distinctions between the prisons may be drawn. This section will include, bit by bit, an essay by Moazzam Begg; one by Houshang Asadi, a leftist once held at Tehran's Evin prison; accounts from Abu Ghraib in the Saddam era; and from Seydnaya and Tadmor in Assad's gulag; and from the prisons of Egypt, Yemen, Morocco, and Israeli-occupied south Lebanon, and more. Most movingly, the French journalist Nicolas Hénin has written for the IPM the first public account of his abduction, imprisonment, and abuse by ISIS. After his release, he wrote a razor-sharp book on Syria – *Jihad Academy* – but he didn't tell his own story. He has told it now at last, at some emotional cost, through the IPM. It's a remarkable piece of writing, crystal clear and painful to read. It describes the human desire of the captive to survive, and break free, and the equally human desire of the captor to hurt and humiliate his victim.

The psychic story of the ISIS phenomenon is a story of desire overflowing in all directions. There's the desire for total control over the streets, and over hearts and minds. There's the desire for revenge. There's the desire to destroy, a Khmer Rouge type lust to erase all that passed before, hence the smashing of museum pieces and the dynamiting of ancient architecture.

That vandalism arises also from the desire to shock. Then there's the desire to accumulate wealth, hence the battles for oil fields before military checkpoints, and the fines and confiscations, and the generalised looting from 'enemy' communities. A desire which energised the little men, perhaps humiliated formerly, who joined the organisation in order to lord it over others, was the desire to upgrade their status, to be somebody. One of the chief Hisba interrogators in Raqqa was a character who called himself Abu Seif. Locals say he was unemployed and known for his problems with drugs before his sudden reincarnation as a guardian of public morals. Audio recordings of his interrogations are kept in the IPM archive. His gratuitously detailed questioning of a man charged with *zina* betrays a good deal of perverted desire. The archive also holds reports made to ISIS by members of the public in which neighbours implicate neighbours, brothers point the finger at brothers, parents at children. These informer reports imply a multitude of petty desires, jealousies, and resentments.

Such are some of the desires that ISIS has worked with. On the other hand sits the IPM's desire to do something positive with all this negative experience. First, the IPM desires, through its investigations, to establish as much of the truth of what happened as it possibly can. Second, it wishes to put the victims, rather than the perpetrators, at the centre of the story, and to amplify the voices of the survivors.

Next, the IPM wishes to assist the survivors, the bereaved, and the relatives of the disappeared to achieve some degree of closure. To this end it is providing a platform – called the Jawab platform – for the families to join up with each other as well as with investigators and legal experts in the search for answers concerning their loved ones. Jawab means 'answer', and the families will have special access to the IPM database. When prisoners scratched their names on walls they were acting on a desire to record their existence before it was snuffed out, and in some cases to communicate with their loved ones across time and the prison walls. In that respect, the IPM is delivering letters.

As the IPM responds to the desire of relatives for knowledge through the Jawab platform, it responds to people's desire for justice by providing a legal tool for international accountability mechanisms. And in Syria and Iraq it serves the desire for a 'national memory' by documenting and analysing the ISIS period, and by putting it in context. In this way it aims to give Syrians and Iraqis a further tool with which to reflect on the calamities that have befallen them.

Finally, the IPM wishes to respond to the desires of journalists, researchers, students, and the general public, for greater understanding of the ISIS phenomenon, and of the Middle East, and of our twenty-first century.

This is a positive set of desires beamed against the walls of the world prison. Because – especially for Syrians and Iraqis – the world remains a prison. Most of the IPM team will be anonymous, for security reasons. ISIS still exists in the shadows, and frequently reaches out of the shadows to assassinate those it disapproves of. The conditions which allowed ISIS to seize power – illegitimate rulers, chronic instability, foreign occupations, traumatising violence, sectarian oppression – all still exist. Nowhere is free of the tyranny that will torture people to death. Which means that all of us to some extent or other are surrounded by walls of fear. And that many of us who are not formally prisoners are nevertheless imprisoned. Some live in Turkey, and these days have to think twice about leaving their rooms – rooms which become cells – for fear of racist mob violence or forced deportation. Syrian and Iraqi refugees are shot at from the walls of Fortress Europe, and imprisoned and abused by Libyan militias or Tunisian police, both funded by the EU. Lebanese authorities deport Syrians back to Syria where Assad often arrests them immediately, then murders them in his prisons.

Finally, Syrians and Iraqis are imprisoned by the imaginations of much of the rest of the world, which insists on seeing them not as human beings but as unwanted migrants, terrorists, CIA-dupes, jihadi savages, and so on. Or which pays attention to them only when they are represented via high-production murder video, or in similar brief bursts, and not with any compassion born of holistic understanding.

We desire to break out of prison, and away from the shadow of prison. We hope the ISIS Prisons Museum will prove a key.

AFTER THE ARAB SPRING

Mohammad El Sahily

Sexual liberties remain one of the most controversial and contested freedoms in the Middle East. Despite the mild normalisation of open expressions of sexuality in popular culture, sexual liberties can never be taken for granted anywhere in the region. The 'debate' concerning sexual liberty flares up in moments of transition or sociopolitical upheaval, the most notable of which was the Arab Spring, and the crushing disappointment that followed as the counterrevolution took hold everywhere.

It would be ahistorical to assume that the regional conversation on sexual liberties, especially coming on the heels of the 1960s sexual revolution and second-wave feminism, only began during the Arab Spring. Intellectuals and activists have debated issues of gender, sexuality, suffrage, and personal liberties since the days of the Arab Nahda (renaissance) which took place in the late nineteenth and early twentieth centuries. At the time, women were among the pioneers of social reform and criticism regarding the state of women's rights, and writings by early Arab feminists highlight a surprisingly progressive streak given the social conservatism of the time.

In contradiction to the mainstream talking point which states that Arab feminist thought developed as a result of European influence during the Nahda, Arab intellectuals of the period, from Mary Ajami and Nazik Al-Abed to Qasim Amin and Butrus Al-Bustani, were pioneers in their calls for female emancipation, primarily through education. In the Levant and Egypt, there was room for intellectual and social debate which did not exist in other parts of the Ottoman Empire. The Empire was already experiencing political and economic decline as it slowly began to lose territory in Europe and North Africa to expanding European colonial empires. As Arab states gradually gained independence from colonial powers, namely the United Kingdom and France, the prevalent cocktail of Arab nationalism and socialism facilitated the gradual (but to some extent incomplete) entrance of women into mainstream society, initially through education and sometimes in the public sector of state-sponsored cultural and social institutions. In the classic top-down approach adopted by the mostly authoritarian states of the region, there were the tidings of a muffled feminism, which was never political and was always attached to the state; whereas in Lebanon there was a civil society movement centered on suffrage and legal equality.

After the Arab defeat in 1967, Arab intellectuals found themselves questioning everything related to their political and social history, recognising that there were regressive aspects of their social makeup that were obstructive to progress. This shift gradually led them in two directions: either towards an intense renunciation of tradition, or to a deeper identification with Islam. This, coupled with the global sexual revolution which began as part of the American counterculture movement, would further push the conversation about emancipation and personal liberties into the mainstream, ensuring that no conversation on social reform could take place without addressing these personal liberties.

As globalisation gradually set in, the Overton window - range of policies acceptable to the majority of citizens - expanded, allowing more discussion regarding personal liberties, and all associated topics such as abortion, rape and harassment legislation, and perhaps most controversially, LGBT rights. As a 'new left', one which centered its political praxis on social justice, began to take shape globally, Arab intellectuals and progressive activists would also join in these currents, ushering in conversations of their own. Initially, these discussions were left to the privacy of homes, muted academic discourse, and the occasional media think piece. This would remain the status quo of expression of sexual liberties and feminism until everything unraveled.

There is perhaps no event as transformative in modern Middle Eastern history, politics, and society as the Arab Spring. Even thirteen years after its start, and after its monumental collapse, it has opened doors for us like no watershed moment in our history has before. In the area of sexual rights and liberties for everyone, we now have more societal input and thought than ever before. What before seemed impossible now appears to be within reach. The transformative juncture we found ourselves in at the start of the protests has changed our lives forever. However, at the critical junctures which Arabs have been faced with several times, this 'hope', which seemed to suddenly rise would just as suddenly dissipate as counterrevolutions introduced new infringements on personal and civil liberties.

While the Arab Spring has altered the public conversation in a plethora of ways, few alterations were as pioneering and groundbreaking as that in the discussion of sexual liberties and feminism. A new generation which came of age during the Arab Spring – in turn inspiring and educating generations to come afterwards – has taught us to be [or find a synonym, to avoid redundancy with 'freedom' unyielding in our pursuit of liberty and freedom], for ourselves and for everyone else. The impact of these implanted ideas, despite everything, will continue to be felt by future generations who won't hesitate to call for liberation.

However, the counterrevolution has imposed new forms of horror and despotism on the individual and society as a whole. We will not dwell on why the counterrevolution won out, but for now, what once appeared possible has been confined to the realm of the imagination, or the impossible. Today Sisi rules Egypt with an iron fist, Saied has suspended the constitution in Tunisia, and Libya is a scene of endless war. As for Syria, the country most bloodied by repression, nearly a million people have died, while Bashar al-Assad remains in place.

Intellectuals, while generally regarded as progressive (at least in the Arab World), have sometimes fueled homophobia and paranoia towards the LGBT community in the region, if not outright homophobia. Take Joseph Massad for example: in his book *Desiring Arabs*, he warned of a 'gay international,' a euphemism he uses to refer to international nongovernmental organisations that are portrayed as introducing 'values' to the region which are either in alignment with colonial or imperial interests, or are meant to cause societal shocks to the region. Massad's postmodern and anti-imperial intellectual arguments have been used by many anti-modernist reactionaries to justify their homophobic arguments.

Another intellectual who may have inspired similar trends, despite being openly gay, is the French philosopher Michel Foucault. When the Iranian Revolution emerged victorious, Foucault traveled to Iran and penned a series of columns which stressed the progressive and anti-imperialist tendencies of Ayatollah Khomeini. This has unfortunately shaped anti-imperialist legitimate aspirations in the same mold as reactionary politics, therefore contributing to viewing LGBT rights as a product of Western imperialism.

In this essay, I strive to do two things: to highlight how the Overton window for the public debate on sexual liberties expanded during and right after the protests which toppled many seemingly invincible Arab tyrants, and how the repression of this conversation became a strategy of the counterrevolution against the Arab Spring. For brevity's sake, I will be focusing on Egypt, Tunisia, and Lebanon. Lebanon might not have been part of the 2011 protests, but it was affected by the wave which engulfed the region, not to mention having a loud and vibrant activist culture of its own.

Let's start with Tunisia, where the first protests broke out. After Mohammad Bouazizi set himself on fire to protest harsh living conditions, protests erupted demanding the removal of Zine el-Abidine Bin Ali, who had ruled for the previous two decades. Decades of corruption, state violence, economic decline, and policing of civil society were contested in Tunisian streets. Gradually, the domino effect spread to Libya, Egypt, Syria, and nearly all other Arab countries.

Tunisia's 17 December 2010 uprising was a moment of liberation from a very long-lasting dictatorship, and it brought with it a mass of feminist demands. Its main slogan – 'Work, Freedom, Respect' – was chanted in the streets by women of all ages, because the revolution was a mixed, secular uprising supported by young female bloggers and human rights activists from different generations. The uprising broke out in the public sphere and altered the country's fate, leading to the issuance of a new constitution, adopted on 27 January 2014 by the National Constituent Assembly.

Tunisia's democratic transition enabled Islamists to return to the scene after they had been pushed aside from power for a long period by Bin Ali. Restoring their political legitimacy necessitated the establishment of a political duality in which secularists and advocates of political Islam confronted each other. This battle would appear during the formation of the National Constituent Assembly (November 2011 – January 2014) in a parliament dominated by the Ennahda Movement (Islamists) The idea of relying on *sharia* as a source of law returned strongly during the formulation of the new Basic Law. This laid the way for one of the largest crises that Tunisia's parliament would ever experience, when in August 2012 Ennahda representatives proposed an article on 'complementarity' between women and men that clearly contradicted the principle of gender equality. This mobilised components of civil society, causing women and men to flock in large numbers to the city centre of Tunis on 13 August, Tunisian Women's Day (and the anniversary of the adoption of the Personal Status Law), to protest the initiative. In the face of these popular objections, the majority withdrew its project from parliament.

The final version of the constitution sided with equality between men and women (Article 21). However, there were still many gray areas: the choice of words was quite vague and highly politicised, and the variations in expression left the room open to manipulate the principle of equality, which was still incomplete. This 'incomplete' equality must be linked to the 'original ambiguity' that Tunisian political culture has directed towards women since the nineteenth century.

In parallel, the issue of parity has advanced significantly in Tunisia, and the issue of equality in inheritance is still on the table after a draft law was submitted to the House of People's Representatives by President Beji Caid Essebsi, in August 2019, but it has not been approved to date. In the end, Tunisian women were able to obtain an organic law related to the abolition of violence against women, which the Tunisian Parliament voted for on 26 July 2017. This was the result of a long battle that feminist activists had fought for more than twenty years. Thus, Tunisia has become the only Arab country that has such legislation, and the nineteenth country in the world that consolidates the fight against violence against women through law.

In 2019, Qais Saied was elected president, and it was assumed that a judge would generally continue to propagate the semi-liberal status quo. However, in an interview he gave after his victory to the National Challenge, he made statements in which he urged citizens to respect traditions in public, while they were free to conduct themselves however they pleased in their private spaces. He also made a joke concerning gay relationships: 'does a man agree to another man coming to ask for his son's hand in marriage?' Thus far, there has not been any targeted campaign against either women or the LGBT community, even as Tunisia continues to regress into a police state, after Saied's suspension of the constitution in 2021.

The bloody and brutal outcome of the revolution in Egypt, meanwhile, leaves no room for doubt that the big dreams raised by millions of demonstrators in Tahrir Square in January 2011 through the slogan 'Bread,

Freedom, Social Justice' have turned into terrifying nightmares. All members of society are affected, and progressive feminist movements are still experiencing shock and witnessing a regression in which previous achievements are called into question. Still, the Egyptian state is not actively repressing women, but has focused on the LGBT community instead, in an attempt to attract conservative popular support.

The Egyptian revolution of 2011 began on 25 January, a date chosen by Egyptian youth to coincide with the annual Police Day as an uprising against increasing police brutality under President Hosni Mubarak. The eighteen-day uprising ousted Mubarak after he had spent nearly thirty years in power, and ushered in a brief era in which Egyptians were able to enjoy expanded freedom of expression. The spirit of progress and the realisation of the possible was palpable – the pulse of the street was felt throughout Egypt, including by some of the most marginalised groups in society, including gay Egyptians.

Today, however, many Egyptians feel like they cannot breathe. They are suffocating under the brutal repression of NGOs, independent media, and any alternative voices that challenge the status quo. Since President Abdel Fattah al-Sisi seized power in the 2013 coup, waves of mass arrests in Egypt have targeted journalists, human rights lawyers, academics, and the LGBT community. However, it is a mistake to assume that the democratically-elected Morsi presidency was any better in terms of women's rights and LGBT rights.

Under Mohammad Morsi, there was an increasing proliferation of Islamist rhetoric, especially concerning social and cultural issues. Islamists believed that one of the positive effects of the Arab revolutions was their weakening of 'Westernised' feminist movements, which is the term used by fundamentalist Islamic movements to refer to Arab feminism. This belief stems primarily from the fact that Islamic movements expanded their influence during the revolutions, as in Syria and Libya, as well as from the transformation of the Arab Spring from its promising civil, democratic beginnings to dominance by traditional, Islamist, and counter-revolutionary forces. This alarming expansion of Islamist influence in society, despite remaining within the realm of rhetoric, led the large majority of 2011-era revolutionary society to tacitly endorse the Sisi coup of 2013, a decision which would prove to be a mistake of historic proportions.

The hope of 'progress' did not last long. One of the earliest signs of state-sponsored repression against 'suspicions of moral degeneration' was when the Ministry of Interior's morality police raided a bathroom in central Cairo on 7 December 2014, after a similar raid in October 2013. In both cases, they charged homosexuals with 'debauchery'. The authorities also announced the closure of a café on charges of 'practicing Satanism', and al-Azhar, the Ministry of Youth, and the Ministry of Religious Endowments issued a joint statement launching a national strategy to combat atheism. These are only the most visible symptoms of a relentless effort to reimpose the state's moral authority in the eyes of public opinion.

These developments alarmed Egyptian liberals, many of whom had hoped that the ouster of President Morsi would illustrate the need to curb the illiberal influence of Islamists and pave the way for a more secular Egyptian society. Supporters of military control claimed that the Muslim Brotherhood sought to impose their backward doctrine on various aspects of life. But in retrospect, it became clear that the Morsi administration had not launched a new, ultra-conservative era in Egypt. Instead of imposing moral strictures derived from a conservative reading of Islamic standards, the Brotherhood limited its activity in this context to the educational field, with some interventions in artistic and media production.

Courts in Egypt have defined 'debauchery' as sex between members of the same sex, whether in exchange for money or not, although the law originally concerned prostitution. Drawing on exclusive access to police documents, a report by DAWN MENA last year showed how police in Egypt and violent gangs use the same tactics, setting up encounters on false pretences using dating apps to target, harass, and abuse LGBT people.

The texts from dating apps that DAWN obtained prove that some of the detainees were just looking for love, or even new friendships online. Clear patterns emerge in these texts, as police often attempt to force their victims to agree to exchange sex for money to help them prove a 'paid sex' charge linked to debauchery. But there are also police reports in which there is no mention of any financial dealings. In recent years, NGOs in Egypt have focused on protecting the rights of LGBT people who have been forced to work underground or in exile, but fragile support networks within the community remain.

Perhaps no case illustrates the Egyptian state's repression of the LGBT community better than that of Sarah Hegazy. When the Lebanese band Mashrou' Leila performed in Cairo in 2017, Sarah and tens of others raised rainbow flags during the concert, attracting significant media coverage. Sarah and dozens of other attendees were arrested and held for an extended period under harsh conditions. Sarah reported that she was tortured by police, who also asked other female detainees to abuse her. After her release, she was fired from her job. She eventually managed to flee Egypt for Canada, where she suffered from post-traumatic stress disorder and panic attacks that intensified after her mother's death. That seemed to be the end of Sarah's tragedy, but another devastating chapter followed. In June 2020, Sarah committed suicide.

By banning public discussion of gender and sexual orientation in society, the Egyptian government is effectively ensuring that these concepts remain taboo and, at the same time, a welcome distraction from the broader and protracted crisis most Egyptians are experiencing under Sisi's regime. The state is able to maintain a false narrative that LGBT rights are merely a Western tool to corrupt and even delegitimise its religious and national authority.

Arguably the most liberal (socially and politically) Arab country, Lebanon was seen as a bastion of personal liberties and sociocultural progress. In the three decades before the civil war of 1975, Lebanon was the closest place to a zone of cultural and social liberty in the Middle East, surrounded by a sea of repressive regimes and political instability. This has made the debate on personal liberties, especially sexual liberties, much easier and more versatile than in other Arab countries, despite the public being conservative in its large majority. While Lebanon was not part of the 2011 protests, it experienced an uprising of its own in 2019, one which subsequently failed, at a significant moral and sociopolitical cost.

What was novel in Lebanon's 17 October protests was that it took a personal dimension for women, who have suffered historic institutional and societal discrimination for the longest time. We saw women confronting with their bodies (bodies which, before the revolution, were the reason for their persecution) the attacks of the 'shabbiha' (thugs) of the ruling parties, and we saw how they stood as a human barrier in front of the military to protect the men of the revolution, contrary to the stereotypical social concept. The protests which swept the country from the north to the south were dominated by women – on the platforms, in the tents set up in the squares, in the media, in the chants, and leading the demonstrations, women took the lead, and were able to minimise the possibility of the protests turning to violence. In the Lebanese Women's Candlelight March, we witnessed how Lebanese women rushed into the streets spontaneously. Without waiting for anyone's signal to start, they held candles in one hand and pots in the other. The symbols were to teach us that this being who came out of the kitchen has the ability to illuminate the darkness of the entire world.

The Lebanese women in the revolution revolted alongside the man, and at the same time they revolted against their oppression. The squares witnessed marches of mothers demanding their right to pass on their nationality to their sons and daughters, women who spoke about gender discrimination in politics and the economy, and women who spoke of their personal torment due to the deeply unjust civil status laws governing marriage, divorce, domestic violence, and custody.

The Lebanese revolution also represented an opportunity for a large number of mothers of the Shia sect to make their voices heard, after they had been stifled by the laws of Ja`fari courts and Shiite society. This society often sanctifies masculinity and enshrines in people's minds the image of the heroic man and the subservient woman who must accept crumbs of rights.

However, as the Lebanese elite re-asserted itself, women's voices were actively ignored. No genuine demands were ever met, and the political elite, figuring that actively obstructing women's rights activists would be problematic, simply ignored them, assuming that patriarchal social norms would eventually reassert themselves. True to form, we have seen rising crimes against women, blatant cases of rape, domestic violence, custody denial, and general discrimination across the board. To distract from their failures, the Lebanese political and religious authorities turned to the next weak link in Lebanese society: the LGBT community.

Human Rights Watch (HRW) released a video report titled *If Not Now, When?,* describing the empowerment the LGBT community felt when the protests erupted. The report conveyed stories of hope and solidarity told by queer women and trans people participating in the protests. By taking their struggle to the streets, through chants, graffiti, and public debate,

LGBT people have moved their rights from the margins to the centre of discourse in a country where same-sex relationships are punishable by up to one year in prison, and trans people face structural discrimination.

For queer and trans people, walking the streets of Lebanon requires a process of self-censorship, as they are forced to hide their identities in their daily lives. Less than a month before the demonstrations began, a conference on gender and sexuality that had been held annually in Lebanon since 2013 was moved outside the country for the first time, following the General Security's attempt to stop the 2018 session. The General Security also prevented non-Lebanese LGBT activists who attended the 2018 conference from re-entering the country indefinitely.

Despite steps taken during the protests and by the emergent activist class to accept LGBT rights in society, LGBT people will continue to live on the margins as long as the Lebanese government maintains Article 534 of the Penal Code, which punishes same-sex relationships. The government is yet to enact legislation that protects LGBT people from discrimination and upholds their fundamental rights to dignity, bodily autonomy, socio-economic mobility, and the freedoms of expression, association, and assembly.

In June 2022, Lebanese authorities illegally prevented peaceful gatherings of lesbian, gay, bisexual, and transgender people. The ban violates LGBT people's constitutional rights to equality, freedom of expression, and free assembly, as well as Lebanon's obligations under international law, and comes during an economic crisis and in a deteriorating climate for LGBT rights in the country. Interior Minister Bassam al-Mawlawi sent an urgent message to the Directorates of Internal Security and General Security instructing them to ban any gatherings aimed at 'promoting homosexuality'. The letter includes very vague and broad reasons, and does not mention any legal basis for determining that these gatherings violate 'customs and traditions' and 'the principles of heavenly religions'. The Minister of the Interior said that this decision came after the ministry received 'communications from religious authorities rejecting the spread of this phenomenon'.

Such obstructions conflict with Lebanese jurisprudence on same-sex relations as well as with international human rights law. In July 2018, a Lebanese appeals court issued a groundbreaking ruling that same-sex sexual conduct is not illegal, and dropped charges against people under Article 534 of the Penal Code, which criminalises 'all sexual intercourse contrary to nature'. The judges condemned the law's discriminatory interference in people's private lives and declared that homosexuality was not against nature. The ruling came after four lower court rulings since 2009 that had refused to convict gay and transgender people under Article 534.

In 2021, during the Universal Periodic Review at the UN Human Rights Council, Lebanon approved recommendations to guarantee the right to peaceful assembly and expression for LGBT people. The Lebanese Constitution guarantees freedom of expression 'within the scope of the law'. The International Covenant on Civil and Political Rights, which Lebanon ratified in 1972, stipulates that every individual has the right to freedom of expression and freedom of assembly and association. The UN Human Rights Committee, which interprets the covenant, has clearly stated that it prohibits discrimination on the basis of sexual orientation and gender identity in the application of any of the rights protected by the treaty, including freedom of expression, assembly and association.

However, the establishment was much more aggressive. Hezbollah Secretary General Hassan Nasrallah launched a social and cultural battle against the LGBT community in Lebanon, considering it a battle that goes beyond 'a party or a sect', to 'a battle for all of society, Muslims and Christians', stressing 'the necessity of confrontation by all means'. This public speech by a cleric who is considered the primary political actor in the country, and the mandate to his followers to act against what he described as homosexuality without specifying how to do so, gave a religious, political, and societal cover for the violence practiced against the community. On the ground this translated to bullying, verbal and physical violence, and even murder attempts.

Later that summer, in August 2023, a group calling itself Jnoud el-Rab attacked a Beirut night club called Madame Om when it was hosting a drag show. Had it not been for the reluctant arrival of the security forces, visitors to the club would have been harmed. Jnoud El Rab is a nascent Christian group which claims to be on a mission to purify society and rid it of 'maladies'.

In the Middle East, sexual liberties have long been the punch bag of social and political upheaval. Given the unfortunate conservatism of society, it is hard to advance progressive visions for people's liberty to live their lives as they choose, when the pace and possibility of political change are fragile, unpredictable, and likely to run into extreme pushback, if not outright repression. One thing we should understand, however, is that the personal is not insulated from the openness of a society, but is rather inextricably linked to it. The depoliticisation of basic human rights leads to their absence from national conversations about enacting political change. Had it not been for the courage of thousands of individuals, who had the will and imagination to dream of a future in which they can live their truth in a region like ours, the conversation on sexual liberties would not even see the light of day.

What many people fail to realise, unfortunately, is that liberty is not a one-time concept to be projected on what we deem to be socially acceptable. Our intellectuals have failed to properly communicate the universality of liberty, and its importance as an eternally applicable principle, if not the primary principle, in the construction of a democratic society. There is always a strange willingness to compromise on liberties deemed inappropriate, anachronistic, or incompatible with the 'public mood', or even mildly offensive or critical of long held traditions. This is an abject failure of Arab political opposition movements.

DISGUISES AND DESIRES

Boyd Tonkin

Constructed out of steel rings, two giant human figures – one male , one female – stand on the seafront. Periodically, the two halves of this eerie outsize couple, each eight metres tall, move slowly towards each other. Briefly, the rings interlock and the figures fuse. Then, inexorably, they glide apart again.

Forever united, forever divided, this pair of metal lovers has since its installation in 2010 become one of the best-loved, and most photographed, landmarks in the resort and port of Batumi on the Black Sea coast of Georgia. As I watched their stately dance of coupling and parting, a steady stream of young visitors (several head scarved women among them) posed for phone snaps in front of the mobile artwork. Once ruled by medieval Georgian dynasties, then by the Ottoman, Russian, and Soviet empires, Batumi now welcomes crowds of tourists and investors from across its region. Already a hub for Black Sea trade and naval power, the port became the terminus of the Transcaucasian Railway in 1883 and, in 1907, the end-point of the oil pipeline from Baku on the Caspian and a crucial conduit for Tsarist (and later Soviet) black gold. In the old town, neo-classical villas, churches and palaces remember Imperial Russia's heyday as colonial overlord. But no one culture has ever monopolised Batumi; today, Muslims still account for about a quarter of the city's people. Lined with show-off hotels and apartment blocks built by Emirati or Turkish developers, the seaside promenades increasingly resemble a lusher offshoot of Dubai.

Georgian artist Tamara Kvesitadze originally created her 'kinetic sculpture' for the Venice Biennale. In Batumi, its booming popularity as an Instagram-friendly backdrop has made it her best-known piece. 'The main message my work conveys,' she has said, 'is that being together is possible for only a little time'. Desire endures, but union does not. On this spot where conflict and rivalry has for centuries pushed people together and then pulled them apart (across the Black Sea's waters, Russia wages war in Ukraine), this monumental but tender image of fragile longing touches hearts as public sculpture seldom does.

What is the work called? Kvesitadze first entitled it simply 'Man and Woman'. Soon, though, it picked up another name. Someone dubbed it 'Ali and Nino' and the appellation stuck. Diplomatically, the artist told the BBC World Service that 'people have their own very nice versions' of the figures' identity. Now, whatever her intentions, it has turned into a tribute to the favourite romance of the modern Caucasus: a tale of two lovers divided by faith and clan but drawn together by irresistible desire, and separated only by the fatal shocks of war.

Popular consensus has determined that these circling steel colossi should commemorate a love story that, in the southern Caucasus and far beyond, has come to vie with other classic narratives of boundary-crossing passion: Romeo and Juliet and, more pertinently, Layla and Majnun. (The great Persian poet Nizami Ganjavi, who around 1190 wrote the most influential epic version of the love-maddened Majnun's longing for the unattainable Layla, came from Ganja, not far from Georgia's southern border with Azerbaijan.) Ali and Nino's mutual longing has taken its place, in this part of the world, as an equally legendary instance of undying love pursued against the grain, and across the lines.

However, in the lovers' hinterland lies a stranger, more elusive tale about stories of desire – and the stories we desire. This now-proverbial affair dates not, like Layla and Majnun's, to seventh-century Arabia, nor, like Romeo and Juliet's, to sixteenth-century Italy, but to no earlier than 1937. In that year a novel entitled *Ali and Nino* appeared, in German, from a publisher in Vienna. Set mainly in Baku on the Caspian Sea, between 1914 and 1920, but with episodes that take place in Persia, Georgia, and Dagestan, the novel is narrated by a young Azerbaijani nobleman, Ali Khan Shirvanshir. Ali, a Muslim, recounts his love for a Georgian, Christian girl, Nino Kipiani. He recalls the growth of their love and their adventures before, during, and after the First World War. The conflict shatters cosmopolitan Baku, convulses the Caucasus with political and ethnic strife, gives birth to a short-lived republic in Azerbaijan, but eventually results in the Soviet Russian seizure of these oil-rich territories. Ali dies defending the bridge at Ganja (Nizami's home town) from the invading

Bolsheviks, with this testament of enduring love recovered from his bullet-ridden body.

The author's name on the title page was 'Kurban Said', an attribution which still features on editions available today. *Ali and Nino* did not cross into English until 1970, after the translator, Jenia Graman, had come across a copy by chance on a Berlin bookstall. Legal documents, however, had identified the author as 'Baroness Elfriede von Ehrenfels'. Other editions ascribed the work to one 'Essad Bey', ostensibly a German-language writer of Azeri origins. Much loved in Azerbaijan itself, *Ali and Nino* has acquired in that country another supposed progenitor: a writer named Yusif Vazir Chamanzaminli, who apparently perished in Stalin's Gulag in 1943. Those who trust Wikipedia, for instance, will read there that Vazir is the 'primary core author' of *Ali and Nino*.

Many people, many interests, have claimed a stake in this classic romance over the eighty-seven years of its existence. It's not hard to understand why. Captivating, picturesque, action-packed, the story brims with hypnotic evocations of culture, custom, and location – not just in Baku itself, but the forests, deserts, mountains, seas, and cities of the territories surrounding it. Asia and Europe, Islam and Christianity, 'East' and 'West' meet in a galloping dream of desire, sensuality and, ultimately, violence across a gorgeously imagined Caucasian paradise. This 'bridge between the two worlds', where creeds and cultures meet, spar – and love – without consuming one another, is depicted on the brink of its extinction. One, Armenian, character thinks of the Caucasus as a kind of beneficent crossroads, 'receiving from East and West, and giving to both'.

Later, during a short postwar period of British military control in Baku, a veteran diplomat tells Ali that 'it is a great pity to see the old solid forms of oriental culture crumble'. *Ali and Nino* turns those crumbling forms into a lavish, bejewelled, fast-moving pageant: a story of desire between doomed star-crossed lovers, but also of desire for a world of unity-in-diversity that had ceased to exist – and maybe never did exist. Questions of authenticity aside, *Ali and Nino* has gained the status of a sort of 'national novel' in Azerbaijan.

However, the book was not written by Yusif Vazir Chamanzaminli, nor by Elfriede von Ehrenfels, nor by anyone called 'Kurban Said'. And if a certain 'Essad Bey' did stand behind the novel, that's only because the real author chose that imposing title as his long-term pseudonym when he began to publish articles and books in Weimar-era Berlin. Kurban Said, and Essad Bey, was the journalist, historian, and novelist Lev Nussimbaum, born in Baku to Jewish parents and (after 1922) a Muslim by conversion. Nussimbaum/Essad Bey, as part of his wholehearted self-invention, claimed to be the offspring of a Muslim nobleman of Turkish and Persian ancestry and a Russian aristocrat. In reality, Abraham Nussimbaum – one of the many businessman with Russian papers who made a tidy fortune from prewar dealing in Baku's oil – was born in Tbilisi, Georgia. His family had moved there from Ukraine. As for Lev's mother, Berta Slutzkin, she came from the 'Pale of Settlement' for Russian Jews in today's Belarus.

The investigative writer Tom Reiss has explored and explained Lev Nussimbaum's origins and career beyond reasonable doubt, first in a 1999 *New Yorker* article and then in his 2005 biography *The Orientalist*. Born in 1905, Nussimbaum spent his childhood in Baku, where oil derricks and Russian imperial monuments flanked an ancient Azeri-Persian city which Lev wandered spellbound, as if in an enchanted labyrinth. The family fled during the post-revolutionary years of chaos. Azerbaijan's infant republic stumbled, and Turkish and British military hegemony gave way to Soviet domination until 1991.

Lev's mother took her own life in still-mysterious circumstances. Her death became a family taboo. Lev and Abraham moved briefly to Turkestan, then Persia, then Istanbul, then Paris, and finally, in 1921, Berlin. Precocious and persuasive, armed with the adaptive gift he lends to the fictional Ali ('a monkey's instinct for languages and dialects'), Lev became a prolific journalist and 'expert on the East' for *Die Literarische Welt*: the eminent review whose pages Nussimbaum shared with writers such as Walter Benjamin.

Even as a schoolboy at Berlin's Russian gymnasium, he had enrolled for classes in the university's Seminar for Oriental Languages. He joined Islamic societies and, in 1922, formally converted in the presence of the Turkish embassy's resident imam. Reiss points out that his declaration took place during the final months of the Ottoman Empire, which he nostalgically revered, and the Caliphate. Thus he 'traded one dying identity – son of a Jewish cosmopolitan from Baku – for another'. As the House of

Osman fell, the rising ethnic nationalism of Muslim circles in Berlin quickly, and predictably, repelled him.

'Essad Bey' wrote fast and fluently. In 1929, *Blood and Oil in the Orient* mingled memoir with political analysis: its colourful, idiosyncratic evocations of Baku clearly presage *Ali and Nino*. Some fifteen further books followed. They ranged from potboiler biographers of Lenin and Stalin (about whom, in 1932, he harboured no illusions; his subtitle is 'the career of a fanatic') to books about the oil business ('Liquid Gold'), Tsar Nicholas ll, Reza Shah, White Russian exiles, and even a life of Muhammad. After the Nazi takeover in 1933, Nussimbaum left Berlin for Vienna, and lived for a short time in New York with his American in-laws. In 1932, he married Erika Loewendahl, whose Leipzig-born (Jewish) father had become boss of the Bata shoe firm in Berlin.

The marriage soon foundered in gossip and scandal. 'Essad Bey', treated as an 'authentic' voice of the opaque and turbulent Muslim Middle East (which, in so many ways, he was), had become a celebrity pundit whose triumphs and mishaps snared headlines in Berlin and – for a while – New York. In 1931, the exiled Leon Trotsky had asked in a letter 'Who is this Essad Bey?' (Trotsky, born Lev Bronstein, was no stranger to self-disguise.) He returned to Vienna, where friendship with the Baroness and her husband (also a Muslim by conversion) allowed Elfriede Ehrenfels to act as a front-woman for the work of Lev Nussimbaum in Nazi Germany, and to collect royalties on his behalf.

In 1938, this inveterate border-jumper made his final crossing, to Positano on the Bay of Naples in Mussolini's Italy. There, a few weeks short of his thirty-seventh birthday, he died in September 1942 – near-penniless, deprived of proper medical care, almost forgotten – after agonising complications from Raynaud's syndrome had caused progressive necrosis in his legs. In his last years the supreme literary cosplayer had even hoped to write an approved biography of Mussolini: a quixotic plan hatched just as the Fascist dictator, who had stubbornly resisted anti-Semitism for years, decided at Hitler's behest to play along with Nazi racial ideology. In Positano, neighbours referred to – and remembered – him simply as 'the Muslim'. That would have pleased Essad Bey.

Reiss's sleuthing in Baku brought him into contact with a police agent, and enthusiast for local history, named Fuad Akhundov, a devotee of *Ali and*

Nino who reported that 'this novel made me discover my country' and 'the whole world that lay beneath my feet, buried by the Soviet system'. Many Azeris feel the same, even if official media enthusiastically endorse Yusif Vazir Chamanzaminli's unlikely role in the book's genesis. In 2011, an entire edition of *Azerbaijan International* magazine championed the Vazir attribution.

Little about these far-fetched claims withstand independent scrutiny. Lev Nussimbaum/Essad Bey/Kurban Said might have been a scavenger, a parasite, an impersonator, a great pretender; as Reiss puts it, 'an ideological Houdini... a racial and religious cross-dresser in a decade when race and religion were as fixed as a death sentence'. (And then became an actual death sentence: Abraham Nussimbaum probably died in the Treblinka extermination camp after deportation in 1941.) But Lev certainly wrote *Ali and Nino*.

This is a story about desire: not just the allure of a transgressive romance in which permeable barriers between faiths and cultures nurture both mutual attraction between lovers, and the obstacles that sharpen that longing, but the desire of readers for paradigmatic tales that give voice to their own needs and wishes. Azeri nationalists evidently find in *Ali and Nino* a model portrait of sumptuously rich local customs and traditions – from music to poetry to hospitality – menaced by war and change but still founded securely on an Islamic base. For neighbouring and faraway admirers, in Georgia and beyond, the book hymns the virtues of hybridity and convergence. Nino, the daughter of the Georgian, Christian 'woods', finds fulfilment with Ali, son of the Muslim 'desert'. 'I love woods and meadows,' she tells him, 'and you love hills and stones and sand'. Together they may forge an idyllic geography; a fruitful landscape of inter-cultural harmony. Nino is pregnant by the time of Ali's death.

For readers outside the Caucasus, the true author's progress through names, masks, and identities may now serve as a source of attraction in itself. Nussimbaum the protean shape-shifter emerged from, and celebrated, a city that flourished (in Reiss's words) 'beyond rigid ideologies and religions for a thousand years'. Later, he would come to imagine 'the Muslim and the Jew united in their struggle against the West and its mass violence'. As a chameleon storyteller whose life and work alike deny 'essentialist' categories, Nussimbaum may also look in hindsight like a forerunner for the sort of creative many-sidedness that now appeals as a challenge to communitarian dogmas. 'Kurban Said', that genius of heartfelt and idealistic masquerade, can himself be an object of attraction for refugees from the prison of politicised 'identity'.

Was Nussimbaum a hoaxer, and does *Ali and Nino* count in some sense as an imposture and a fraud? As Reiss argues, the novel's author 'thrived on hiding in plain sight. The whole point of his secret was that it wasn't really a secret.' In Berlin, many friends and colleagues knew that Lev Nussimbaum had become 'Essad Bey' and built a literary career under that flag. Enemies and sceptical reviewers could attack him (and did) for being too Jewish, too Muslim, too 'Eastern', too 'Western', too Russian or too German. *Blood and Oil in the Orient* had made him 'the *bête noire* of a loose association of anti-Semites and Muslim nationalists'. Later books often provoked a ritual unmasking of this 'story swindler' who seemed to change cultures as others did their shoes.

In a deathbed manuscript that Reiss found, a fictionalised memoir entitled *The Man who Knew Nothing about Love*, Nussimbaum describes his 'wretched life' as 'typical for our days and our time, for this time of upheaval and cataclysm'. Regarding the exchange and multiplication of aliases, he was certainly correct. Through the twentieth century, as ideologies of ethnic exclusion in Europe and Asia forced long-settled communities to flee their homes, millions adopted masks simply to stay alive. Essad Bey may have converted necessity into a profession, but he also swapped personae as an act of defiance, a refusal to let the world 'put him in the cage of its latest modern barbarity': a unitary identity. The 'Kurban Said' who published *Ali and Nino* in 1937 was indeed a Baku-born Muslim (since 1922) steeped in the life and lore of old Azerbaijan. He was also the Ashkenazi Jewish Lev Nussimbaum, child of the Russian imperial twilight.

Besides, it takes two – or two million – to tango. In literature especially, cases of so-called 'hoaxes' or impostures often reveal a willingness among readers (not to mention publishers, agents, and critics) to join and sustain the game. In fiction, in autobiography, and in various branches of 'autofiction' that blend memoir and invention, we seek access to distant worlds – of place, of class, or belief or of experience – guaranteed by some stamp of authenticity. Even in made-up narratives, readers supposedly crave the truth: the truth of a congruence between the nature of the story and the nature of the author. This 'autobiographical pact' only emerged, in the nineteenth century, as fiction both rose in its social and artistic status and became associated with sincere self-expression by known individuals. In the age of traditional storytelling, few cared about unique creative identities. A hoary classicists' joke tells of a scholar who proudly announced his discovery that the *Iliad* and *Odyssey* were composed not by Homer but by another poet of the same name.

Impersonations and performances crowd the bookshelves. They range from the hugely influential 'Ossian' poems of the 1760s, when James Macpherson maintained that he had translated ancient Gaelic bardic verse that he had himself composed, to outright frauds such as the forged 'Hitler Diaries', and innumerable confected memoirs, such as James Frey's fake addiction testimony *A Million Little Pieces*. For three centuries, literary culture for a broad public has prized the authority of individual selfhood but at the same time bred an insatiable appetite for fictions of every variety. Ventriloquism – the ability to express the voice and being of others – lies at the heart of the literary enterprise. Yet modern personhood (including the personhood of authors) requires stability, solidity, and continuity. From this bed of contradictions bloom a hundred doubtful and disputed flowers.

In well-developed publishing milieux, this double scale of value inevitably operates as a breeding-ground for frauds, masquerades, or hoaxes. When the demand for 'authentic' first-person accounts of dramatic or extreme experience exceeds the supply, the ranks of impersonators may enjoy a bonanza. Hence the alarming, but illuminating, proliferation of fake Holocaust memoirs after the 1980s, when the numbers of actual survivors able to call out impostures and inventions began to diminish. The most flagrant examples, such as Binjamin Wilkomirski's *Fragments: Memoirs of a Wartime Childhood* (1995), sometimes put the author's actual plight into a fictional, camp-based form. Wilkomirski really had been traumatised by childhood abuse in Switzerland that had nothing to do with Nazi genocide. The publishing business had created a template for reported early suffering that commanded universal respect and attention. So he made his singular misery fit the bill.

Publishing hoaxes endlessly surface, and endlessly fascinate. As the literary editor for a national newspaper, I understood that only a few kinds of book-related story would have news editors clamouring for an article to run on the front page. Almost more than celebrity kiss-and-tell titles, rumours of million-pound advances, or bitter feuds between prize-winning literati, hints of a hoax got the newsdesk adrenaline flowing fast. Readers evidently enjoyed these pieces. I concluded that some of this delight stemmed from a suspicion that the entire literary racket amounted to a scam, fraud, or con of some kind: an ancient judgment that possibly dates back, beyond religious objections to made-up stories, to Plato's rejection of art (in the *Republic*) as deception and distraction from the truth.

At the same time, a curious ambivalence came into play. The unmasking of a literary stunt, either by detective work or an insider's disclosures, often led to ritual punishment and penitence – as when Oprah Winfrey, who had raved about Frey's counterfeit confession, then righteously flayed him on her TV sofa. However, exposure alone frequently failed to kill an ostensibly fraudulent or deceptive book. *A Million Little Pieces* still enjoys scores of glowing reviews on Amazon. As does *The Education of Little Tree*, the entirely fabricated 'memoir' of a Cherokee upbringing published in 1976 by 'Forrest Carter' but written by a former white supremacist and Ku Klux Klan member, Asa Earl Carter. As does *Sarah* by 'JT LeRoy', the white-trash hillbilly sex-worker persona sustained for years by Brooklyn artist Laura Albert; she even had a friend repeatedly act in public as LeRoy. In these and multiple other cases, readers' desire for plausible, dramatic, and moving stories from exotic lands – psychological, cultural, sexual – outlived the shame of unveiling. The temporary disgrace of a hoax's revelation need not mean permanent oblivion.

Lev Nussimbaum never put in any performance on that scale. By 1937, he indisputably counted as an Azeri-born Muslim. So it's hard to classify 'Kurban Said' or 'Essad Bey' as anything other than pen-names of the sort that many writers use for a variety of purposes. Still, because of his origins and background, the taint or thrill of literary transvestism persistently attaches to *Ali and Nino*. I cannot locate any recent edition that names Nussimbaum on the front cover or title page, although some do identify him in the blurb.

Severe readers might accuse him of the type of impersonation that Christopher L Miller, in his book *Impostors*, labels an 'intercultural hoax'. Here, authors 'pose as people they are not, in order to (mis)represent a foreign, ethnic or other culture or class'. With his primary focus on the long-standing and murky French tradition of literary impersonation, Miller argues that such pretences in print 'cross a boundary from a realm of greater privilege to one of lesser privilege'. Among the many spectacular instances he dissects, none made a bigger splash than the extraordinary stunt pulled by the Lithuanian-born French writer Romain Gary (born Roman Kacew in Vilnius). Having already won the Prix Goncourt under his own name, and so barred from future competitions, the ageing and insecure Gary triumphed again in 1975 with a novel submitted under a false name: *The Life to Come* by 'Émile Ajar'.

A classic 'intercultural hoax', it told the first-person story of a French-born North African beur youngster in the multi-cultural Belleville district of Paris. Critics, and a million-plus readers, adored the vitality, audacity, and indeed the 'authenticity' of this underclass voice, even though Gary further stirred the plot by presenting his hero Momo's story as having been written by an Algerian-born doctor called Hamil Raja. Further Ajar novels followed before Gary unveiled himself in a book-length apologia in 1979. Despite the play of masks and facades that accompanied its publication, *The Life to Come* remains one of Gary's strongest novels. Momo's voice does indeed convince. However, he spins a yarn – about his tender friendship with an elderly Holocaust survivor, Madame Rosa – which slots neatly into an orthodox French narrative of shared republican values as the solvent of superficial ethnic differences. In the late 1970s, and subsequent decades, a mass audience in France and elsewhere yearned to have that story confirmed. A deep desire for feelgood social harmony (Miller calls it a 'making-cute project') absolved the sin of deception.

In *Ali and Nino*, Nussimbaum looks not so much down, from power to penury, or out, from mainstream to margin, as sideways: from one vulnerable community on the fringe of tottering empires to another. He did not grow up as an Azeri nobleman from a venerable Persian house, although he sounds as if he wishes he did. But by the time of the novel's publication, he wielded no authority but eked out a precarious living in Vienna as an exiled man of letters from a people about to undergo a genocidal slaughter. Not much detectable 'privilege' attaches to his project, but an awful lot of romantic longing and lyrical nostalgia for a semi-imaginary domain. 'Kurban Said' endures because readers still desire that name with this tale. If not a hoax, *Ali and Nino* endures as a kind of gloriously costumed drag act. Such works, as Miller writes, 'continue to tell stories that people want to hear'.

Ali and Nino might have begun as a supreme exercise in wish-fulfilment. Just as ethnic and political doctrines erected barriers all over Europe and the Middle East, Nussimbaum concocted his bewitching romance about Caucasian cousins, of disparate clans and creeds but bonded by a shared heritage: 'Born under the same sky, by the same earth, different and yet the same'. In fact, the novel – for all its ecumenical reveries – enacts in its plot the tensions that its author tried so hard to hold at bay. Those words are spoken by Ali and Nino's Armenian friend Nachararyan. Radicalised (as we would now say) by pogroms against his own people, he turns traitor, attempts to kidnap Nino, and symbolically perishes when Ali, on horseback, overtakes their motor-car and exacts his revenge. 'Essad Bey' might have dreamed of cross-cultural amity fuelled by friendship and desire. But even in his signature fantasia of unifying love, he shows division's power.

Ali and Nino by Kurban Said – rather than Lev Nussimbaum – survives, and thrives, as an object of desire and a pole of attraction. It turns out that institutional as well as individual readers feel its lasting pull. In 2016, generous Azerbaijani funding lay behind the release of a lavish adaptation of the novel directed by the British film-maker Asif Kapadia, whose previous subjects, as a documentarist, include Amy Winehouse, Ayrton Senna, and Diego Maradona. Among the film's executive producers were Layla Aliyeva, daughter of Azerbaijan's ruler Ilham Aliyev. Palestinian actor Adam Bakri played Ali, María Valverde from Spain was Nino, while Mandy Patinkin – the veteran Hollywood and TV star known for supporting cross-community peace initiatives in Israel-Palestine – took the role of Nino's Georgian father. For Azerbaijan's dominant dynasty, 'Kurban Said' has played his own small part in their overseas charm offensive. Who can say that Lev Nussimbaum, whose own erratic politics embraced devotion to the Ottoman Caliphate and a deluded vision of Mussolini as a just, non-racialist Caesar, would not have nodded in approval?

Ali and Nino, and other such long-cherished works, both narrate a romantic desire that breaches boundaries – and satisfy their readers' own desire for consoling or uplifting stories from exotic parts. For Christopher Miller, the power dynamics of global publishing plant a susceptibility to fraud and pretence at the centre of this genre: 'the very unfamiliarity of the foreign, ethnic or minority culture makes faking possible and, indeed, seems to invite it.' Yet, as the critic Jaime Hanneken explains, literary impersonations threaten to drive the market for such faraway tales down. After all, 'the value of minority literature' rests on reliable attribution to 'the real life of a free, inalienable subject, who is free and inalienable because he or she made and sold the story'.

Take away the gold standard of the 'free, inalienable subject', and you undermine the exchange-value of their product. Scandal, outrage, lawsuits – and considerable public mirth – may ensue. Rebecca F Kuang's entertaining if heavy-handed 2023 novel *Yellowface* feeds these questions into a pointed satire of 'intercultural' hoaxing. Failed writer June Hayward acquires a manuscript about Chinese workers in the First World War when her friend Athena Liu dies, and proceeds to remake it as the work of 'Juniper Song'. As for Percival Everett's savagely funny 2001 novel *Erasure* (recently filmed as *American Fiction*), its hyper-intellectual, avant-garde African-American writer decides that his only route to success in commercial publishing lies in acting the part of a semi-literate ghetto thug. He duly does so, fabricating a supposedly autobiographical testament entitled 'My Pafology'. It storms the charts and wins a movie deal.

Both novels skewer the book trade's voracious hunger for ethnic minstrel shows. They chose their targets well. Recent acts of literary cross-dressing often come with a cargo of cynicism, manipulation, calculation – or desperation. Miller argues that the potential 'harm' in hoaxes includes not only the 'cultural appropriation' of others' experience but damage to the mental health of their perpetrators. Romain Gary was released from his fears of career decline by 'Émile Ajar', but only able to celebrate his comeback in secret. He committed suicide a year after he had stripped off his mask. In comparison, *Ali and Nino* seems to belong to a more innocent, if not exactly guileless, age. In his Berlin heyday, hostile critics routinely denounced the phoney Essad Bey – the 'fake sheikh' of Weimar literature – but Lev Nussimbaum carried on regardless. For he had, more or less 'authentically', become the character he forged. What did for him was not imposture, but Nazism and war.

Meanwhile, Tamara Kvesitadze's steel lovers glide gracefully into and through each other on Batumi's seafront as a hundred smartphones catch their fleeting trysts. Whatever the sculptor planned, the metal couple's dance of love and loss has become another iteration of Ali and Nino's grand but doomed romance. That story's creator imagined a love that vaulted over difference just as he longed — in his person, in his writing — to embrace and entangle separate worlds. Such ambition, such attraction, may well leave the door ajar for masquerade and mimicry to slip inside. But beloved stories will withstand their makers' vagaries. The dance of desire goes on.

BOLLYWOOD DESIRES

Rachel Dwyer

While Indian cinema has often been celebrated as a cinema of love and of the family, it has its own ways of showing desire. Filmmakers seek to avoid their films being cut by the Board of Certification, informally called the Censors, and they also want to reach the greatest possible audience by getting a general certificate of release, thereby allowing them to make a film that families can view together. Thus popular Indian cinema has developed ways of appealing to audiences by showing desire in its own particular manner.

While desires may be instincts they are also about culture, the greatest single resource for imagining desire is cinema, which is, after all, an industry of desire. The films pick up on existing cultural trends, as well as borrowing from all available sources, to create their own style. They draw on other cultural elements, including from literature and song, to create a new language of desire, in terms of language itself, visuals, music, gesture, situations, locations as well as showing who or what is desirable.

Hindi movies are most famous for their song and dance sequences and their melodramatic style. These are major resources for the depiction of desire, with the melodrama foregrounding emotions and articulating them in great detail, providing their own logic of networks of desire. Desire as part of romance and love is a key part of popular cinema and in Hindi cinema the heterosexual couple desire one another but the plot sets up obstacles, such as the family's wishes for marriage, creating a wide variety of situations which extend the moments and expressions of desire.

Desire without love or good intentions may be indulged for young men, although some of the older films would likely be unacceptable to a generation wise to the implications of #MeToo, although the drifting bachelor may well be tamed later in the film. The vamp and the villain, though (sadly) found less often, were often those who desired or sought to be desired, without seeking love, although the vamp would often reveal that was her real desire just before dying. The 'item girl' who appears for a sexy dance is guilt free as she has no logic in the story and vanishes after her song.

The films make clear the physicality of desire. Much of this is found in the conventions of Indian literary traditions, where the physical sensations of desire are described. These may be the sweating, horripilation, heart beats, sleeplessness, inability to concentrate and so on. Desire itself is often translated as thirst (best exemplified in the 1957 Guru Datt's *Pyaasa,* the thirsty one) and metaphors abound of the natural ways of desire from the moth desiring the flame to the bee seeking nectar in the flowers.

Bollywood films invite the touch, an actual touch of desire, with the desirous on screen being electrifying. But often the desirous one has to use other senses, so may have to smell the beloved through the perfume of breath or touch and smell a discarded item. The allegedly forbidden touch of lips on lips in the kiss, is a taboo, which has its own complicated history.

However, one of the main loci for desire is the look. The audience collectively desires the stars, while the spectator watches alone. The characters on the screen exchange looks with themselves and with the audience or with the camera which the filmmaker themselves uses to look.

What do we see? We see the ideal of beauty at the moment of the making of the film. We look at faces, we look at bodies, we look at everything that is held within the frame. One of the glories of Hindi cinema is the face, the perfect faces of the film stars. The women of course, but also the men. In the older films, bodies were usually covered and were not shown to be exceptionally worthy of desire as desire was focused on the face. This was particularly true of the most beautiful women who featured as courtesans. One of the most famous was Meena Kumari as *Pakeezah* (dir. Kamal Amrohi, 1971), where we don't see a single 'naked' part of her body. Only her hands and feet are shown (and we don't see her hand which was damaged in an accident), but they are ornamented with colour and jewels. Her face is made up (and indeed we know it was often a mask).

One of the most striking examples is in *Sahib Bibi aur Ghulam* (Dir. Abrar Alvi, 1962), where Bhootnath (Guru Dutt), a poor but educated man, is summoned by the zamindar's wife, Choti Bahu (Meena Kumari). The camera shows Bhootnath's point of view, as he stares at the carpet, then at her feet. She invites him to look up but he does so only after they have begun talking. He looks at her face, specifically at her bindi and is dazzled, as are we, the audience. The zamindar spends his nights with courtesans so Choti Bahu tries to make him stay home by dressing up and preparing for his arrival but even though she invites him (She says, '*Ek baar idhar to dekho zara. Sirf ek baar.*' Look here one time, please. Just one time.) he is not interested (He says, '*Kya bakwaas karti ho? Main yahan baitha tumhara munh dekha karoon, itni fursat nahin mujhe!*' What rubbish are you saying? I don't have time to sit here looking at your face.) Unlike Bhoothnath and we the audience who desire to see her beautiful face, the husband, the one who should look at her, does not.

The other important sense in film for instigating and feeling desire is hearing. As with many other cinemas, music plays an important role but the film song brings together language and music in its own ways.

The Hindi film uses language in the film to express everything in great detail, augmenting, replacing and contradicting the images of desire expressed elsewhere. The lyrics and the dialogues are often written by different authors and a fairly inarticulate person may switch to exquisite poetry in a song or a speaker of contemporary 'Hinglish' (where English is mixed with the Hindi) shift to flowery Urdu.

The language of the Hindi film has a complex history as Hindi and Urdu have desired each other and merged and separated over the years while English has intruded more and more frequently. The wider cultural frames are also significant with tropes of Urdu poetry elaborating unrequited love, the cruelty of the beloved, the abjectness of the lover, the season for love being spring and the location in a formal garden with roses, tulips and nightingales. For Hindi, there is devotional longing with rain the romantic season, the lotus and the cuckoo. Both traditions also have contemporary styles while Hollywood and other styles have also affected language.

Hindi films have changed and I have grown old so it's not surprising that I prefer the old style of depicting desire. The focus on beauty rather than sex appeal and the poetic longing and its expression are what I enjoy so much. I barely know what Dilip Kumar's body looked like but his charm and desirability are in his wild hair, his eyes, his smile and his overall charm. Shahrukh Khan may be a modern hero but he also has Dilip Kumar's qualities.

I have chosen a few examples to show how desire can be condensed in song sequences with little emphasis on dance. Most of these are available online and I hope you enjoy watching them even half as much as I did.

First, the unfulfilled desire. The song, '*Mitwa*' from *Devdas* (Bimal Roy, 1957) (music by SD Burman, lyrics by Sahir Ludhianvi) is an example of accepting desires that will never be fulfilled. The monsoon skies are dark and a storm is brewing. Devdas (Dilip Kumar) is carrying a gun, and a bird, possible prey, is shown singing in a tree. Devdas is wearing a shirt, scarf and dhoti and sits or walks around among the trees. He is unshaven and the song is mostly in close up of his face or shows him from behind. Talat Mahmood, one of the most celebrated ghazal singers, explores the music and emotion as he sings slowly in a semiclassical style accompanied by traditional instruments, such as the sitar and sarangi. Devdas says he is consumed by fire and his friend (*mitwa*) will never come and he has only tears. Devdas knows he and Paro will never have their desires fulfilled.

Second, full-blown passion! Kishore Kumar, whose playback singing was often for Dev Anand to the music of SD Burman, began to sing for the composer's son, RD Burman, who brought a new style of music to Hindi cinema. His voice was most closely associated with Rajesh Khanna and Amitabh Bachchan. His rich voice and informal style and his ability to act in the character of different actors associates him with this era of a new kind of a more open masculine desire, where language became simpler and the music more funky.

Rajesh Khanna was the first superstar of this post-Nehruvian era and his films featured many of the most popular songs of Hindi cinema, a winning combination of singing by Kishore, music by RD Burman, and lyrics by Anand Bakshi. *Aradhana* (Dir. Shakti Samanta, 1969) turned Kishore's career around as after this he began to dominate the playback scene.

The beautiful young couple, Vandana (Sharmila Tagore) and Arun (Rajesh Khanna), had already seen each other in another song which was a huge hit for Kishore, '*Meri sapnon ki rani*' (the Queen of my dreams'). They fell in love and got married, without witnesses, in a temple. They were then stranded in a log cabin in a thunderstorm. Vandana appears in a carefully pinned orange blanket (or is it a towel?) while Arun shows his hairy chest in a white shirt opened to the waist. A couple in the next room is shown in silhouette as the man recites poetry. Then they seem to hear the song coming from them.

The sequence is a single shot as they stare into each other's eyes and look away, then touch as they go round a fire as if it's a wedding fire but along with crashes of thunder which show the dramatic symbolism of passion, while the lyrics are about intoxication (*mastana, raat nashilee, nasha, sharabi mausam*) and fear of doing something wrong (*bhool kabhi humse na jo jaye*). The tension in the music is increased through the Latin jazz/samba style with the use of saxophone and accordion, while Kishore whispers and gasps before singing at full volume. The tune was by SD Burman but RD Burman gave it the style which makes it so distinctive. The song ends without anything untoward happening but gives the viewer plenty of scope to imagine that there is only one ending. As this results in her pregnancy, the viewer imagined correctly.

Third, the common motif of love and longing in the rain. Rain in a very different way is another RD Burman-Kishore collaboration, '*Rim jhim gire sawan*', this time with lyrics by Yogesh in *Manzil* (Dir. Basu Chatterjee, 1979). The first time we hear the song is Kishore's version where Ajay (Amitabh Bachchan) plays the harmonium at a wedding. Aruna (Moushumi Chatterjee) finds her initial irritation with him changing to attraction. Although Kishore sings of burning love and longing in the rain, the visuals are rather static and the performance doesn't add to them at all. However, with the second full version of the song later in the film, sung by Lata Mangeshkar, the visuals of the couple splashing about in the rain at several South Bombay (as it was) landmarks is more memorable, though again perhaps not exactly the images that the song itself conjures up for the listener.

Fourth, we have the devoted lover. Although he is now finding new success as an action hero, Shah Rukh Khan emerged in the 1990s as the devoted lover, the master of tears and romance. For many of us he will always be the romantic hero who embodied the style of cinema that we call 'Bollywood'. He will go to any length for his beloved. He will stalk and he will threaten (*Darr,* dir. Yash Chopra, 1993), he will win the beloved's family (*Dilwale Dulhaniya le jayenge*, dir. Aditya Chopra, 1995), he will pretend he is not in love because he knows he will die (*Kal ho na ho*, dir. Nikhil Advani, 2003), he will divorce (*Kabhi alvida na kehna*, dir Karan Johar, 2006), he withdraws from life when his lover promises God she will never see him again if he lives (*Jab tak hai jaan*, dir. Yash Chopra, 2012). In *Veer Zaara* (dir. Yash Chopra, 2004), Veer (Shah Rukh Khan), the Indian Air Force officer will appear, at least in his lover's imagination, to comfort her, Zaara (Preity Zinta) when she marries the man her family has chosen for her in Pakistan. He goes to prison to protect her when her husband blackmails him, and he waits over twenty years for Zaara until he is old, carrying her anklet in his pocket until he finally meets her. In the song, '*Tere liye*', the old couple meet again, merging into their old selves.

There are so many other examples one could take. Guru Dutt's *Pyaasa* (1957) is usually seen as one of the greatest of all Hindi films and as the title suggests is a film entirely about desire, for love of poetry, for justice, and is expressed differently in each song where the work of many great artistes is at peak form, or one could look at Raj Kapoor's or Yash Chopra's focus on desire.

But it's not all about the past. *Rocky aur Rani kii prem kahani* (dir. Karah Johar, 2023) is one of my favourite films from recent years, even though it had enough issues in it to be a serial rather than a film. My favourite film pair, Ranveer Singh and Alia Bhatt, are as great a screen couple as the oldies, even if they are a full generation younger than me and their expressions of desire ends in a happy marriage song. However, Sanjay Leela Bhansali's hugely popular Netflix series *Heeramandi* (2024) shows that, as in the courtesan film, beautiful women may desire love and happiness but they rarely find them.

THE OTHER SPACES OF DESIRE

Liam Mayo

Desire is an emotion in the present for something that exists in the future.

When I met Sarah, I desired her. The person, the life we would have together, the family we would share, I desired it all. And we set out to do all the things.

When Sarah was expecting our first child, Cassidy, we spent nine months having all sorts of new and interesting conversations; what type of parent do you want to be? What type of life do you want to live? How big do you want our family to become? And with our second, Patrick; what type of family do we want to become? What type of world do we want to leave our children?

These are conversations loaded with desire.

This is a well-worn path of human experience. Desire is a potent emotion that propels us through life, moving us to pursue goals, a person, an object, or an ideal. It may be ignited internally or inspired externally.

In her book *What IS Sex?*, Alenka Zupančič explores the Lacanian notion that we can get the same satisfaction that we get from sex from any number of activities, like talking, writing, or painting. She argues that sexuality is a short circuit between the ontological (how we exist in the world) and epistemology (how we know the world), meaning that sexuality and knowledge are symbiotic, interconnected in complex ways.

This implies that desire (as a component of sexuality) is not just a biological or personal feeling, but something that interacts with our understanding of existence (ontology) and our acquisition of knowledge (epistemology). It also suggests that our desires can influence, and be influenced by, our understanding of the world and ourselves.

Does this mean that my family is a result of my innate longing to feel connection, purpose, and love? Or did my desire for a family originate with societal expectations, temptations, and cultural narratives? Or is it a little bit of both?

Psychologists believe that desire is of the mind, where it is shaped by our thoughts, experiences, and perceptions. It is in the mind that we form desires based on what we perceive, think and feel. Neurologists link desire to specific areas of the brain, such as the limbic system, which involve emotion and motivation, and the prefrontal cortex which is involved in planning and decision making.

Indeed, desire has been a powerful driving force in the realm of art. It has inspired countless works, from ancient sculptures to modern paintings, music, literature, and more contemporary digital art. Artists channel their desires into their creations, transforming intangible feelings into tangible expressions that others can see, hear, and feel. This process not only allows artists to explore and understand their own desires but also invites viewers to reflect on their own feelings and experiences. This is a cycle of inspiration, creation, and reflection that has been ongoing for millennia and will likely continue for many more.

Regardless, let's agree desire is non-linear in nature. It can ebb and flow, intensify or diminish, and be influenced by a multitude of factors including personal experiences, relationships, and external stimuli. It's not something that can be easily quantified or measured in a linear scale. Instead, it's a dynamic, evolving feeling that can change based on context and circumstances. It's this non-linearity and unpredictability that often makes desire such a compelling and nuanced subject of study.

So, if desire can be entirely non-linear, and all at the same time, internal and external, emotional and physical, how do the spaces we inhabit influence and shape our desires? And by that, I mean, how do the physical spaces like our homes or workplaces, emotional spaces like our relationships and inner-feelings, and societal spaces like cultural norms and expectations, influence and shape our desires?

Pilgrimage

I was reflecting on this recently. I was at a loose-end and, as is often the case, found myself standing at the bookshelf idly thumbing through different books until something jumped out and struck my fancy.

Despite how this may appear to an outsider, this is not an act absent of desire. I have a yearning to create something and am searching for inspiration from the world around me.

I have a little book of poetry by Yeats. I flick through the all-too-small-pages, and something jumps out and grabs me. In the opening stanza to 'The Pilgrim', we find the speaker describing how he has fasted for forty days on bread and buttermilk, a symbol of self-denial and spiritual discipline.

> I fasted for some forty days on bread and buttermilk,
> For passing round the bottle with girls in rags or silk,
> In country shawl or Paris cloak, had put my wits astray,
> And what's the good of women, for all that they can say
> Is fol de rol de rolly O.

This must be our pilgrim!

He suggests that a life of indulgence in worldly desires, of women and drink, has left him feeling empty and dispossessed. He embarks on a pilgrimage to *Lough Derg's holy island*, where, *upon the stones*, he prays *at all the Stations* (a series of devotional stages in Catholic tradition). Now it is spiritual enlightenment that he has turned his desires toward.

Ah-ha! I have found my inspiration. And with Yeats tucked under my arm, I scurry back to my desk.

Lough Dergs holy island is a reference to St Patrick's Purgatory, the ancient pilgrimage site on Station Island in Ireland. According to legend, the site dates back to the fifth century when God showed St Patrick a cave on the island, telling him that it was an entrance to purgatory. This was in response to St Patricks prayers for help in converting the Irish people to Christianity, who were skeptical of his teachings and desired substantial proof of claims he made. The idea was that by showing this place to the people, they would witness the consequences of not embracing Christianity with their own eyes. And by experiencing purgatory the Irish people would understand the reality of the joys of heaven and the torments of hell, and turn toward Christ.

So, St Patrick – guided by God – created a physical space to influence and shape the desires of the Irish toward Christianity.

And whilst St Patrick wasn't the first to speak to the concept of purgatory, the physical representation of purgatory as a cave on Station Island had a profound impact on how Western Europeans thought about life and death, heaven and hell. It framed the idea of purgatory as a physical place rather than an abstract process of purification. And it would go on to be treated as such: a monastery was established by the disciples of St Patrick and medieval texts referenced the site.

Around 1153, a knight named Owen embarked on a pilgrimage to the island. Owen's journey to purgatory was voluntary and driven by his desire for penance and spiritual purification. After giving confession to an Irish bishop, Owen was unwilling to accept what he believed to be an unfittingly easy penance. He was remorseful for his sins and sought to cleanse himself through the torments of purgatory. He fasted and prayed for fifteen days. The monks in charge of the site conducted a funeral mass for him, marking his symbolic death, before leading him into the cave and locking him inside.

Over the next twenty-four hours, Owen faced a series of tests and temptations, torments, and sufferings. The monks informed Owen that regardless of what confronted him, if he turned inward, and called on the name of Jesus Christ, he would be saved.

In this way, it is not merely the pain itself, but Owen's response to his suffering that is of most importance. By trusting in the power and mercy of God to save him in his weakness, Owen is delivered. Eventually, Owen crossed a bridge to a peaceful paradise, where he joined the other saved souls waiting to enter heaven. After a full day in the cave, Owen emerged, purified of his sins after faithfully enduring the cleansing fires of purgatory.

In his desire for atonement, Owen travels to a space to stare into the abyss and returns transformed.

Owen's journey became a medieval blockbuster. The *Treatise of St. Patricks Purgatory* popularised the site as a space of popular pilgrimage, with Christians from France, Spain, Hungary, and Italy traversing profound distances to the most western part of the known world, to repent, to purify, and to bring into focus their mortality through visions of that which exists beyond them. This is desire toward devotion.

And over time, the site of St Patricks cave, morphed and evolved, becoming the space of purgatory through translations and adaptions across continental Europe. Marie de France, the first female French poet, published a popular adaptation around 1190. A scene of purgatory featured in an Italian fresco in Umbria in 1346. Shakespeare's *Hamlet* famously references purgatory. Dante's *Divine Comedy* elaborates meaningfully on *Purgatorio*. And Renaissance-era navigational charts reference Patricks Hole. The site of purgatory, a cave far off in the very top corner of the world, morphs to become a space in popular culture, continuing to influence and shape humanity.

Because spaces are never static, their symbolic meanings and the complex network of relationships they have shift and change over time.

Space

St Patricks Purgatory stuck with me for weeks after I rediscovered it, guided by Yeats.

I have been doing some work with a university in the Netherlands and needed to fly there for a series of seminars and workshops.

The Netherlands from Australia is like the mediaeval journey from Western Europe to St Patricks cave; as far away from home as one can feasibly get.

Earlier that day I dropped Cassidy and Patrick at school. I knew I would not be seeing them for three weeks. They are now old enough to understand that Dad is going to be away for some time – that he will be back – but things will be different for a little while. They asked me to park and walk them to their classrooms. We hug each other tight and long. And I tell them I will try and call as much as I can. And that I will miss them. And I have that horrible hollow feeling in my stomach, a lump in my throat. I know there are others far worse off. Separated from their children for far longer, under much worse circumstance, sometimes permanently. I have perspective. But the irrationality of fatherhood is rooted in the lining of one's gut, and I am grieving for something that has not happened yet.

'When will you get to Amsterdam Dad.'

'In about 30 hours. Tomorrow night. Or thereabouts.'

They scrunch their noses and laugh at my logic. The prospect of travelling through such vast timescales, across such long distances for work seems absurd to them.

They are the Irish and I am St Patrick: 'You're so silly Dad...'

At the airport it is hard to make sense of where the line to check-in is.

There are two types of people who arrive at the departure terminal at any airport, anywhere in the world. There are those who adopt a swift purposeful walk, aimed at achieving the most efficient line between the airport entrance and the gate. And those who assume a meander, often with a luggage trolley, always inexplicably gazing in an upward direction toward the spaces where the walls meet the ceiling. I prefer the former approach.

Quantum physics tells us that space and time intertwine in a continuum. In the vast expanse of the universe this continuum is not just a physical entity, but a container that holds the manifestation of our desires. We desire space, for the freedom it represents, and for time, with all the opportunities it brings. My journey to the Netherlands, like the medieval pilgrimage to St. Patrick's cave, is a quest for knowledge, for growth, and for meaning.

I weave my way through a long labyrinth of queue barriers – those flat black retractable belts suspended between silver poles that stand just below waist height – back and forth, back and forth, the length of the entire check-in desk, edging closer but not quite getting there. I am pulling a suitcase on wheels. Suddenly a dead end. Two rows from the desk. Immediately to my left a line of people waiting to check into the same flight as me. A man dressed in an airline uniform, with a thick dousing of hair gel approaches me.

'Whoopsie.' We laugh lightly and politely at each other. 'You are in the wrong section, sir. Just head back out and join the queue.'

As I turn to leave a woman standing in the queue next to me smiles at me warmly: 'Sneak through here', she says, pulling at black plastic clip to release the tape from a silver bollard and create an opening for me to join her in the line.

'Sir, you must exit the queue and return to the back of the line.'

'But this is the back of the line.' The woman protests on my behalf.

'Sir, please proceed to the back of the queue.' The man raises his arm as if directing traffic. The woman shrugs her shoulders at me with wide eyes and a thin smile. 'Sorry' she says. It is not her fault. I weave back through the labyrinth made of seat belts, am released onto the cold oversized beige tiles, loop back around to another entrance of the seat belt labyrinth and rejoin the queue there. The meanderers have found their way to the queue just in front of me. This is time I will never get back; I think to myself.

As I said, the vast universe, with its space-time continuum, not only holds physical entities but also the manifestation of our desires. It permeates our daily lives, our relationships, and the roles we play. As a father, the space and time away from Cassidy and Patrick is filled with a poignant mix of anticipation and sorrow. The desire to be with them, to share in their lives, is a gravitational pull. Yet, to make the journey I want to make means that space must be traversed, and time must be spent. Is it helpful to ruminate on the notion that every moment of separation is a step towards reunion, every moment of desire, a step towards fulfilment? Or, is it better to marinate the thought that, whether you stride with purpose or meander through the halls of the airport, you are always, in some way, simply enacting your inner desires within the space-time continuum.

Power

Downstairs at customs I am trying to get the automated machine to scan my passport. The passport goes picture side down on a thick clear plastic tray and is dragged backward into a machine. The machine sends it back with an error reading. I try again, and again, and again. I also try to ignore the fact that there are over a dozen immigration officials in uniforms standing behind a clear Perspex screen chatting frivolously to one another, blissfully unaware that I am metres away arm wrestling with a machine that is slowly making their jobs redundant, while I feel myself slowly edging closer to death. One more failed attempt and I step out of line awkwardly, letting the person behind me come through. They manage to make the machine work on the first time and move through. I curse and try again. It works, and the automated gates open to let me through. Time I will never get back, I think to myself as I skate past the crowded booth of customs and immigration officials.

I find a seat at the airport lounge and open my laptop. I am going to try and do some work before I board the plane. And there is a picture of

Cassidy and Patrick on the screen. It feels like it will be a very long time before I get to see them again.

I think about Michel Foucault and his idea of *heterotopia* – 'other spaces' that deviate from the societal norm. These spaces can be physical, like libraries or brothels, or conceptual, like the realm of a novel or a dream. He contrasted heterotopias with utopias, which are idealised, imaginary spaces that lack a physical presence. These *other spaces* exist outside the normal, both real and unreal, as they reflect and contest the world around them.

I think about how airports are heterotopias. Heterotopic spaces are linked to time, either accumulating time indefinitely or celebrating time in its fleetingness. They do this through regulated systems of opening and closing, rites and permissions, that isolate them and make them penetrable.

An announcement comes over the loudspeaker. My flight has been delayed by an hour. More time I will never get back.

Foucault identified two primary types of heterotopias. The first is crisis heterotopias, reserved for individuals undergoing a personal crisis, such as adolescents, pregnant women, or the elderly. The second is deviation heterotopias, designed for those whose behaviour is considered abnormal, such as inmates in prisons, patients in psychiatric hospitals, or residents in retirement homes.

Heterotopia often arise as a response to power structures and can serve as sites of resistance or control. They may, on the one hand, reflect the power structures of society. For instance, a prison, a form of heterotopia, is a manifestation of societal power, designed to control and mitigate the threat posed by crime. But in the same way, they can also serve as spaces of resistance. They can provide a refuge from dominant power structures and offer a platform for marginalised voices and can challenge dominant discourses by providing a space for alternative narratives. They typify how desire often involves a yearning for something different, distant, or 'other'. This longing can lead individuals to create or seek heterotopias as spaces where they can explore and express their desires.

I pack my laptop and find the airport bar. If I am stuck for another hour, I might as well enjoy it.

Repression

On the plane I cannot sleep. I can never sleep on planes.

I cannot work successfully either. I feel too far removed from reality to do anything meaningful. Perhaps it is my relative proximity to death (hurtling through the skies at 900kms an hour, encased in cylinder of aluminium) that leads me to unconsciously arrive at the executive decision to cease the good conscience of life on the ground and focus my attentions on food devoid of nutrition and the hyper-coloured mini-screen half a metre from my cornea.

This is an Emirates flight, with a stopover in Dubai on my way to Europe, so when I turn on the little television lodged in the seat in front of me an advertisement for Dubai plays immediately. 'Welcome to the future,' a voice with an American affectation announces. I am presented with dramatic and cinematic footage of Dubai: grand shiny skyscrapers, corn yellow beaches carved into the shape of a palm tree, and low lean cars driven by very attractive people of ambiguous ethnicity. New residential developments invite me to invest. Dubai is home to the apartments, transport, and restaurants of the future. Some of this is real, a lot of this is not real. Like highly produced computer-generated animations of urban plans directed by Michael Bay. Or Christopher Nolan. Or James Cameron. I think, this is what it must feel like to be in the uncanny valley. Or perhaps that's just the heat from the screen hitting me directly above the bridge of my nose. 'Invest in Dubai, 'we're open for business.' Dubai, the voice declares, is 'the cross-roads of cultures, where tradition meets innovation.' Whatever that means.

Is there desire here? There is certainly satisfaction of some variety it would appear.

I decide early to settle into something that will help me to escape the blandness of the long-haul flight. I'm going to binge watch season four of *Succession*: a television show about an extremely wealthy family who are horrible to one another in their desire to gain ultimate control over the media empire the patriarch has built. Well, that, and their rapacious desire for their father's approval.

I order a drink and then two and get comfy. A plane is a heterotopia too, I think to myself.

Succession is an often a crass demonstration of the human condition in its desire for validation and acceptance. But what is so arousing about its narrative is the way it explores the contradictions of the liberal class, where people long to be seen as virtuous artists and creative thought leaders, even as they simultaneously engage in crude pursuits for money and commercial success. Desire is, after all, a contradiction. We all have a secret self. The duality of desire lies within the conflict between what we want, and our values. Or at the very least how we want our values to be perceived.

The show has been a global hit. And it's not an unfamiliar plot. Especially in the West. King Lear and Macbeth explored the corrosive effects desire and the pursuit for power, demonstrating how actions are often driven by unconscious desires and fears. The Roy children of *Succession*, with their relentless pursuit of their father's approval and control over the family business, are simply manifesting unconscious desires rooted in their childhood experiences. Their actions are not always rational or consciously chosen but are driven by these deep-seated needs and fears.

Roman Roy is an interesting character. He is complex and tormented. He seeks out conflict and pain. His hyper-sexual hyperbole scene after scene feels jarring and violent against his vulnerable and boyish deportment. And his relationship with Gerri Kellman, a senior executive at the family company, is unconventional and inappropriate. His behaviour is a stark juxtaposition to his public persona. He is, in his own way, an embodiment of the desire *Succession* seeks to portray.

Freud proposed that humans are driven by the pleasure principle, where sexual desires and aggressive behaviour are controlled by the reality principle; the restrictions we follow to conform to proper behaviour. Repression occurs when our drive for unbridled pleasure is supressed by the reality principle and becomes sublimated or buried in our unconscious. Repressed desires return to us in things like dreams, literature, or 'Freudian slips.' In essences, repression is a mechanism that transforms our desires into socially acceptable behaviours.

This dynamic interplay between repression and desire is a fundamental aspect of modern psychology: who we are and who we need to appear to be to navigate society.

The elegance of Foucault's heterotopia is that they can either create an illusory space that reveals reality as deceptive or establish a compensatory space that presents a meticulous alternative to the disordered reality. By stepping into the other space, we disturb and unsettle our understanding of the world. Here we may confront and deal with repressed desires. These spaces necessitate a change in our modes of being, disrupting usual interactions and prompting self-discovery. Heterotopias uniquely juxtapose incompatible spaces, leading to new insights.

As such, visiting heterotopias allow us to step outside our normal experiences and perspectives, offering us a chance to see the world in a new light. They challenge our preconceptions and encourage us to think critically about ourselves and the society that surrounds us. Which suggests, I think, that our desires can also be influenced by the spaces we inhabit.

But, as we have established, power is an innate aspect of heterotopia. While heterotopias can serve as sites of resistance and liberation, they can also function as sites of control and exclusion. Power, much like desire, is complex and multifaceted. It's not just about control or authority; it's also about influence, perceptions, relationships, and the ability to shape narratives and outcomes. And power, like desire, is not just a tool or a resource; it's also a burden and a source of tension. But repression, too, is a form of power – the power to deny, to ignore, to push away. And so, the cycle continues.

'Ladies and gentlemen, the seatbelt sign has now been turned on. As we now prepare for landing, we ask that you now return to your seats, stow your tray tables away, turn off all electronic devices, and fasten your seatbelts.'

Ah yes, here it is, right on cue: the airline and its crew hold institutional authority, enforcing rules and regulations for us, the passengers', safety, and comfort. We accept this power as part of the agreement of air travel. The airplane's physical layout mirroring societal class divisions, with different levels of comfort and amenities offered in first-class, business, and economy sections. This reflects economic power and status. And in the confined space of an aircraft, there's a delicate balance of power around personal space; you're invited to recline your seat but to do so you encroach on the space of the passenger behind you. The flight crew controls the flow of information, such as flight updates or turbulence warnings; there are those with knowledge and those dependent on it. Passengers hold power as consumers; their purchasing power can influence airline policies and services, a fact that's more evident now with social media amplifying individual voices.

'Sir, can I ask you to please place your tray table away.' A directive from the towering steward who is suddenly next to me.

'Oh yes, I'm so sorry. Right away.' My repressed compliant child comes out.

Unconscious

If you're from Australia, transiting through Dubai on your way to Europe is not an unfamiliar experience.

I know this trip well. And if I have learned from my years of travel, it is that a good soundtrack aids in traversing the transit experience. Especially one as grand as the Dubai International Airport.

One of my pleasures in life is to disembark the aircraft and navigate an airport with music turned up loud in my headphones. What I do is wait until the seat belt sign is turned off and then I shift the headphones over my ears and hit play, slide out of my seat and into the aisle, and remove my overhead luggage.

At the moment I am obsessed with the album *The Bootleg Series Volumes 1-3 (Rare and Unreleased) 1961–1991* by Bob Dylan. I don't know why. Although, it is not hard to become obsessed with anything Bob Dylan does, great, good, bad, or otherwise. He is, to me, an infinitely interesting artist.

I also happen to have a new pair of over the head noise cancelling headphones, which make for a crisp and clear audio experience. Whatever that means.

In the song 'Series of Dreams' Dylan has a sense he is trapped in a cycle of dreams, where time and pace are beyond his control. The human condition is a series of dreams that, like our desires, seem beyond our control. The 'exit' that 'you can't see with your eyes' is the fulfilment of these desires, which often seems elusive or invisible to us. I think.

I move across the bridge and into the wide bright white shiny corridors of the terminal. I can move fast here, with only a small carry-bag briefcase,

I weave through the crowds of ceiling sniffers, making my way toward the next gate – pause momentarily at the large televisions overhead, find my flight number, eyes move across the screen, Gate 37, Terminal 3. I have four hours before boarding, but it is fun for me to see how fast I can work out where I need to be and when. I don't know why. Maybe it is about having a little bit of control in the space, for the time, where everything is out of my control. I think. Maybe.

Foucault thought that the boat is the ultimate heterotopia. It is a floating and moving piece of space that connects and explores different places and cultures. He says that in civilisations without boats, dreams dry up and adventure is replaced by espionage and police.

Moving through the airport is like muscle memory. Or like reading brail: the hard plastic handrail of long steep escalators, the cold metal buttons light up on the terminal train, soft spongey carpet underfoot, an elevator door closes, the boarding pass between my thumb and forefinger, I double check the flight details, the polyester of a bar stool, a laminated menu, a cup to coffee. And wait.

'Series of Dreams' is a journey into the unconscious mind. Dylan's dreams, where everything remains wounded, are the unconscious mind's way of dealing with unresolved issues and repressed desires. The unconscious mind holds feelings, thoughts, urges, and memories outside our conscious awareness, which can influence our behaviour and decision-making. What he is describing is the vague, undefined nature of dreams.

I think about Dylan's series of dreams and wonder if this is his metaphor for the often-nebulous nature of our desires. Just as dreams can be confusing and hard to interpret, so too our desires can be difficult to understand and articulate. We often describe our desires as something we dream for.

Suddenly, I feel a longing, a hefty tugging at my bowel, already missing my family, knowing it will be weeks before I see my children again. But, all at once, I feel excited about seeing my friends and colleagues in Europe, the work we are doing is interesting and fun. I feel impatient about my journey. I have been travelling for sixteen hours already, it's around another ten before I land. Yet I am now, for this moment, quite contented to sit here at an airport café, with an awful cup of coffee, watching American sports I don't understand on three different large flat screen televisions.

And here, surrounded by strangers with nowhere to be immediately, and nothing really to do, far from home, and far from my destination, in an other space, I experience a visceral understanding of life in all its complex tapestries. This heterotopia delivers me coherence.

Death

The horizon is above you in the Netherlands. Australia is a big country.

Where I live you can stand on the beach and look out over the ocean and see the horizon softly and slowly drop away. Or turn 180 degrees and see the horizon fall behind the broad mass of land. But on a train between Utrecht and Amsterdam, the horizon feels like it envelopes me.

I came to this realisation after a few days of travelling across the Dutch landscape, zig zagging from meeting to conference, workshop to seminar. It's been three weeks now, and I can automatically calculate the time in Australia without needing to count forward on my fingers. I'll call home to the boys in an hour when I get to my new hotel. They'll be having their breakfast. I'll be finishing my day.

In Amsterdam I meet Sietske. We deliver a seminar to a group of CEO's and business leaders who are curious about the work we are doing together. It's a small room, with an oversized projector screen and a long conference table running down the middle. The group is active and engaged. I am deeply interested in the notion that society is moving through a period of significant transition, where modern ways of knowing and being in the world are dying, and new forms of knowledge and existence are yet to be born. I don't have answers for where we are going, or what we will come next, but I do have some ideas about how we can make sense of this transition as a way to more meaningfully navigate it. With health, humility, and humanity.

Its an easy and straight forward case to make. In our media saturated globe, the collective sense of demise envelopes all of us like the Dutch horizon.

Freud believed that the death instincts (Thanatos) exist alongside the life instincts (Eros) in the unconscious. The life instincts, sometimes known as the sexual instincts, are related to survival, while the death instincts include thoughts of aggression, trauma, and danger. Thanatos, for Freud, is rooted in the law of entropy, or the idea that all systems eventually reach their lowest point, and demise. This can be contrasted with Eros, which is focused on the propagation of life.

Meetings, conferences, workshops, and seminars are death spaces. The very nature of my work means I have to spend a great deal of time in these types of spaces. Rooms, large and small. Natural or fluorescent light. The theatre set up or break out tables. Open-aired and air-conditioned. Everything in between. These are spaces where ideas, motivations, theories, and agendas come to die.

And anyone who tells you otherwise, business consultants, keynote speakers, self-described thought leaders, are lying to you and probably themselves.

I am guilty of this myself. I speak at conferences, facilitate workshops, chair meetings, and deliver seminars, espousing innovation and an emerging perspective. But afterward I feel empty and somewhat fraudulent. In my early career important people would say to me, we love what you do, we love your energy, if you could just emphasise this, do more of that, and water down this, you will have a wonderful product to sell to the market. And so I did, and gosh I felt horribly conceited.

In the pursuit of knowledge creation and distribution, the concept of death is transformative. It signifies not an end, but a necessary metamorphosis - the letting go of the old to make space for the new. Yet, our meetings, conferences, workshops, and seminars often resist this transformation, despite what they profess. They have become incubators for ideas, motivations, theories, and agendas that should have been allowed to die. Instead of fostering the birth of new insights, they cling to what is familiar, often repackaging old concepts with new sexy terminology. Oh, and the punters are happy to buy it. Consume it. Celebrate it. This is hyper-capitalist Communion.

The true misstep of business consultants, keynote speakers, and self-proclaimed thought leaders is not their inability to generate new ideas, but their unwillingness to let go of the old ones. This is where desire comes into play. The desire for comfort, for the safety of the known, often overshadows the desire for true innovation. It prevents us from embracing the uncomfortable yet essential process of dismantling outdated paradigms to clear the path for fresh perspectives. This is exacerbated by our desire for money and commercial success. What a crass conundrum within which we have found ourselves. Not unlike our friends from the television show *Succession*.

So how should we think of these spaces? These graveyards of ideas.

Foucault is again helpful here. He speaks of cemeteries as spaces within society that are real, but not ideal, and so must be contained and controlled. Cemeteries mutate with their function dependent on their specific historical period. In eighteenth century France, for example, concerns for hygiene and the rise of the idea of 'death as disease' removed the dead from the crowded sacred spaces adjacent to churches to new cemeteries on the outskirts of cities. Cemeteries are also spaces that enclose an absolute break with traditional time, in the sense that what constitutes the loss of life for an individual is also a 'quasi eternity in which he perpetually dissolves and fades away' Foucault, 1998: 182.

American musician and founder of the band Nirvana, Kurt Cobain, in his suicide note, left the words 'it's better to burn out than to fade away.' He was paraphrasing Neil Young's 'Hey Hey, My My (Out Of The Blue).'

I fantasised about suicide a lot as a young man. And I don't mean for that to sound macabre. But it was all around me, everywhere. Many people I went to school with took their lives. As did many of my heroes. Normalised through school assembly's and news broadcasts, but never spoken about around the dining room table. When testosterone and social maladjustment come together, suicide seems like the most romantic gesture of all. Which is another way of saying that the social structure of neoliberalism nurtures, if not revels in the destruction of self.

In fact, if you look closely enough at the last decade of the last millennium, and the first decade of this millennium, you can see the high-water mark of modernity. *Friends*, *The Sopranos*, and *American Idol*. *The Matrix*, *American Pie*, and *Fight Club*. The internet of things and mobile personal technologies. Processed food, swine flu, and mad cows. Globalisation and the dot-com bubble. 9/11 and weapons of mass-destruction. The Spice Girls and Eminem. Twenty-four-hour news cycles and video games. Toxic masculinity and material excess. Desire and instant gratification.

When I think about this now, as an adult with children of my own, I can understand why we cannot collectively overcome the things that need to be overcome to create a better future for everyone. The generation before me ushered in the sexual revolution, the socialisation of recreational drugs, and rock and roll music. They then invented the internet and flooded it with pornography. The war on drugs has resulted in the legalisation of some drugs, and an epidemic of others. And rock and roll music has exposed itself as peak commercialism rather than the art of renegades it pretends to be. What I witnessed was a generation who had become aware of the paradoxes of late-stage modernity, who became hell bent on burning the whole thing down. Now my generation is taking their opportunity to peddle their own snakeskin oils, to fulfill desires that appear far closer to the desires of their fathers than we would care to admit. Collective suicide, it would appear, is a lot easier to deal with than life. Better to burn out than to fade away, it would seem.

After the seminar, Sietske and I meet a group of the participants at pub close by. They want to buy us a drink. They've enjoyed the seminar and want to keep the conversation going. I mention my epiphany; that the horizon here feels like it is above you.

'Well, I am sure you know about the dykes.'

I do know about the dykes; the complex system of natural sand dunes, constructed dykes, dams, floodgates, drainage ditches, canals, and pumping stations that prevent around two thirds of the Netherlands from going underwater.

'Dutch engineers are the best in the world. We trust them to keep us safe and secure from the water.'

We talk about society and its relationship with the natural world. We talk about the prevalence of natural disasters and the ongoing impact this has on our way of life. Just last week I was stuck in Rotterdam because of an unusually severe storm that halted the train network. I tell them my family in Australia have lived through floods and been evacuated because of bush fires. And yet, I continue to watch as large sprawling suburbs are developed on huge parcels of land that should not be built on.

'I think there is an interesting point to make here,' one of my new friends interjects. 'I think the difference between us here in Europe, and you in Australia, or the United States, or Canada, or even New Zealand for that matter, is that we went through a renaissance. You didn't. There is some truth in the idea that we are the old world. So, we have a knowledge of the world, of the things, that the new world hasn't quite developed yet.'

There are some idle and casual nods from the group. It's an interesting, but perhaps not well developed, observation.

I tell them about the advertisement I saw on the plane to Dubai. Dubai has created palm tree-shaped islands using advanced technology and engineering by dredging the sand from the Persian and Arabian Gulf floors. The Ancient Arabs gave us algebra, the pointed archway, and water wheels used in irrigation systems.

'I heard that it was actually the Arabs who developed windmills in the form we use them today.' Someone else jumps in.

There is a general sense of interest around this statement.

'You know. I live not far from here. My house is on stilts.' Another member of our group joins the conversation. 'My wife and I paid over a million euros for this house. We love it, but we knew when we brought it, it was well below sea level, and that it would only get worse. We always talk about how we will keep up with rising insurances, the shifting building code compliances and government regulations.'

I think that Kurt Cobain misunderstood what Neil Young meant in his song 'Hey Hey My My (Out Of The Blue)' where he contrasts the vibrancy of life and creativity with the inevitability of decline and obscurity. His reference to the king (Elvis Presley) and Johnny Rotten illustrates his idea that while rock and roll may endure, individual artists often struggle to maintain their relevance. Whilst the line 'it's better to burn out than to fade away' has become iconic as the calling card for the idea that it's preferable to leave a lasting impact rather than slowly become irrelevant, to burn out doesn't necessitate the loss of life.

Maybe, I wonder, if rock and roll will never die, as Neil Young claims, it too is a heterotopia, representing an absolute break with traditional time, a piece of quasi eternity in which the music perpetually dissolves, and slowly fades away. And thus, it is the art form that fades away, not the artist. The artist exists forever

Maybe, Kurt Cobain wanted to kill grunge music, not himself. He just didn't know how. Or he wanted to kill a version of himself, but didn't know how.

Navigating the death of the old, the birth of the new, means we must align our desires with the needs of the times. The death of the obsolete is to yearn for the discomfort that comes with unlearning and relearning. However paradoxical that notion may feel, when self-love is so great, to perpetuate oneself, one must initiate one's own self destruction.

This is not to say that all that is old is obsolete. Or all that is obsolete should be forgotten. As we transition to a new normal, we must excavate the relics of modernity and find within them something holy to believe in. Marshall Berman argued that to be modern is to experience personal and social life as a maelstrom, while to be modern is to find a way to feel at home within it, to embrace its rhythms, and to seek out reality, beauty, freedom, and justice amidst its chaotic flow. If we are at the end of the modern world, how we align our desires with the needs of our times will ultimately determine how we navigate our transitional age. Because memory is not just a passive recollection of the past but an active and dynamic process that influences our present and future actions.

The king is gone but he's not forgotten.

Memories

The following day is Saturday. My last day in the Netherlands. Tomorrow, I fly home.

Amsterdam is the best city in the world to get lost in. You can trace the curves of canals through different little humming city squares, but always find yourself back at a landmark from which you can orientate yourself. Here I surrender to the time–space continuum; I become the dreaded airport meander in narrow-cobbled streets. But this is my desire to enact, I think.

I find myself in the Museumkwartier district and decide to have a look around the Stedelijk Museum. I download a free app that allows me to take a guided walk through the museum and use the QR codes next to each piece of work, to learn about the artwork and the artist. This is the paramount heterotic experience.

I amble from room to room, making the time to engage with each piece of work. Some are incredibly interesting, others I do not care for. But I have no place else to be, and time is on my side here. The ritual and order

of the museum space lull me into a deliberate reflection. And I feel a sense
of purpose.

A few hours in and I round a corner on the second floor and enter a
different exhibit. My eyes fall to a painting on a wall at the far side of the
room. And I feel the breath leave my torso.

'Wow.'

I remember this painting. I know this painting. It feels so familiar. But I
don't know why. I am at a stand-still across the room, fixated on the reds
and the greens and the yellows, the brush strokes, the movement, and the
depth.

'Where do I know you from?'

I make my way across the room, suddenly feeling very aware of all the
other people around me. I try to act casual as I lean in to read the wall
label next to the painting.

WILLEM DE KOONING
(1904 – 1997)
Montauk IV, 1969
Oil on paper on canvas
Acquired in 1969

'I remember you!' I think to myself.

High-school art history. A long time ago. I learned about abstract
expressionism, and I learned about Willem de Kooning.

'De Kooning,' the audio in my headphones tell me, famously noted,
'content is a glimpse. This suggests that the painting is not a literal
depiction of a thing, but rather an emotional and psychological response
to it.'

I find the long timber bench in the centre of the room and sit and watch
Montauk IV. I'm seventeen again, at high school, a raging mess of ambition
and desire. I like abstract expressionists because they evoke raw emotion
and deep, primal feelings through their use of colour, form, and
movement, bypassing the need for representational clarity. I like de
Kooning because of his aggressive brushstrokes and chaotic yet agreeable
palette. I like him because people like my parents say things like, 'that's not
art' 'anyone can do that', 'give me a tin of house paint and canvas and I'll

knock you up one of those right here, right now.' And I scoff at them and tell them they're stupid. And they tell me I am just a kid, and what would I know. And I promise myself I will never think like them. It all feels very intense and feels real to me.

'Montauk IV' draws me in deeper. Each brushstroke records a moment in time, a moment that is gone as soon as it is captured. This fleeting nature of existence is vividly portrayed through de Kooning's work, embodying his play with notions of destruction and rebirth. Abstract expressionism is death and rebirth, an escape from the confines of traditional art forms established by the grand masters. It forges a path toward something new, something different, allowing for a continual cycle of dissolution and creation, mirroring the ever-changing landscape of human experience and desire. And here, it is memory that transcends. Like a rudder through the maelstrom of existence.

I have a friend who often says to me, 'it doesn't matter where you go, there you are.' Which is a kind of bullshit way of saying you can't ever escape what you really are. That in the space-time continuum within which we exist, memory will always outstrip us.

When she says this, I think of the song 'Blues Run The Game' by Jackson B Frank, which says that it doesn't matter where you go, the blues are all the same.

Which is an interesting way of saying that there is a shared human experience, that we may call the blues, and it doesn't matter where you are from or where you go, it's all the same. Which in turn implies that the very experience of being human, of living, of loving, of longing and of losing, is shared. That in the blues, we find solace, at the very least, in the fact that the experience is shared, and that we are not alone, and that maybe, all it takes, is for all of us to hang in there, grow a little older, and know more about the world, be wiser. Maybe.

This, I find interesting. This contains inspiration.

I raise my phone and take a photo of Montauk IV. I'll show Cassidy and Patrick when I get home. And then I think to myself, no you won't, they're not interested in a picture on your phone of a painting in a museum in Amsterdam. I put my phone away.

No, that's a memory for me, just me. To remind me. My own personal desire.

COMPLEX DESIRES

C Scott Jordan

Is it fate, or algorithms? Either way, it seems as constitutionally necessary as my morning cup of coffee for my feeds to be saturated with images and videos of maimed Palestinian children. I do not slouch into my social media apps as casually as I used to. I even err on the side of caution when checking my WhatsApp messages. Now, I only really use the app for its messaging capabilities, but I have lived long enough in Malaysia, where gossip and conspiracy are coveted commodities, to think twice before opening any old notification. Sometimes you find yourself opening a typical uncle-propelled conspiracy theory video or fake news article with a salacious, click-bait headline that has already been dishearteningly 'forwarded many times'. Yet other times, more intense shared content comes about, often without warning. I once received a video of two politically noteworthy men in a hotel room engaged in what could have been mistaken for Olympic Greco-Roman wrestling. The veracity of this video certainly puts a new spin on the term 'deepfake'. On one occasion I received a shaky video taken in a crowded public area where it quickly became apparent, I was witnessing the last moments of a young man's life as he plunged six stories to his gruesome end on the concourse level of the famous KLCC mall. The amateur snap-zoom in on the young man, lifeless at the site of his impact, dispels any mystery of what I had just been involuntarily thrown into witnessing. Tragic and traumatic as that one was, another video has really stuck with me lately.

One evening as I was winding down for the night, a notification flashed upon my mobile. Unsuspectingly, I tapped upon it. The scene was a rather placid, overcast blue body of water. A distant head popped up through the surface. The head bobbed calmly, without much movement. Shouting was heard, but it is unclear if the shouting came from the head or elsewhere. This prompted me to increase the volume. The head suddenly shifted from

looking left to looking right as the man's shoulders breeched the surface.
A fin, slightly larger than the head, also pierced the surface. Then a tail fin
preceded the white splash of disruption to the right of the head. The
shouting was definitely coming from the head. What dug down to my
bones was how the shouting changed. The sound lost what can distinguish
it from a howler, roar, or squeal, attaining an inhuman pitch. It is the
utterance a human makes only when they are at the precipice of mortal
fear. Something many actors have tried, but never quite get right in the
movies. The utterance cut through but was drowned out by the phrase 'oh,
my, God' repeatedly draining from the mouth of either the camera woman
or an onlooker beyond the camera's frame. The head and the pair of
shoulders beneath it lifted up out of the ocean before falling into a
descending wave which is torn through by the snout of a shark as it leapt
atop the victim. For an instant, all is below the water's surface. Suddenly,
the head and a fin broke through the surface, only to synchronously
resubmerge. The shark's tail flailed in and out of the water. Then, an instant
of calm. The ocean is again placid just as a man leaning over the edge of a
small motorboat sails into frame. The man on the boat prepares a rope in
futility. Only a red mass stared back at him. One more faithless 'Oh, My,
God' is heard before the screen faded down and a centred swirl arrow
asked if I'd like to view all that again.

I tried to make sense of what I had just witnessed through the low-
quality video and the randomness of the event. Nevertheless, I was the
definition of uncomfortable. Believing there had to be more to this, I was
driven to learn that the head in the water belonged to a twenty-three-year-
old Russian named Vladimir Popov. Vladimir, along with several others
were at a resort just outside Hurghada, Egypt. The place was called Dream
Beach on the Red Sea. Not the first place that would come to mind if I
thought of likely shark attack spots. In fact, only twenty-four unprovoked
shark attacks have occurred in Egypt in the last one hundred years.
Vladimir and his girlfriend, Anastasia, were swimming in a popular area,
marked by distinct water slides often used by children who frequented the
area, when he was attacked. As the shark was focussed on Vladimir,
Anastasia managed to swim safely back to shore where she was dragged
from the sea by others on the beach. The shouting at the beginning of the
video were clear cries for his 'Papa', Vladimir's father Yury, who stood

helplessly on the beach as his son was killed in a matter of seconds. I recall, several years ago, when I suffered a serious injury that by some miracle, I have no memory of. I was told that, in my shock-induced stupor, I cried out for my 'Mommy'. And this was not the first shark attack I have had described to me in more detail than I cared to receive. At some point, the omniscient algorithms learned of my deep fear of sharks and the open ocean. It is as if they delight in haunting me with the occasional recommendation of sharky images and videos slid in-between those of mutilated children, cute cat antics, and the latest influencer trends. Even reflecting on the quality of the video and distance from the incident it took as its vantage point, it was a far cry from watching a remastered print of the 1975 film *Jaws* in 4k. Of course, reality and fiction are two very different things. I also didn't walk blindly into the over two-hour film. I do not know Vladimir and I have yet to have been on a beach in Egypt. But more than I have with any film, which are tailored to make me feel, I felt this short, forwarded video. I was really quite shaken. I did not sleep well that night and even after a day or so, it just did not sit right.

And yet, I callously scroll past the umpteenth video of a parent cradling a wad that was once their living child, or a child crying alone tethered to the body of their lifeless parent, or of blow off limbs, rubble drenched denizens, and other such images that accompany the eradication of a people from this planet and from history. And yet Harambe, the seventeen-year-old silverback gorilla who was shot to death in 2016 when a three-year-old child climbed into his enclosure at the Cincinnati Zoo in the US, got a candlelight vigil in Hyde Park, London, attended by thousands. Now, back in October 2023, the first images of the truly innocent being the collateral damage were very very troubling. And 2023's giving way to 2024 was underscored with some serious themes of depression. I recall one video of an Israeli trooper condemning Palestinians who were, to him, nonhuman and sentencing them to hell along with their religion and their prophet before throwing an explosive through the window of someone's house. Only a few instances later, the wall around that window was completely blown out. What was even more troubling is that he spoke in English and bore the accent of a stereotypical New Yorker. But even before 2023 — the latest season of this horror show — we have been watching the road to genocide in Palestine, week after week for quite some time. It had the ratings of a hit HBO show. And much like *Game of Thrones*, it feels as though, in the later seasons, that the writers have really lost the plot. In fact, they were jumping the shark. Maybe it is the randomness of the shark attack that gave me pause. And that I knew one man was now dead and a family, a community plunged into disarray. It is not easy to get my head around that. As numbers climb in Palestine, body after body, the mind cannot comprehend it. And heartache and depression do not follow mathematics. Depression plus depression does not necessarily equal more depression. What does it even mean to be 'more' depressed. Everyone has a different threshold for this sort of thing after all. In Palestine, the situation is much more complex. It has history and omnipotence. But then they say its beyond religion, or beyond politics, or beyond history because there isn't a nice simple answer to fall on. When the conflict is human versus human, each side has a different story even before we get into the notion of post-truths. Thankfully, sharks have yet to master the art of fake news. There is an understanding that there are innocents and there are belligerents and although it is sometimes hard to determine who is who, either side must have their reasons for their actions, right? We cannot place a similar dichotomy on a shark attack. Or at least we don't have to. They are one of those things that statistically never really happens, so when it does, we see it as this great tragedy. And tragedies have victims and victims must be the result of some evil. And because I know we have a collectively warped sense of justice; I knew that 'justice' would be pursued because we can see it done simply and quickly. Deep down, I knew that shark was going to have to pay for his 'crimes'. That 'maneater' would pay the price of his nature.

Let us think about this. What are we even doing in the ocean in the first place? And for 'fun'? And that shark was only there because climate change, that big existential tyre fire that we have and continue to contribute to, deprived sharks of their natural ecosystem and forcing them to seek new waters to do what they do. And yet we are surprised when they do what they do, and things go wrong for us. Interestingly, when it is man versus nature it is nature versus us, and us are the innocent victim. That us is conveniently absent when the conflict is man versus man. Had Harambe killed the boy, intentional or not, the conversation would be the tragedy of underestimating the wildness of a wild animal. Since Harambe was the one to die, he takes the victims place but since some tragedy had occurred, justice still must be demanded for the evil that took place. Whom do we blame? It depends on who you ask. Some say the boy's parents, some say the zoo staff, others blame American gun nuts, one opinion probably claims that you and I are somehow complicit in this 'crime'. At the end of the day, it is easier to empathise over a man being eaten alive by a shark or a gorilla being gunned down in a zoo than with the plight of the Palestinians. And that empathy exists in spades. But why? Does complexity dull our sympathies?

In the 2019 Netflix docuseries, *Don't F**k With Cats: Hunting an Internet Killer*, we witness an internet mob of strangers come together and hunt down a man who posted a video of himself suffocating a cat to death. Regardless of your feelings on the matter, it was a bit terrifying how effective they were at finding the culprit. If half of the madness that compelled that internet mob were directed at the situation in Palestine, the genocide would already be a short chapter in history. It doesn't make much sense. Then again, social justice warriors, of all flavours, are not famed for their adoration of reason. But there is something to explore in the phenomenon that results when a person or a group is willing to enact questionable approaches to justice on account of an animal. We can anthropomorphise certain animal companions to the point where we attribute to them the worth of collective defence and protection, even human rights. Yet more and more, it is hard to do that for beings that are already human.

Anthropomorphism is an incredibly powerful literary tool that, even in its most amateur applications, allows us to empathise in unexpected and unimaginable ways. I unabashedly adore it. This love affair has come, unfortunately, with no dearth of hardships, especially for one who read philosophy at university. For anthropomorphism is the attribution of humanness not just to animals, but also to other aspects of nature and even ideas or concepts. On reflection, I now know what my retort should have been to those staunchest critics of my anthropomorphic tendencies. You see, the practice is purely a linguistic, literary mechanism for articulating relatability or empathy for an idea. At the very least, it makes higher concepts a hell of a lot more readable, if not entertaining. This mood for love is perhaps why I so easily gravitated towards non-western philosophies.

Few can anthropomorphise like the Chinese, be they philosopher, scientist, politician, or parent. But this too is the other side of the extreme, and it has given rise to hokey astrological cosmologies and an overabundance of 'cute' consumer rubbish. Obviously, the tool must be applied with care and, importantly, a dissociation of the subject being observed from the humanistic constructs placed upon it must be performed before a truth claim or logical move is attempted. Most do not think to do this last step because to anthropomorphise is comfortable and can be a sense making process. But if I were a gambling man in our world of extremes, I'd rather people be over-attributing humanity to things where denial of humanity is the rule of the day. We are in a dire, sorry state of contemporary affairs. A right mess, really. My favourite -ism might just be a stepping stone towards figuring out how we lost the capacity to care. As it stands, solidarity is dead and our ability to sympathise and even empathise have become victims of our extreme times. Forget about compassion, not just for our fellow humans, but for much of anything on this planet.

Fast-forwarding eight months after the night of the man-eating shark, I was logged into a Zoom discussion that was part of World Futures Day. Each 1 March, Teach the Future, a global endeavour aimed at promoting futures thinking in youth and pre-university education, brings together young and not-so young futures thinkers for a twenty-four-hour long conversation that begins in New Zealand and ends in Hawaii. Each hour was given a different theme and this one's was the futures of human rights. While it was not directly said, an uncomfortable truth haunted the not always stable WIFI that was holding us all together: how could one speak of the futures of human rights when nothing of the sort seemed to exist or garner any respect in the present. You may not be surprised to find out that we didn't get very far with the futures of human rights. Resigned to the farce, we instead reassessed our aim. The rest of the conversation took a step back, focussing on the rights of the rain forests and the planet's flora and fauna. Regardless of what rights we discussed, at least we could feel confident that no plants would see themselves as more equal than others. The takeaway was that we needed collective will and collective action if we are to have any hope of moving forward.

Events these days have a talent for magnifying details we might otherwise leave out. In Palestine, we are seeing the catastrophic failures of collective action, dysfunctional attempts at solidarity, all of which is leading to a self-sabotaging pursuit of justice.

The collective, if I can be so bold, has rallied behind compromise after compromise, only to be defeated by a simple yet persistent, and nigh evil, veto. From 'Freedom From the River to the Sea', to ceasefire, to something/anything, to please at least stop murdering children, attacking hospitals, and turning safe zones into warzones as effortlessly as you flip a light switch. Veto, veto, veto proudly proclaimed as though they actually think they are on the right side of history on this one. The response is the putting forward of well-reasoned arguments accusing the Israeli authorities of war-crimes, human rights violations, and genocide. These are not knee-jerk reactions. Not nothing. And while I have never been one to see protests as a productive expression of political power, it is a bit ridiculous how the most noble demonstrations are cast aside with the clever application of the words 'antisemitism' and 'wokeness' — words that like sticks and stones can actually break bones and hurt you. Of course, these valiant efforts are undermined by the boycotts which illustrate the masses inability to appreciate or cope with complexity. Boycotting of certain brands, particularly those already in the business of millions and billions, in their most effective, only hurts those on the lowest rungs of the ladder while executives and fat cats will gladly continue building thrones out of the high-quality mortar the corpses of nameless, minimum wage exploited labourers make. Add to this the complexity of franchising. Add to this the complexity of the global economic system that frankly positions us so that no matter where you spend it, every dollar, and quite likely, every pound spent goes back into the machine, overall benefiting the state known as Israel.

And then there are the TikTok videos. Destructions and mutilated bodies of children. And thanks to our technodependent lives, all of it is quickly dismissed as fake news from both sides. Add to this the use of AI generated art to depict the inhumanity of refugee camps, the plight of the Palestinians, and even to portray the true story of Israeli soldiers setting loose dogs to attack a Palestinian woman. First, such a lazy approach to inform the masses underlies a special level of uncaring. The old effortless form of sympathy was to simply post 'thoughts & prayers' for whatever the tragedy of the week was and then carry on. Now we just ask ChatGPT. Is protest art even still a thing or just the stuff of AI hallucinations? Second, the uncanny valley only muddies the post-truth waters of this conflict. The mundanity and oddness of AI generated art makes it easier for '#EyesOn' fill in the blank to quickly become an image that exists everywhere, but that we no longer see in the maddening fray of it all. It is the unforgivable epitome of undermining one's own efforts. Why shoot yourself in the foot when you can just cut the appendage off?

And then we have some who even forgive, perhaps so they may forget and get on with their self-righteous lives, these atrocities through the despicable application of the label 'martyr'. How disgusting do we human beings have to be to justify – and yes it is justification – the dismemberment and torture of children by claiming that they should be proud to be martyrs for the evil of other humans. And folks wonder why I have not thrown my hat in any particular religious ring. I ask a man why he boycotts a brand that will result in a young, Malay Muslims losing their job while the CEO buys a private jet and he responds saying, 'worry not, their hardships will be rewarded in *Jannah*'. And I ask an auntie, how do we cope with all the dead children, and she says 'worry not, all martyrs go to *Jannah*'. Sorry, that's disgusting. Completely unacceptable. An abhorrent crime is committed when religion justifies the evil acts of man through the promise of some paradise few, perhaps none, actually deserve.

If you listen to both sides, then everybody is raping everyone else while, perhaps simultaneously, murdering children. All with a smile on their faces. And where compromise and middle of the road are seen as weakness, either you stand on the side of Israel in the name of historic guilt in an eternal battle against manifested antisemites, or you side so deeply with the Palestinian people, in an extremist form of compassion, that you actually take their pain and it becomes yours, you dispossess them of their pain and even their identity in a hubristic attempt to be a social justice warrior. Worse of all, we all seem to be just fine with that. Two major wars accentuate the daily news and countless other 'civil kerfuffles' remain unfit for print. Sorry says the UN. No peace or end in sight. But if it ain't man bites dog, it ain't gonna trend on X formerly known as Twitter. Sun goes up, sun goes down. Meanwhile the 'conflict', a word that does no justice to it, is like a washing machine that cannot get past the first wash cycle.

The clothes only appear and smell clean, while remaining impossibly damp. High chance for mildew. Events, my dear boy, events! It is all just too complex. Unable to conjure compassion for our fellow man we demand justice for hedgehogs, foxes, gorillas, kitty cats, and puppy dogs. Maybe it isn't such a crazy idea to reacquaint ourselves with the art of anthropomorphism.

From the fables of the ancient Greek storyteller slave Aesop to the collected folklore of the nineteenth century German academics Jacob and Wilhelm Grimm, we can see the capacity anthropomorphism has for articulating simple themes and morals. Beauty is only skin deep, be weary of strangers, cooperation and planning can get you out of some truly sticky situations, and the list goes on. These sorts of stories are rather straightforward and illustrate a simple, yet often profound, message. Interestingly, us humans are rather good at this process. But I wonder if the tool can be taken further. I wonder if anthropomorphism can help us to appreciate, perhaps even navigate the complex. You see, us humans are rather useless when it comes to complex systems. Complexity confounds and entraps the human mind, rendering it in a sleep paralysis that only grows in strength the more we struggle. Can upright walking, talking animals in human clothes come to the rescue and help us solve this Chinese finger trap? We may just need to go beyond nursery rhymes in order to get there.

Anthropomorphic stories are often hidden in the contradiction of being kids' stuff that's not really for kids because of how they address themes we may consider 'adult'. E.B. White's 1952 novel *Charlotte's Web* has a soft, yet not sheltering approach to the complexity of change, loss of innocence, and death. Even Arnold Lobel's well dressed and well-mannered *Frog and Toad* were not afraid to confront the complexity of friendship throughout their 1970s series of books. And few novels, anthropomorphic or not, have demonstrated such a masterful investigation of complexity than George Orwell's stand against totalitarianism in his 1945 novel *Animal Farm* or Richard Adam's 1972 novel *Watership Down*, where a rag-tag band of rabbits navigate tyranny, freedom, reason, faith, individualism, and communalism as they seek out a new home.

More recently, the English writer Neil Gaiman admirably plays at this through his masterwork *The Sandman*, a DC Comic series running between 1988 and 1996. Not once, but seven times Gaiman anthropomorphises a complexity into a character in this series. Collectively, they are known as the Endless, and aside from the titular main, Dream, Gaiman personifies Destiny, Death, Destruction, Desire, Despair, and Delirium. They are further anthropomorphised into being siblings of a typical non-traditional trope-defying dysfunctional American family of the late 1980s.

The task is fraught as anthropomorphism of complexities comes awfully close to simplifying complexities. Indeed, in simplifying complexities, the complexities cease to be or grow untenably in their deepening complexity. With either result, you are in for a world of hurt. Yet, the best characters are rather complex, and with postmodernism in its heyday at the time of this series, Gaiman retains complexity in their anthropomorphic forms rather well. The character Dream, for instance, is given the space to unpack his rich complexity across time, cultures, and the morality spectrum.

Where Dream and even Death are indicative of Gaiman's successful application of anthropomorphism onto complex concepts, the closest he comes to failure, and the concept given the least justice in the series, is the character of Desire. But this is not for lack of effort. The character is meticulously crafted. Desire is, of course, androgenous. Not just this, but in the artwork, Desire accentuates both traditionally male and traditionally female attributes from frame to frame. Just when the reader has an idea of who this figure is, it changes – sometimes both genderless and genderful simultaneously. Desire is sometimes referred to as 'sister-brother' and 'sibling'. Desire even resides within a giant, flesh and blood, replica of itself displaying the carnal nature of desire and its narcissistic tendencies. Each of the Endless has a sigil to represent them. Desire's is a glass heart, representing fragility but also openness and freedom. Desire even has a twin sister named Despair and are interestingly the closest pairing of the seven siblings. Yet, in all the steeped potential for a complex study of Desire, they are characterised as the lead antagonist to Dream and often fall into the trap of a cartoonishly evil bad guy. But this may say more about us than the complexity that is desire.

An interesting cross cultural commonality is found in how, across the globe, desire is cast in a dark, uncivilised light. In fact, the society where all are free and driven by their desires is a common caricature of civilisation, the bastard opposite that condemns humanity to the antiprogress that is nature or, heaven forbid, anarchy where, in the end, they ultimately destroy themselves. Along the way, desire has been equated to sin and generally there is a social expectation that we resist our desires lest we shatter the delicate Victorian shroud we throw on to pretend we have moved on from the eighteenth century Genevan philosophe Jean-Jacques Rousseau's primitive state, pleasure palace. It is a fatal misstep to allow this simplification of desire. We must not lose sight of the fact that Rousseau's state of nature also includes the English write Clive Barker's cenobites, Caligula (both the historical and mythical character), and amphetamines.

Desire is a complexity. It is perhaps the first brush we humans experience with the truly complex. Desire breaks the mould, taking us beyond our more infantile feelings of hunger, pain, fear, comfort, or joy. Desire is complex as it is not only subject to change but also competing against other desires, both to the self and in relation to the desires of others. And then of course there is the colonising nature of desire. To appreciate complexity, it must be grappled with. And thanks to our lacking predilections towards complex thinking, we need to keep trying new ways of navigating complexity. Comprehending the global economy is hard. Wrapping one's head around Palestine is difficult. And, fair enough, it is somewhat programmed in our biology. We are tool using beings and once we invent a hammer, it is hard not to see the world as anything but a series of nails waiting to get pounded. Our incredibly sophisticated eyes pluck patterns from obscurity and our fingers are set at untangling the wonders of the world. We are master simplifiers, even unto our own undoing. To move forward, we must resist such attitudes and keep ourselves open. We can still analyse without breaking down by following art museum etiquette's 'look, but do not touch'.

We can begin with the aim. Indeed, the aim of complexity is unity. The centre need not hold, but the systemic structure must demonstrate a reassuring solidity. Complexity disbanded is simply oblivion. Desire, in the same vein, seeks a unity of sorts. A unity of wants, concentrated in what we might describe as, for lack of a better term, a happy person – at least a content one, balancing desires requires some delicate sacrifice. That balancing in itself is incredibly complex. Especially as our desires are not always our own, but those placed upon us by others, conscious and unconscious, as well as those we ourselves place on others. Like it or not, conscious or otherwise, our desires actually tie us together. Desire serves as an inception point for networking. We can add to this an interesting feature: desire is largely frowned upon or expected to be tempered or repressed. Desires are then hidden and left unevaluated or examined except for by certain psychologists that we might prefer kept their desires to themselves. When something is sidelined from public discourse it rarely goes away. Instead, it festers and ferments. Desires supressed or denied become monsters of our own creation. If they are kept out of the light of reflection or public discourse, judgements are not passed, and anything goes. Desires unchecked are allowed to come in all shapes and varieties and can even be counterintuitive. The aim of desire to be a united happy person or connected happy people is dead on arrival. And if we attempt to think of anything but desire, when we are faced with it, we simplify it and undermine the complexity. Simple wants undermine desire and the whole project falls apart. All in the same boat, we wonder how true crime, often unintentionally idolising the evilest that humanity has to offer, carrying out the most unimaginable crimes, is so popular. The strangest things bring us together.

Postnormal times theory adds another dimension. Complexity is highly susceptible to chaos which further complexifies the complex. New branches and new impacts can take us for quite the ride. In the cascading complex impacts chaos delivers, we find contradictions abound. Things once thought impossible stand there staring us in the face. Desires, either not understood (especially in their complexity), or denied, or supressed, run amok. Eventually certain desires arise that are counterintuitive to other desires. Yet the complex machine must find that balance and some messed up attitudes, believes, and actions result. And then, were desires in and of themselves ought to be bringing us together, they are rather tearing us apart. In some cases, bringing us together in tearing us apart.

The cherry on top of the dementing of desire is found where it interplays with extremism. The complexities of desire and the chaos of extremism are the fire and gunpowder that have propelled the assassin's bullet through the flesh of solidarity. And solidarity looks in no position to take advantage of this situation for a photo op or to tell its followers to 'fight'. And this gunman was no lone-wolf isolated event. Extremism was underestimated. It was a way religious and political fanatics conducted themselves. Let the counterterrorism experts handle it. It has worked so well in the past...

But extremism is a cancer and cancer can come for any good intentioned cells. Desires are spectral, this is how we can meet in the middle and experience comradery, even if the degrees are not precisely the same. This supports a move for greater intersectionality. But extremism is a binary. For or against, the middle ground need not apply. Furthermore, extreme is seen as strength and stability while moderation is seen as weak and wobbly. Not a good approach to holding water. In sloshing off the minutiae – the middle ground – the cascading complexity of desires, which once united us, now divide and divide further. Desires move to become wants and now go a step further, becoming needs. And it is very hard to go back from that point. Reason is tossed out the window as needs are not just a part of the unity of the being, they become an existential. And this can become very dangerous as the existential is easily threatened and with all else in the valley of extremism, stereotypes and gross generalisations, become the grammar by which we navigate the everyday. If you cannot have what you consider existential, you might as well raise the white flag and kiss all that you hold dear goodbye.

Let us see how this happens. A perfectly reasonable desire is to be brave. Now bravery is an incredibly vague quality taking on numerous definitions and with even more ways to demonstrate it. Bravery can range from the kid who stands up to the schoolhouse bully, to a person facing down rejection to ask another on a date, to a person who speaks out against an injustice while others remain silent. Bravery has many faces. And that's great because then more folks have access to what we may call bravery. A community of the brave may just take root!

One definition of bravery is to persist in spite of fear. To quickly break this down, in order to be brave, one has to have a fear of something and an enduring strength, which may ground its fortitude in the physical or mental. Reasonable application of this notion of bravery presents no inherent problem. But if we take the value of bravery as an extremism and make it existential, something very troubling arises. Two things happen immediately. First, the complexity of bravery is reduced in its most extreme form to the definition we are considering. Second, bravery as a complexity can exist as a nascent potential or kinetic form, but when reduced to an extremism, this bravery now requires demonstration. To exude bravery, it must constantly be exhibited. Is a knight who is not constantly saving helpless maidens or slaying ruthless dragons one you can call brave? Then we look at the particulars of the definition. It requires fear. And fear is a funny thing that when it is faced down, it loses its scariness with repetition and practice. So, an extremist bravery requires constant construction of fear lest the bravery demonstrated lose its shine. The other particular requisite is strength which, in order to maintain the bravery's authenticity requires a regular raising of the stakes. If you lift the same 20 kilogram weight over and over, you will become quite good at lifting 20 kilograms, but not necessarily be getting any stronger. So, in order to maintain both the requisite strength and requisite fear, the fear you are constantly creating has to be successively scarier. After all, one wouldn't want their bravery questioned.

A hint of forward thinking quickly shows this to be an unsustainable approach. But as we have seen with other forms of extremist thought, an idea does not need to be sustainable in order to cause a lot of devastation before it burns itself out or collapses. Sometimes we burn the whole house down in the process. Nevertheless extremisms, like revolutions, eventually burn out. A revolution can only exist when it has something to revolt against. This was the problem with various communist revolutions, in order to retain power, they needed to find a new group to revolt against. Eventually, the hope is wiser header prevail and you find a new way, otherwise, the cycle repeats itself. Some last longer than others. China's present advantage is that it has a ridiculously large population and that affords you a lot of different folks you can feed the next wave of revolution with. So, the moral of the story is check the fine print terms and conditions on your next communist revolution. But if stars must too collapse into blackholes, it makes sense the same fate awaits extremism.

This is the present predicament with identity. More accurately put, this is the condition of desire for identity. Desire is already complex and identity itself is a different complexity. Now there is an infinitely diverse complexity if I've ever seen one. It is almost like there are as many identities as there are combinations of given and surnames, in fact more, seeing as certain culture's naming conventions are quite limiting. And many of us spend some fraction of a century trying to iron out what that identity actually is. Because its complex. And why shouldn't it be? It is after all informed by where you were born, the languages you speak, the stories you were told, the history you were born into, everywhere you've been, everyone you've talked to, all that you've sensed, and a whole lot of other internal and external factors. Identity is also organic or plastic. In saying this I mean that identity is subject to change and growth. We are indeed not the same people we were five years ago. The complexity of having multiple facets and being a living and changing concept means that all identity is constructed. This is not to be confused with the claim that all identity is socially constructed, I just mean to iterate that all identity is being built. This is also not to say that certain aspects of identity do or do not have greater permanence than others. That is not really the concern here. What I want to look at is that some identities are imagined. But just because they are imagined does not mean that they are good, bad, or otherwise in comparison to what we might call more authentic identities. And just because an identity is imagined does not mean that it is not real or that it can be ignored. Even imagined identities pose issues that we must address lest we undermine the complexity of one's desire for identity — something that is truly a universe unto itself.

The idea of imagined identities borrows from the late Irish historian and political scientist Benedict Anderson's notion of the imagined community but expands the concept slightly. Anderson was concerned with nationalism, something I completely agree is an imagined identity, that has been an incredibly problematic artefact of modernity that requires address. When reflecting on Anderson, I cannot help but recall the American comedian George Carlin's famous warning: 'never underestimate the power of stupid people in large groups'. And then I feel bad for Milwaukee, an American city that I had never really had reason to sympathise, as it was overrun with folks in red MAGA (Make America Great Again) hats adorning Van Goghian bandages over their ears during the 2024 Republican National Convention. I might be tempted to agree that nationalism and political identity are more towards the worst-case scenario of imagined identities, but no less complex and certainly no less real than other identities. They are imagined because they are not innate. Nationalism and political identity presuppose a nation-state global order and a particular political context in order to make any sense. But there are many other imagined identities. They exist as a spectrum. Take for instance the refugee. Refugee is an imagined identity not because I am refusing their existence, but because a refugee can only exist if there is a nation-state global ordering. But in say nomadic, pre-nation-state ordered societies, there weren't refugees as the identity did not need to exist. Again, although imagined identities, and even if they too are a nasty byproduct of modernity, they are still real, and they are human beings, and they need to be given due dignity and their problems respected as our problems because we will only be able to transcend our problems together.

To see how the corruption of the desire for identity has led to the death of solidarity, I want to focus on three imagined identities that have risen in prominence in recent times: race, class, and gender. Race is clearly an imagined identity as it is based in biology that is simply incorrect. Yes, we know that now, but that doesn't undo its long and brutal history. Race is imagined, but it damn well sure exists and millions of people have been affected by its existence. This is the difference between the post-race folks who would prefer that we admit it was wrong, but now let's move on because actually we are all equal and the antiracist folks who want to escape the racialised worldview, but we simply cannot as it has had some serious long-term impacts on equity. Intimately related to and complexly interconnected to race is class. With class we can also include caste as the same dynamics are at play. Again, imagined but also very real, perhaps the most real of the three I will discuss here and the one that can 'fake it until it makes it' through vitriolic political rhetoric. Classes emerged out of hierarchical systems that persisted through incorrect notions of genetics, archaic notions of ancestor worship, and more recently with the rather grotesque need for divisions within economics systems. The elephant in the room everyone is ignoring being capitalism. The third imagined identity is not as historically interlinked as the first two. It is gender. Gender is very intricately interwoven with another complex identity, sexuality, and is the one most directly under attack from various right-wing forces. Although it scares many to death, gender is very real, requiring collective respect and address. It is imagined as it is a troublesome product of a culture of necessary dichotomies, labelling, and the assumed, simplified binary identities of man and woman. These, of course, are not the only three identities that have run up against a resurgence of extremism creating a very troublesome predicament, but looking at these three might give us some valuable insight into what is going on.

So postnormal times finds us between the old paradigm and what comes next. Increasing complexity is witnessing higher frequencies of chaos that are laying bare more and more contradictions that are tearing down the walls of stability we took for granted in the past. Whether or not its where we came from, we are in something damn close to the state of nature described by the English philosopherThomas Hobbes in his 1651 work *Leviathan*. We are shaking in our boots, terrified the next bloke we come across will be the one to do us in, and we will give anything for a social contract. Our traditional security blankets are crumbling as we desperately search for anything resembling stability. Since identity is as much personal as it is communal, also open and rather complex, this is where many are doubling down. Ideally, the scenario could play out quite nice. Some introspection and critical thinking have us really fluffing up and analysing the complexity of our multitudes, finding new ways for commonality and maybe even bringing to life a new social paradigm grounded in wisdom communities built on intersectionality. But, don't forget we are rather bad at complexity. So, this isn't what is happening.

Two Americans are having a doozy of a time trying to cope with what is actually going on. In the space of race and class is the writer and investigative journalist Asad Haider and in the space of gender is the feminist philosopher Judith Butler. Both are keenly aware of an important observation: the right – Conservatives, Republicans, Evangelical Christians, Old People, Donald Trump – is on the warpath. Haider notes how the right has coopted solidarity. Where it once existed as a method for bridging similarities between different, yet commonly aimed groups – often justice was a good common object that made certain opposites come together – to form a bond of siblinghood, the right now uses it as a call to either 'join us or let them execute you', not surprisingly reminiscent of 'you are either with us or against us'. Haider observes antiwokeness as the ultimate simplifier of the left's rich, complex diversity. Identity is reduced to identity politics and standard populist tactics make for a quick checkmate. Butler observes that the right has turned gender, the word itself already a complex mystery for most, into a 'phantasm' or a made-up boogieman that threatens their families, their bodies, their beliefs, and their children. Fear is the simple emotion that silences the complexity of nontraditional identities. Both Haider and Butler construct expositive and well-reasoned prosecutions against the Trumpian sensation/movement, the unholy alliance of the Catholic Church and Evangelical American Christians, and the unabashed racists, homophobes, and xenophobes who hide behind emperors who have no clothes around the globe.

Afraid in these uncertain times, many are looking to race, class, and gender for stability. Yet, extremism is the rule of the day and not only undermines the complexity of our desires for identity, it dispossesses that complexity. Anything that does not fit into the boxes of one extreme or another is not only socially cast out, but policies and laws are created to attempt to control the complexity of identities. Those extremist identities allowed are then seen as existential threats to one another. Identity becomes ideology and identity politics, armed with justified offensive stereotypes, is the only way to seek recognition and thus the protection and opportunity being a citizen of a state used to come with. In the absence of the complex minutiae of our true identities, imagined or not, there are few points of commonality to be found. Meanwhile identity fades from a desire, into a want, into a need. And this is clearly not sustainable. Extremisms by definition must continually become more extreme. In terms of identity, this means identities get weirder, but also more militant, eventually becoming nothing more than a weapon that just might kill the others before they kill you. At this point, the only solidarity you might hope to find is a most bastardised form that unifies the self. As this scenario will likely be accompanied by more than a few instances of psychosis and if you run out of others to fear, why not fear the other selves in that head of yours? Xenophobia in all its faces from homophobia to Islamophobia will be so normal, the various words will not require mentioning. After all most of the phobia's targets will be terminated either through the quick death of state sanctioned violence to the slow death of denial of access to education, healthcare, society, basic human needs, and eventually, existence. It of course will not hold, but are you so confident any of us will survive that fire?

At the precipice, postnormal times theory calls for policies that navigate as opposed to controlling complexity, anticipating as opposed to ignoring chaos, and for transcending as opposed to solving for contradictions.

Erring on the side of caution calls for us to not further complexify, if we can, while attempting to not give way to the conditions that give rise to chaos and to always be thinking towards new approaches where contradictions arise. This is a good general policy, but in confronting the death of solidarity and the inhibition on the desire for identity we need to go further. Butler argues for revamped education, awareness after all never hurt anybody, complete with solid curriculums in critical race theory and gender studies along with other yet-to-emerge disciplines, while in the meantime it is our duty to simply call people out when they are wrong and especially when they are being hypocrites, denying rights and access to others. Haider proposes a move towards what he calls an insurgent universality, a universalism that instead of presupposing some abstract bearer of rights – which tends to end up being white, male, and 'civilised' – seeks to highlight the agency of individuals. He also still believes in the power of the masses of which I remain suspicious. These are all fantastic ideas and should be pursued, but what is missing is a need to become comfortable with complexity and to think in that space.

The American civil rights advocate and scholar Kimberlé Crenshaw made a startling observation: in the US, legally, black women do not exist. Crenshaw carefully studied a large sample of cases where black women argued that they had been discriminated against in a variety of situations. American judicial systems were found to be incapable of commiserating with complexity. Black women either had to argue they were being discriminated against on the grounds of sex or race, but not both. While women in general face innumerable inequalities in comparison to men, to say all women, black, white, or otherwise stand on equal ground is as absurd as saying black men and black women stand equal to one another. And what of black trans individuals? It is not easy to change legal systems, but it is not an unheard-of phenomenon. And since times do change, laws need to be readily plastic to adapt to what may come. And it speaks volumes to the weakness of a legal system if it is unable to even engage a duality, let alone the deeper complexity its citizenry actually possesses.

So, instead of erring towards caution, I think we need to embrace complexity. To truly navigate our way through increasing complexity, we need to unlearn that which holds us back and to explore strange new worlds and boldly go where no one has gone before. In doing this we should critically engage our identities in all their spectral complexity weighing tradition and culture with new ideas and ways of being. This requires facing certain fears and knowing, even loving one another. This means pledging a respect for the dignity of others. It can be as simple as trying each day to get the pronouns straight – which even as a member of that supposedly woke millennial generation, it is difficult to break from the old, often oppressive structures that otherwise refuse to die. It is difficult to resist the temptations of false and destructive simplicities and the allure of populist, extremist ultimatums. Indeed, it can be as strange as accepting an identity that may sound absurd to you but that, at the end of the day, has no impact on your life and can be everything to that Other. And in doing this do not give into the fallacies of slippery slopes or outrageous situations that magically and ridiculously turn ourselves into the victims of some fictitious wrongs, which speaks more to our own shortcomings than the shortcomings of others. In doing this all of our infinite complexities can be realised and actualised and who knows, we may just find unthought intersections in those complexities, new ways to build communities. And then finally the complexity of desire can reach its aim, that of unity. Maybe, just maybe we can then stand together in a reborn solidarity where collectively we can navigate the future ahead agreeing not only that it is a good idea to be careful stewards of the natural world, but to uphold that due to all peoples, access to human rights and dignity.

The American poet Althea Davis has one poem that is constructed as a prayer to God for a better afterlife for all the animals who have been killed by humans for simply doing what they naturally do. The last line strikes a lasting feeling. 'If I am killed for simply living, let death be kinder than man'. Following Vladimir Popov's unfortunate encounter on the shores of the Red Sea, a band of fishermen tracked down the tiger shark who had killed and partially eaten him. After the tiger shark was caught, the army of fishermen were greeted by applause and shouts of 'Allahu Akbar' as they dragged the animal to the shore. On that Egyptian beach an assembled mob proceeded to bludgeon the animal to death. Video and grotesque images are available for inquiring minds. The leader of this delivery of justice was none other than Yury Popov. He wailed and wept as he threw his full force behind the wooden rod he used to strike the lifeless thing that was once a tiger shark. Meanwhile, a young man smiles as he poses for a selfie with the mangled, blood and sea water bloated carcass with its jaws extended for maximum monstrosity. If we must strive to separate man from beast, then that line is our complexity. The irony is that we have failed to enable ourselves to live with complexity. Let death be kinder than man.

ARTS AND LETTERS

EXILE IS A HARD JOB

Marjorie Allthorpe-Guyton

The celebratory mood at the Venice Biennale 2024 was muted by the pressing reality of current wars in Europe, the Middle East, and Africa. The agenda is evangelical, forcing a revision of values and of histories. Even the sponsors seemed less bent on display; just one super yacht was moored alongside a super catamaran, ArtExplorer, the project of the businessman, philanthropist, mountaineer, and grand patron of the Louvre, Frédéric Joussett. He sees his boat museum as a campaigning Greenpeace project bringing the experience of museum quality art to new audiences 'everything we do for the audience is free'. For the Biennale punter this Biennale offers few quick pickings of 'emergent' artists for the market. There is a strong focus on the 'indigenous' artist who may be part of collectives or families of artists; the work is culturally specific, and unfamiliar, demanding time and knowledge.

There are eighty-eight national pavilions this year and thirty collateral events across the two main sites of the Giardini and Arsenale and the palaces of the City of Venice. Asia and the Middle East have a stronger presence. Africa has thirteen countries represented, up from eight in 2022, New entrants are the Republic of Benin, Ethiopia, United Republic of Tanzania, Democratic Republic of Timor Leste. Morocco was due to debut this year, but canceled; Nicaragua, the Republic of Panama, and Senegal have their own pavilions for the first time. The Holy See has a project in an active women's prison on the island of Guidecca, but without Vatican pre-registration many preview visitors were turned away. Israel's pavilion remained shut, under guard by the Italian army. After a petition signed by 23,000, the artist and curators refused to open their show until hostilities cease. For less privileged artists, with few opportunities to show in their own countries, dissidence may not be an option. Russia's pavilion, closed at the last Biennale, is given to its longstanding partner in Latin America, impoverished Bolivia. The commissioners state 'the project brings together artists from Bolivia and friendly countries in Latin America... an opportunity to share and demonstrate the brotherhood and joy that unites us ...the common ground of our indigenous origins and the vocation to "live well" in harmony and equity among ourselves and with our "Mother Earth"'. In 2023, Bolivia signed a $450 million lithium deal with Russia.

While political agendas and dubious compromise prevail, the 2024 Biennale is a determined attempt to break free of premises which have defined Venice, the archetype of Biennales, since its first edition in 1895. The ground was laid by the foundational Havana Biennials of 1984 and 1986. They focused on Latin America, Africa, the Middle East, and Asia challenging the hegemony of the global north, the representation of the nation state, the notion of centre and periphery, and the idea of an international art language which precludes the local, the artisanal, and the outsider. There have been sporadic reforms during Venice's long history and the 2022 Biennale, curated by Cecilia Alemani, was a game changer in its restitution of women artists. The curator this year, Adriano Pedrosa, the Brazilian artistic director of MASP, the Museu de Arte de São Paulo Assis Chateaubriand, is the first to be both from and based in the global south. Eurocentricism and global inequality were unequivocally laid bare by the late Okwui Enwezor, Nigerian-born curator of the 2015 Biennale, but Pedrosa is the first to so wholeheartedly embrace global modernisms and indigenous and marginalised art practices. He describes his inclusion of artists working in the twentieth century in Latin America, Africa, the Middle East, particularly South and Southeast Asia, as speculative, a provocation. Overall, this year there are three times as many Asian artists showing.

Biennale Arte 2024, Venice
Curated by Adriano Pedrosa
Giardini / Arsenale / Forte Marghera
20 April – 24 November 2024

Pedrosa's project in the central pavilion in the Giardini and the Arsenale includes 312 artists in two parts, historic and contemporary: *Nucleo Storico* and *Nucleo Contemporaneo* . The title, *Stranieri Ovunque-Foreigners Everywhere,* is appropriated from a Paris based collective, Claire Fontaine whose neon words in over fifty languages, except English, bookend the exhibition. It is an ambiguous, multivalent carrier for Pedrosa's diverse subjects from the diasporic artist, the migrant, expatriate, émigré, refugee, to the queer, the outsider, the self taught, and the indigenous artist. Their many histories, identities, cultures, and practices are in danger of being subsumed, even homogenised by the rubric. Can Pedrosa claim to be what the French Martinican poet and philosopher Édouard Glissant called an 'assembler of the dissimilar' embracing the opacity, the chaos of a diasporic contemporary world? And a future where 'there will be no more cultures without all of the cultures'? While Pedrosa's exhibition can claim complexity, his vision is ultimately failed by the Biennale format which remains fixed on national representation, however upended.

There should be surprises, even some horrors, but Pedrosa's show, which aims to propel a march to a more connected future, is in content and in presentation a revisionist museum proposition with few of the bells and whistles, the theatre of previous Biennales. It also has to compete with the showier spectacles of some of the national pavilions and over thirty collateral events. The *Nucleo Storico*, from 1905–1990, has two hundred artists grouped in two sections, portraits, abstractions, and a third, devoted to the Italian diaspora, in the Arsenale. Brazil has the largest Italian diaspora in the world. With each artist represented by just one work, this survey is both too wide and too narrow to fully assess quality or significance. Of the portraits there is every modernist expression by artists from Asia, Africa, Latin America, the Middle East, and beyond. From the Afro Cuban of Wilfredo Lam to the metaphysical surrealism of the Oxford-

based Sudanese artist Ibrahim El-Salahi, to the symbolism of the Iranian
Bahman Mohasses. There are some standout works alongside the canonised
Mexican artists, Frida Kahlo and Diego Rivera, such as a muscular portrait
Cabeça de Mulato 1934 by Brazilian Candido Portinari (1903-1962), born
into an Italian immigrant family from the Veneto, whose subjects were
black immigrant farm workers.

Nil Yalter b.1938, *Exile Is a Hard Job 1973-ongoing*; mixed media, detail.
Photo: Theo Allthorpe-Mullis

There are few large sculptures and a glaring absence of digital media in
the Giardini central pavilion. This might come as a welcome relief, but the
prevalence of paintings and drawings over film, video, and installations
gives an unbalanced view of contemporary practice, including that by
indigenous artists some of whom happily work across traditional materials,
painting, drawing textiles, wood, skin, and clay to iPhone, iPad, and video.
Easel sized paintings and small drawings also make other demands, they
need close attention and reflection – as well as the reading of labels which
the museum can offer but is nigh impossible in the monstrous scale and
jostle of the Venice Biennale. It is hard to linger over the Italian paintings
beautifully displayed on suspended glass screens in the Arsenale's
colonnade when the throng moves on relentlessly to the next bay and the
next. After the quiet portraits, the smaller abstract section in the Giardini
heralds a more contemporary vibe with exuberant paintings by

Mohammed Chabaa, Mohammad Melehi, and Mohammed Hamadi of the Casablanca School, part of the Moroccan new wave post independence. Their work fuses modernist abstraction with motifs from Arabic writing and tribal Glaoui carpets. Paris-based Turkish artist Nil Yalter shows *Pink Tension* 1969 one of her early abstracts influenced by Russian constructivism.

Nil Yalter, an untrained and fearless artist now in her eighties, is a pivotal and powerful presence in the *Nucleo Contemporaneo* with two of the most resonant works which mark her feminist and political activism and her focus on migration. Born into a Turkish family in Cairo in 1938 she moved to Paris in 1965. She says in a recent interview 'I'm a nomad, an immigrant, a Mongol, a Jew from Salonika, I come from all of these places. They are part of me, my family, my history...my father is a Muslim from Bosnia and Herzegovina'. *EXILE IS A HARD JOB* 1973-ongoing is a long-term project with refugees, in Istanbul, Paris, and New York; video and fly posters document their lives. The title comes from *Sofya' dan'* 1957 by the Turkish Poet Nâzim Hikmet who was exiled to Russia. *Topak Ev* 1973 is a whole room installation, a circular space with walls of posters and videos of Turkish and Portuguese immigrant workers, with a central Bektik tent traditionally made by nomadic brides in central Anatolia. Yalter, like most of the artists in Pedrosa's project has never been shown at the Biennale. She is a recipient this year, alongside the Brazilian Anna Maria Maiolino, of the Biennale Golden Lion for Lifetime Achievement.

Yalter and many artists in this Biennale are transnational citizens, indeed *foreigners everywhere*. Bouchra Khalili, French Moroccan, living in Austria, shows *The Mapping Journey Project*, eight large screen videos in the Arsenale where tortuous journeys of migration drawn in real-time make a simple but powerful statement. National pavilions in the Giardini have made strenuous efforts to answer Pedrosa's call. France shows multimedia artist Julien Creuzet, born in the French overseas island territory of Martinique. Germany shows the Israeli Yael Bartana, of Berlin and Amsterdam, who represented Poland last time and Jeffrey Gibson, of Cherokee and Choctawa origin, is the first indigenous artist to represent the United States. Corralled in the national pavilions, these artists are a Biennale Trojan horse, at the vanguard of a growing movement which resists nineties globalisation and nationalist parochialism, to confront the historic and continual exploitation of the global south and the now deepening poverty of many in the global north. The *Immigrant Movement International Manifesto* of the dissident Cuban artist Tania Bruguera describes the diasporic experience: 'we have been called many names. Illegals. Aliens. Guest Workers. Border Crosses. Undesirables. Exiles. Criminals. Non-citizens. Terrorists. Thieves. Foreigners. Invaders. Undocumented.'

Jeffrey Gibson b.1972, *Be Some Body* 2024; glass beads, thread, buttons, steel.
Photo: Marjorie Allthorpe-Guyton.

Khalili Bouchra b.1975, *The Mapping Journey Project 2008-2011*; video.
Photo: Marjorie Allthorpe-Guyton.

The diasporic is, then, a wide semantic term for domains of experience where past, present, and future are entangled. As Stuart Hall wrote in *Familiar Stranger: A Life Between Two Islands* 'no identities survive the diasporic process intact and unchanged'. Hall was a close collaborator with the British Ghanaian artist John Akomfrah who represents Britain in a formidably ambitious and dense work of film, music, and poetry which may test the commitment of many Biennale visitors. Akomfrah's work is a political and aesthetic project which draws deeply on visual, literary, and philosophical ideas. *Listening All Night To The Rain*, the title from poem 83 by the eleventh century Chinese poet Su Dongpo, is conceived as a work of image and sound in eight parts inspired by Ezra Pound's *The Cantos* 1925. Multiple narratives of modern war, migration, resistance, and activism are interwoven with Akomfrahs' spare poetic images of watery landscapes filmed on the Isle of Mull, Scotland and in Yorkshire. In the Romantic tradition, a solitary figure stands by the water's edge. The embedded screens are framed like retables in an altarpiece. The spaces echo the abstract colour fields of Mark Rothko. With the poetic texts and the metronomes, multiple sounds from archive speeches, field recordings, popular music, and jazz, the work becomes a threnody, a lamentation for the world. Akomfrah talks of 'the idea of listening as activism in mind. I sense that one can know the world – that you can find a name, an identity and a sense of belonging-via the sonic'. Akomfrah's film installation for the inaugural Ghanaian pavilion at the Biennale in 2019 was supremely visual, in *Listening All Night To The Rain* the visual marries with philosophical concepts of sonic materialism where sound is a primary force in the world and in human perceptions. The multiscreen, multilayered sonic experience is, though, not well served by the claustrophobic divided spaces of the British neo classical pavilion.

Sound is nowhere more potent than in the Polish pavilion. *Repeat After Me 11* stays in the mind as one of the most conceptually original and powerful works of this Biennale. It was chosen by the Polish centrist coalition to replace the nationalistic history paintings originally selected by the previous right-wing government. Curated by Marta Czyż, this film project by the Ukrainian collective Open Group is described as a 'workshop on empathy'. It gives voice to the victims and survivors of Russia's invasion of Ukraine now displaced to Poland, Germany, Austria, Ireland, and the US. They are filmed in two videos made in 2022 and 2024. Speaking the language of war, they recall and imitate the traumatic and defining sounds of firearms, artillery shelling, missiles and bombs, helicopters and warplanes. Microphones are set up in front of the screens, the audience feel compelled to participate in what is a profoundly disturbing military karaoke: 'repeat after me: 'TUTUTUTU BUKhKhK'... Visitors can take a leaflet 'What Else Should You Know When Under Fire' translated from Ukrainian guidance given out before the invasion. The three artists are themselves nomads, Yuriy Biley lives in Wroclaw and Berlin, Anton Varga in New York, Pavlo Kovach, from Lviv, returned to join the Ukrainian army in 2023.

Scattered on the gravel paths of the Giardini were small red posters calling for an end to the other war uppermost in the mind. The army presence and pro Palestinian protests by the Art Not Genocide Alliance threw into focus a compelling, restrained collateral exhibition which presents works created in the South West Bank by artists in Palestine and their allies. The projects of Artists + Allies x Hebron and Dar Jacir for Art and Research in Bethlehem are stories of art and life on what sustains a homeland: family and community, the growing and sharing of food, care for the earth and for agricultural and cultural traditions. This is a rich and nuanced expression of Palestinian identity, exemplified by Baha Hilo's *PRESERVE 2022-24* on the cultivation of olives which supports more than 100,000 Palestinian families. Adam Broomberg's and Rafael Gonzalez's photographic book project *Anchor in the Landscape*, documents the olive trees precariously surviving Israeli occupation which has destroyed 800,000 trees since 1967. The magisterial Al-Badawi tree is 4,500 years old.

Art Not Genocide Alliance, 2024; petition posters. Photo: Theo Allthorpe-Mullis.

Occupation and colonial violence are the predominant themes of this Biennale. One crowd puller is the work of internationally acclaimed Wael Shawky in the Egyptian pavilion. Egyptian born and living between Alexandria and Philadelphia, Shawky's multifaceted practice is presented with film, video, sculpture, and ceramics. The set piece is *Drama 1882*, a 45 millimetre film, a quasi–operatic recasting of Egypt's nationalist Urabi uprising against British imperial rule, crushed by Britain's bombing of Alexandria. Produced in an historic theatre in Alexandria, Shawky sees the work as a challenge to the historic record, not as theatre but as a moving painting, an inversion perhaps of the classical commemorative history painting, but *Drama* is unquestionably a performance, a mesmerising but mannered costume piece with toy town painted sets, the singing actors bending and bowing, with English subtitles. It recalls the work of radical forbears such as Tadeusz Kantor, the rascal Polish artist whose staged visual economy delivered a more savage emotional punch. Kantor knew the power of objects and could magic a machine gun from a cardboard prop camera. For all its ambiguity and interrogation of historical 'truth,' Shawky's *Drama 1882* is disappointingly literal, no match for the visual seductiveness and political power of his earlier epic performance trilogy *Cabinet Crusades, The Secret of Karbala* with his handmade grotesque animated marionettes.

Baha Hilo, *Preserve 2022-2024*. Photo: Theo Allthorpe-Mullis.

Wael Shawky b.1971, *Drama 1982*, film. Photo: Marjorie Allthorpe-Guyton.

British imperialism comes again under fire in Nigeria's debut national pavilion *Nigeria Imaginary* which is a triumph. The eight artists acknowledge past and present realities. Ndidi Dike's *Blackhood, A Living Archive,* a room-sized rack of police batons with name tags of victims is a bleak *memento mori.* Fatimah Tuggar's *Light Cream Pods (Excerpt)* lifts the spirits, celebrating a living rich culture with animatronics and vitrines of Kora, traditional calabash musical instruments, which viewers can see played on their phones using an AR (Augmented Reality) app. The exhibition, with a large-scale model of the Museum of West African Art (MOWAA) now under construction in Benin City, Edo State, is inspirational and forward looking, although hedged around with thorny issues of restitution. This is confronted head on by Yinka Shonibare's terracotta pyramid piled high with clay facsimiles of the pillaged Benin bronzes in British collections and a bust of the British military commander who led the 1897 attack. *Monument to the Restitution of the Mind and the Soul* 2024 is an impressive departure from Shonibare's signature works with textiles. In 2019, he established a visionary non-profit Foundation to promote cultural diplomacy, education, and to provide artists residencies in Lagos and on a working farm in Ijebu, Ogun State.

Nigeria Imaginary is a curatorial tribute to Enwezor's Biennale *All the World's Futures* and a manifesto for a new Nigeria, opening a wider critical agenda for the representation of African countries at the Venice Biennale and a more meaningful engagement with African contemporaneity. This is not to underestimate the financial and political hurdles facing African artists and the fact that 'the assumption remains that to exist in the (art) world, one must leave Africa'. That assumption is overturned by the Congolese artist collective Cercle d'Art des Travailleurs de Plantation Congolaise (CATPC) whose macabre effigies coarsely carved from Lusangan clay and cast in cacao and palm oil give off a sickly smell, purposefully contaminating the white cube minimalism of the Dutch pavilion, fittingly next door to the Belgian. *The International Celebration of Blasphemy and the Sacred* is a strong but conflicted project made in collaboration with a Dutch artist and a curator. The CATPC live and work in Lusanga to make art to buy depleted palm oil plantation land to regenerate for their impoverished community. Their bitingly witty film *The Judgment of the White Cube* underlines their ambivalence to the art world. CATPC's white cube gallery, built by the Dutch in Lusanga, is swiftly convicted and beaten with palms in retribution for the evils of extraction, the Unilever confiscation of land and of brutal Belgian colonial rule.

Manal Aldowayan b.1973, *Shifting Sands: A Battle Song 2024*; wood, Tussah silk, ink, acrylic, sound. Photo: Theo Allthorpe-Mullis.

It is not hard to share their fears, as a CATPC member says 'we are not sure that good intentions will really lead to a Sacred Forest. In reality, we are at the very beginning...'

Circumspection is also prompted by Saudi Arabia's pavilion which declaims 'a powerful vision of womanhood in Saudi Arabia today'. *Shifting Sands: A Battle Song* is an imposing installation of sound, sculpture, and text by Manal AlDowayan whose multimedia work has long focused on collaborative workshops with Saudi women. A dark stage set with towering black edged leaves is inspired by the singing sands of Rub' al-Khali, the Empty Quarter and the elusive and ephemeral desert rose, weird crystalline petals melded by heat. These 'roses' bear texts about Saudi women from news media and two central leaves are screened with women's drawings and writings in response. Voices in unison are heard, Bedouin battle songs traditionally sung by men. A hopeful call to arms for women to come together in a country where the transformative power of the voices of most women remains unacknowledged and untapped. The pavilion petals look charred, and the sun has not yet risen.

Dana Awartani is a Palestinian–Saudi artist who also works collaboratively, learning textile dyeing with artisans across the Arab world and India. In the Arsenale she has hung yards of silk dipped in brilliant yellow and orange natural medicinal dyes, the multiple panels have tears marking sites destroyed by war, the latest in Gaza; each tear she laboriously darns as an act of healing. *Come, Let Me Heal Your Wounds. Let Me Mend Your Broken Bones* is a haunting testament of loss. The work of Abdullah Al Saadi in the United Arab Emirates pavilion also bears witness to the spiritual force of homeland, of landscape and the natural world. *Sites of Memory, Sites of Amnesia* is one of the most memorable experiences in this Biennale. The work, modest scrolls, drawings and objects documents a lifetime's journeys around his Khor Fakkan home which Al Saadi archives in biscuit tins and metal trunks. He is a reclusive founder member of the Emirati *avant garde* of the 1980s and 1990s and holds to the value of work being seen in the context of where it is made. To emulate a pilgrimage to the artist's remote studio, on request two actors will relate stories from each scroll. This was not the discomforting experience expected, the performer was a compatriot of Al Saadi, understood the work, quoting effortlessly from classical Arab poets.

Al Saadi's life and work is a counterpoint to the nomadic international artist and to that of some of the widely exhibited and travelled indigenous artists in this Biennale, raising questions of the contested position of the 'indigenous' artist, and of the contradictions and complexities of indigeneity. These are borne out by the differences, of tradition and modernity, of some of the work. The hallucinatory monumental mural painted on the façade of the Giardini Central Pavilion by the father and sons of the Brazilian Huni Kuin Artists Movement (MAHKU) is visually and conceptually rooted in Kaxinawa song and ayahuasca visions and dispenses with western pictorial convention. While the *Takapau,* which spans the Arsenale entrance by New Zealand's Mataaho Collective and awarded a Biennale Golden Lion, is a minimalist architectural structure woven of gleaming modern synthetic fibre. Its creators, four Māori women artists, Erena Baker, Sarah Hudson, Bridget Reweti, and Terre Te Tau, integrate Maori craft customs with a modernist aesthetic. Archie Moore, a First Nation artist claims he is 'presenting', not representing Australia, experiencing the double consciousness of being both an Aboriginal and an Australian. His work *Kith and Kin* has a pristine white platform, laden with orderly stacks of white paper documenting the redacted bureaucratic horror of the incarceration of Aboriginal peoples. It hovers above a pool of dark water. The blackboard wall and ceiling are covered in a densely inscribed chalk family tree of Moore's complex ancestry: Kamilarol, Bigambul, British, and Scottish, including 3484 people over a 65,000+ year time period – in the Kamilarol understanding of time reaching endlessly into the future. It is a resolutely contemporary memorial: as sombre and modernist as the Rothko chapel. *Kith and Kin* was awarded the Biennale Golden Lion for best national pavilion.

The Biennale, a European institution still wedded to the nation state, inevitably reinforces a 'repressive authenticity' which denies the hybridity of the art made by peoples who are identified as 'indigenous'. It commodifies and fetishises the work detracting from the diverse contemporaneity of indigenous experience and its manifold epistemologies; it is not enough to just showcase indigenous artists as somehow trapped in time. As US artist Jeffrey Gibson says 'I've existed in many narratives'. Pedrosa's exhibition with its pluriverse world view has divided opinion, but, like Enwezor's in 2015, his is a necessary Biennale throwing down the gauntlet to a neo liberal market economy and a myopic Western art world. It remains to be seen whether it is a bedrock for a future truly global Biennale. The Italian leadership has replaced the Biennale President, film producer Roberto Cicutto with the provocative right-wing journalist Pietrangelo Buttafuoco, a recent convert to Islam. Will he be minded, or able, to build on Pedrosa's vision?

READY OR NOT

Maya Van Leemput

'Welcome to Postnormal Times'. The first words inviting visitors into The Postnormal Times MADANI Exhibition in Kuala Lumpur (26 May–10 November 2024) are the same as the title of the 2010 paper by Ziauddin Sardar. The seminal text initiated the development of a future oriented approach to address the changing nature of change. Postnormal times thinking sees the speed, scale, scope, and simultaneity (4Ss) of our globalised, digital, networked environment drive increasingly complex, contradictory, and chaotic (3Cs) accelerating change. This perspective situates our era between the no longer and the not yet. Uncertainty and ignorance follow, characteristically affecting actions and choices available to us in our personal or spiritual lives, in our lives as citizens, and in policymaking too. To orient and move forward in such an enigmatic present, managerial and solutionist mindsets must be shed. The real task in front of us is to jointly navigate the massive challenges people, communities, nations, and organisations face; and to negotiate our way towards a more equitable and just tomorrow. To continue as normal is to put ourselves, our communities, cultures, and the planet itself at peril. We will have to count on diversity, on values, and on imagination if we are to make it through.

The Postnormal Times MADANI Exhibition, curated by Ziauddin Sardar and C Scott Jordan, organised by the Centre for Postnormal Policy and Futures Studies.
Designed by Effusion LLP, installed by Rock, Paper, Scissors Sdn Bhd.
Berjaya Times Square, Kuala Lumpur
26 May 2024 onwards

The exhibition is divided in three parts to bring these ideas across in an accessible and engaging manner. The opening section highlights the confounding realities of postnormal phenomena, some of the major issues we face today: from misinformation and the AI revolution to genetic manipulation, climate catastrophe, the impacts of the COVID pandemic, and degrading governance. Next, the exhibition offers a lens through which we may more clearly discern and understand what is really going with a view on enabling mutual work towards a preferable state of affairs. The third and final section of the show presents how postnormal times thinking informs the values driven policy of the current government of Malaysia, the SCRIPT/MADANI framework and plan for reform, a compass for action in the present based on six central values: sustainability, care and compassion, respect, innovation, prosperity, and trust.

With national policy – literally – in the spotlight at this exhibition, it is suitable that the show was opened, on 26 May, with a viewing by Malaysia's Prime Minister Dato' Seri Anwar Ibrahim. Along with him came a big flock of journalists from local, regional, and international media outlets. The Malaysian leader is not just a champion of postnormal times thinking, he is actively implementing it, putting forward SCRIPT/MADANI as a national vision and a navigational plan. At the press conference that followed his guided tour, he called for as many people as possible to see the exhibition and to get talking about our changing world.

The show site is the Berjaya Times Square complex in central Kuala Lumpur. It is an ambitious production, a massive expansion on previous exhibitions produced by the Centre for Postnormal Policy and Futures Studies (CPPFS). A tremendous amount of work has gone into its realisation, beginning with the development and elaboration of the postnormal times approach itself in papers, workshops, and polylogues by members of the CPPFs and a broader network of postnormal thinkers and practitioners around the globe. Then followed the labour of translating this work to an attractive and fathomable exhibition format for an extended peer community that includes all sections of the diverse Malaysian population as well as policymakers and intellectuals with a taste for forward thinking.

Photo: bram goots

In September 2023, a pre-figuration of the current exhibition was presented at the KL Jazz & Art Centre, a modest venue with ample gallery wall and floor space and an atmospheric dark basement. With a well-developed popular science approach in a contemporary arts venue, this 'not your normal exhibition' already was impressive in its detail, contextualisation, content choices, and clarity of design. So impressive that the crew received encouragements to scale up; six months later they were ready to present an even more striking new exhibition at the tenth floor of Berjaya Times Square. Every section of the plentiful current show uses multiple video and infographic screens. Visitors are invited to interact with the content and displays. In the 'Tunnel of Truth' in the Post-Truth section, they can walk through a series of tight beam sound showers, a jumble of historic and current affairs sound bites. Another audio installation draws attention to how misinformation takes hold in the echo chambers of social and mainstream media. Visitors put their head into one of two small cubes filled with repetitive audio for an embodied sensory experience of the reverberations of beliefs and opinions in our filter bubbles. One corner resembles a hall of mirrors in which images of the self are distorted. In the

Photo: bram goots

area dedicated to AI, there is a game for guessing who in a series of portraits is the real human being and who is an AI creation. Nearby, a smart CCTV display shows any visitor approaching the monitor, a live stream of their movement back to them, against a checkered background repeating the message 'Smile! You are being judged'. Further into the visit, in the theory section, viewers can add their own answers to the question 'what are you uncertain about?' to one of the exhibition panels. The Prime Minister wrote 'the economy', someone put simply 'my life', one thinks of finding love another of finding employment. Such is the variety of the postnormal condition.

Photo: bram goots

It is a good thing that with all the effort and attention that has gone into creating this exhibition, it remains unfinished. Not that there are notable loose ends in what has been put together. No stone has been left unturned in the treatment of all the various elements that represent issues and phenomena of our intermediate era and how they might be understood or addressed. Each idea is illustrated with salient examples as well as explanatory texts. Still, by itself the material of the Postnormal Times MADANI Exhibition is unfulfilled. Only the visitor can complete the exhibition. As such, this expo is an open work in the true sense that

Umberto Eco had in mind. The curators, designers, and production team put in a strong and multifaceted creative intention. The makers' intent by itself integrates multiple meanings and levels of granularity. Crucially, it is not final, it does not determine the one and only true meaning of the content or the form. It can only land with the readings and interpretations of visitors. And surely this too is intentional.

Given the ambiguities of the subject matter, exemplified amongst others by an 'AI gambling wheel' that has two pointers which always land on one positive and one negative potential impact of AI, it is appropriate that the exhibition leaves space for viewers to find their own perspectives on (and responses to) the topics at hand. There is ample opportunity for the viewer

Photo: bram goots

to choose their own way through the different sections and subsections. For some the physical wayfinding may be somewhat disconcerting, not as perturbing as navigating postnormal reality, but certainly an experiential reminder of its challenges. At the main entrance to the exhibition a well-crafted signalisation points the way. Once inside, here and there arrows indicate the general direction for following the narrative. Having visited or simply crossed the exhibition multiple times, I never chose the same trajectory. I often found myself questioning where to go next, how much to take in before moving on, what to skip and what to revisit.

Photo: bram goots

If you follow every path the curators and designers have provided, it will take you far. You can go find the books and magazines on display here and take them home, read and watch the referenced news features online, or take in the full text of the SCRIPT/MADANI document. Not every visitor will dive in so deep, and every visitor will make something different of what is shared in this open work. It matters if the viewer is the PM or an MP, one of a group of Islamic futures students accompanied by their teachers, a gallery assistant, a futures consultant, a policy analyst, or a housewife, the minister of education or a member of her cabinet. This exhibition is not the same if you are a resident of Kuala Lumpur - a KLite, a regional visitor or an international traveller, a tourist who came across the flashy promo clip elsewhere in the Berjaya Times Square complex, or someone working nearby just using their break for a quick visit. Certainly, the way I see this exhibition will not resemble any of theirs. My perspective is that of a privileged witness with a lot of background in postnormal times theory and practice. Having hosted the CPPFS in my hometown Antwerp, as co-curator and fellow exhibitor of the group exhibition in the Museum of Contemporary Art of Antwerp entitled *A Temporary Futures Institute* in the year 2017, that same year I became a senior fellow of the CPPFS. Later, part of the postnormal exhibit from Antwerp travelled to Barcelona where I joined a group of CPPFS fellows for the Blanquerna Summer School. I have written about postnormal times, given talks on science days in Belgium, and facilitated and contributed to workshops in Brussels, London, Istanbul, Sarajevo, and Kuala Lumpur. In other words, I know the challenges of bringing across to different audiences the essence and nuances of the postnormal times approach.

This biases my perspective towards the popular science aspects of the effort that was put into the Postnormal Times MADANI exhibition. From that point of view the well-crafted show is exciting. The question 'so what is going on' central to the second section of the exhibition is not an easy one. It leads essentially to a presentation of postnormal times theory's key concepts. The transition into more notional reflection after the numerous thought-provoking examples of postnormal realities in the first section is smooth. In a large more open space where the visitor can recover from the myriads of impressions and sensations in the colourful and fast paced 'what just happened' section, a large projection slows one's racing thoughts down. This room is filled with the white light of the background of a many metres long projection with soft black and white images of swans, elephants, and jelly fish quietly gliding across the wall. The big letters of keywords, the single sentence prompts, and the explanatory texts or audio have been left aside. It is a relief to the by now overstimulated senses.

The wall across the spacious projection is dotted with a series of small frames in the signature aqua colour that saturates most other parts of the expo. The most important question one reads here is 'what are we not seeing'. The visitor must lift the aqua frames covering short explanatory texts to reveal what might be missed when thinking about the Covid-19 pandemic, the war in Israel-Palestine, or pollution, to name just a few. The meaning of the three animals in the projection is explained with these provocations. Only after crossing this space, we return to a multitude of examples and explanations to illustrate postnormal theory. The questions 'what is the elephant in the room', 'what black swans evade our focused gaze', and 'what chaotic jellyfish are about to bloom' feature in an installation that hides typical exemplars inside. Then, in no particular order, the visitor can explore instances of postnormal change, demonstrating how speed scope, scale, and simultaneity bring about the forces of contradictions, complexity, and chaos, leading to ever deeper ignorance and uncertainty. At the end of this section a series of timelines compares how all these elements taken together define postnormal times as distinct from classic, modern or postmodern times. Finally, a panel asks 'where now'. I can barely imagine what other viewers responses to the open question 'what future would you like to create' might be or whether at this point they would even be inclined to address it.

Photo: bram goots

Ultimately this exhibition offers more than popular science or a diagnosis of our time. It shouldn't be seen separately from the specific political context for which it was developed. The contemporary affairs content, the abundance of examples of the weirding of our world, pressing matters all, underpin the idea that a response is indeed required. SCRIPT/ MADANI is one such response, a strategic framework for policy in the face of all the urgent matters that Malaysia must address. This policy programme relies on the specificities of Malaysian society and its diverse cultures with trust in a set of key values that are undeniably virtuous.

Photo: bram goots

The addition of this section casts a whole other light on the show and the makers' intentions. The entire effort now can be seen not only as science communication but also as a form of marketing. The banners lined up between the theory section and the policy section, featuring images of the national leader, Malaysian environments and people, are unmistakable. There is no hidden agenda, the partisanship is explicit. In that context the question begs to be asked if besides being informative, educational, and triggering; this exhibition is persuasive too. Surely, this depends again on the starting points of the visitors. It would be surprising if a visit to this exhibition would sway members of the conservative opposition to accept the merits of the more progressive take on the needs of Malaysians and the nation that can be found in the discussions of the SCRIPT/MADANI section. A more detached viewer on the other hand, might be interested in understanding not just from the short introductory text by the Prime Minister in the brochure accompanying the show, but inside the dynamic three-dimensional affair itself, how postnormal thinking got to be embedded in the current government's programme. Is this something that could be done in my own country too, I wonder. What would be required? How do concrete policies engage in navigating postnormal times? Perhaps this section might also have benefited from the same kinds of examples of specific measures, actions, and behaviours that are omni-present in the previous sections. Even so, the show strikes the difficult but important balance between persuasion and openness to interpretation well by setting up the presentation of the MADANI values to include the voices and imaginaries of artists rather than politicians.

As I participated in the events and activities at the KL Jazz & Art Centre in the fall of 2023, what stood out to me was exactly the absence of artists. The significance of the roles of artists and their creations in postnormal times has been highlighted in more than a few pieces of postnormal times literature. These creatives can reframe, re-orient, trigger learning and un-learning, impress and inspire. It was good to see that in the Postnormal Times MADANI exhibition six Malaysian artists from different backgrounds and regions contribute to evoke the values that are the drivers for the SCRIPT/MADANI framework. Of course, the artists do not exactly describe policy aims, criteria, and measures in the domains of economy, institutions, education, social, cultural, urban, and rural sectors. Instead, they provide an open-ended introduction to the core values of the programme from their lived experience. Their work is far removed from the slick and often superficial copywriting of more common formats for political messages and campaigns.

This section wants to convince but it also provides some surprising re-interpretations of the values that it presents. The artists' representations of the six drivers in six separate booths that make up the last stretch of the show, serve to implicitly bring across the framework's openness and preserve the shows character as an open work. The first booth features the multi-disciplinary artist Anju, who treats 'sustainability' with attention for the throw-away culture of our time. The small paintings on the walls, invite a closer look to reveal they have been composed with items collected from trash. To look more closely at these elegant yet slightly disturbing pieces, the viewer must walk underneath a collection of plastic garbage items dangling from the ceiling, seemingly having risen from the bright orange bin in the centre of the space. The accompanying wall text casts sustainability as a process, a collective effort that pertains to rural and urban communities and people and their families as well as the natural environment. In the next booth, the artist Fakrhul Zaman presents minimal collages and sculptures, small toy-sized objects casually arranged on a table and shelves to address the second driver of 'care and compassion'. This is a friendly piece, the small imaginary creatures on the shelves and table have a childlike naïve quality that softens the heart. Here it is easy to feel the love for others unlike ourselves and for nature that is so essential to how we live and go forward together.

Photo: bram goots

The highly original description of 'respect' in the third booth is eye-opening and well accompanied by graphic designer Stephen Menon's set of stirring prints with strong human figures against evocative backgrounds and by the artists thoughts on the relationship between self-respect and empowerment. Next, Peter Jambai Anak Albert Bangau shows a video of a single digital artwork in the booth that is dedicated to 'innovation'. Here, the MADANI explainer connects the idea of conscious design to planning and creativity. The artist in turn examines technological progress with a critical eye. He proposes a video game in which the player's decisions guide the evolution from one civilisational level to the next. The piece itself is presented as a small projection in an otherwise empty booth. No more than the growing, evolving silhouette of a plant, it almost disappears against the background. The 'prosperity' booth with sculptor Liu Cheng Hua's bamboo structures covered in gold paint is quite the opposite. It is heavy with the 'Golden Shafts' that reference shaft mining techniques, pointing at the extractive nature of mining and the impact of globalisation. The final driver, 'trust', is presented with a well-conceived piece by the artist Azizan Paiman. It stands in stark contrast to the post-truth section that opens the exhibition. The accompanying text describes trust as a vow of earthly, divine, and spiritual moral responsibility, highlighting also that the Malaysian notion adds faith and the principle of reciprocity to this interpretation. We are not only morally responsible for building trust, but also for honouring the trust put upon us. The artist's modest glass cabinet that encases unreachable quotes related to trust, serves as a metaphor for the delicate balance between trust and scepticism in political leadership, is a worthy endpoint for the show.

The SCRIPT/MADANI section opens with a banner stating 'ready or not, postnormal times is here'. Any visitor of the exhibition will have plenty of material to ponder the question.

For me, impressed by the utterly self-referential nature of the inordinate breadth and depth of this exhibition and the staggering amounts of ideas, images, and content it presents, it was hard to answer with an unequivocal yes. Even more so because the exhibition's physical setting adds a disturbing paradox. It takes place in the centre of one of the fastest growing metropolitan regions of Southeast Asia, itself bursting with colourful moving advertising panels, a consumerist feast with wares and goods on display everywhere, whether in street markets or in shiny, over-lit shopping malls. The show can be found on the tenth floor, right above one of the most prestigious of these malls, at the heart of the Berjaya Times Square complex. A few floors below is the largest indoor theme park in Malaysia, a five-storey bonanza including a roller coaster for the public's entertainment and distraction. The exhibition has a view over the theme park. The entrance to the show is flanked by a wall sporting a huge Starbucks logo. To explore the nature of the troubles of our time in the midst of the trouble itself, with the background of deep drone and rattle of the attraction next door conducted through the concrete and steel bones of the building, and the screams emanating from the rides, sounding of both joy and fear, layer upon layer of overwhelming sensory overload, it is unclear if indeed we will be able to untangle ourselves from the path we are on and navigate through the imbroglio of our unique in-between era.

It is indeed an act of bravery that the curators of this exhibition, and leaders and policymakers who embrace a postnormal times approach, have put so much into guiding us towards the insight and intention we need for a glimmer of hope.

Photo: bram goots

MY LOVE FOR YOU

Amenah Ashraf

At last the beautician is done working her magic onto my face. 'I have to say, Nadia,' my sister Sadia gushes softly at my reflection, 'she's turned you into an ethereally enchanting version of yourself. The make-up is not hiding you under its cosmetic weight, it's…bringing you out, somehow.' She places a reassuring hand on my shoulder and meets my eyes in the mirror, a sheen of pride swimming in her orbs. All I can do is smile lightly as I blink to push the tears away. I have no words to describe how much I'm going to miss her.

I'm getting married tonight. To a man who found me to his liking in an online picture of his cousin in which I figured. I'm ashamed. I'm not talking to that friend of mine anymore; the one who's his cousin. One Snapchat story and I've caught someone's fancy. If that isn't a stupid enough reason to marry, I don't know what is.

My face was out there in the open for I don't know how long, and that terrifies me somewhat. Marriages don't happen this way; they *shouldn't* happen this way. If fixed in this Haram manner, their very basis is a prevalent but abhorrent practice. Who knows when another friend off his cousin's Snapchat story or WhatsApp status catches his fancy, and I'm left fending for myself?! I pray that *that* doesn't come to pass. My thoughts of the future, however, are exceptionally grim. The internet's a dangerous place. Doesn't even take a second to lift your pictures off it. My privacy is busted one day and I can't take back my photo from a stranger's phone, sitting a thousand miles away. God knows I may find it one day stuck onto some licentious body, floating around on the World Wide Web, just like that.

According to common standards, my husband-to-be is slightly above average, looks wise. Some may even call him 'handsome'. I've met him twice now. His behaviour was decent, I admit. I wouldn't have agreed otherwise. He has a logistics firm of his own in Pune. He was probably looking around when he saw me. And the rest is history.

To be honest, I don't really dislike him. He just doesn't happen to fit my criteria of a man I'd want to marry. He doesn't always pray, his Qur'an recitations are rickety, at best. He can't recall the five pillars of Islam at once, doesn't have a beard, and sunnah trousers have never been his thing. And lastly, he doesn't know even half of the 30th Juz by heart. Believe me, I asked him all of that. A man lesser in Deen than yourself is hard to respect.

'I shall help him learn things' – is now my life goal. I don't want my children growing up away from the religion I know to be the truth. I had meant to elevate my Iman through my better half. But things haven't really turned out in my favour. Life's like that, I guess.

My other sister, Hadiya (the only one with a 'y' to her name) comes bustling into the room, her dupatta flying about in her wake, my mother in tow. 'Are you ready, aapi? Mustafa Bhai's people have sent the car!'

It was agreed that the car taking me to the hotel venue would come from their side. Ours would be too outdated and mar their reputation, apparently. There's a rush of lush fabric at the news as we all simultaneously stand up.

'And my, what car!' Hadiya exclaims chattily.

'Am I looking okay, Mamma?' I fret.

'You're looking lovely, Nadia! Quit worrying.'

'Thanks, but I can't help it! Sadia, please get me my abaya from the almirah there,' I instruct my more responsible sister.

'Do you know what car they've sent, aapi?' Hadiya goes on, blissfully unaware of my nerves. I'm in a state of utter and complete panic and all she can talk about is the model of the blasted car.

'It's Land Rover, aapi!' she informs us all. 'I have never even seen one in this city before. Do you think they sent it to show off?' she asks, suddenly sceptical.

'Most likely,' I reply, sneering beneath my glamourous mask. The girl's talking after my own heart.

As I get out of the car in front of the gates of the venue, I can't help thinking of the amount of money Baba has splurged on this event. My dreams of a simple Nikah all turned to dust the moment I came to know I'd be getting hitched at a hotel. Mustafa's parents were insistent, and Dad gave in. My fists clench at my sides the more I think of the amount of money my father is throwing away on this place. Just to match their status. Grand is the word that fits the hotel best. And accidentally, that's also a part of its name.

There's a regality to the building that makes it stand out amongst the structures in the vicinity. Its stark white walls are bordered with gold and sparkling golden chandeliers grace the ceiling. The white-marbled stairs make me feel like I've landed in a Disney fairytale. The ostentatious aesthetics make a mockery of my simple teenage fantasies – of marrying a long-nosed, square-jawed angel in white, with a good amount of dark facial hair gracing his features. He'd send his signatures from the Masjid as I would sign the Nikah papers from home. And when he'd come to see me for the first time, lo and behold! We'd be all that the other could have ever wanted. End of story.

Not!

As I mount the marble steps, I can hear my dreams getting crushed beneath my branded heels that match my dress to the t. Sigh.

I'm taken to the ladies' side of the sitting area, which is being continuously infiltrated by male waiters and family members of the groom. They've arrived early, I see. I ask my mom to tell them to clear out or else I'll keep sitting in my Naqab at my own wedding.

The men do so reluctantly, eyeing me distastefully. The ladies of Mustafa's family have hoisted their perfect eyebrows. There's a muffled murmur of disapproval but I don't care to acknowledge anyone with any sort of apology.

Right as I settle myself along with my dress into the plush sofa for two, a man comes up on to the stage and starts clicking away his camera busily. Probably came with the hotel package…or maybe Mustafa engaged his services. Who knows?

But how dare he!?

I put a hand up to stop him, and then proceed to gesture to him to go away too. He looks at me with an unreadable expression on his face and then saunters off, looking back every few seconds. I probably seem to be an alien bride in his eyes. Suits me just fine.

This is an absolute nightmare. Can't I sit in peace for a few minutes? The Nikah hasn't even been done yet, and I'm flustered!

Thankfully, people let me be for a while, as I attempt to breathe in my dress. Sadia comes and sits beside me, keeping me company and making small talk, eventually soothing my nerves.

After fifteen minutes or so, our local Imam begins the Khutbah and I listen, my mind far, far away. It's only when I see my dad, coming over to me alongside the Imam and a few of my relatives as my mother wraps a large dupatta around me, that I break out of my reverie.

I say that I 'accept' thrice upon being asked as many times, signing the papers along with Baba and others as witnesses, and the Nikah is done. The same must have gone on over at Mustafa's side.

After the party has left, I release a spurt of tears at short notice, and my parents huddle around me, pulling me close, shushing me, trying to prevent their own tears from spilling out. This catharsis was storing up inside me for a while now.

The mother and sister of the groom arrive on the scene shortly after, their faces a mixture of slight aversion, some surprise at me not turning out to be a Bridezilla, and most importantly, plastered smiles that look more like grimaces. The sister seems less scary than the mother, however. If given the chance, the latter won't pass up the opportunity of judging the shape of my toes even, it appears from her keen eyes that seem to look into my soul.

'May Allah bless you, my daughter. You look like the Moon itself,' she utters a bit monotonously, gently caressing my cheek. Not bad for first words, I think. The acting's pretty good too. Or maybe she genuinely cares, I shouldn't be assuming things here.

The sister then comes forward to shake my hand, dropping a quick kiss on it before letting go. 'Mama is right, Nadia di,' she reiterates, smiling.

After all the formalities are performed by Mustafa's mother, he himself is seen making his way towards the stage, flanked by both our fathers at his sides. He raises his head to look at me. And right there and then, my heart stops.

He's wearing a cream sherwani with a brown saafa and looking directly at me, his gaze searing. Beneath the turban, a heavy stubble graces the lower part of his face.

I quite visibly gulp. The look in his eyes has made my temperature rise and I'm hyperventilating a bit. Okay, not just a bit. But I hope I can be normal by the time he comes to sit beside me.

Turns out, my heartbeat only escalates the moment I feel the warmth radiating off his body. My hands shake. Mustafa or My Husband looks at them and gently takes one into his own.

His hands are warm and reassuring, a sort of balm to my soul. The magic is in the Nikah, I believe.

People around us are milling about. A large enough crowd of family and friends have gathered near our seat and I can see what is coming next.

The photographer I sent away comes sauntering back, looking much too pleased with himself. He has a faint smirk of victory upon his face and for a brief second, he looks to me like shaytan, that spawn of the devil!

A sense of inevitable helplessness courses through me and I quietly bear the photography session with the family. Mustafa probably senses my discomfort and rubs the back of my hand that's still in his hold. I feel thankful for his concern but it's completely inadequate.

I'm probably being too critical of him, and unjustly so. But I can't help blaming him for every darn thing. If he understood me completely, he'd have sent the man on his way, but he didn't.

What comes next positively horrifies me. The photographer has signalled the family to move away. It's time for a couple-only photo session, I'm guessing. For a minute, we remain in our seats, holding hands and me gazing down mostly. But then the man tells us to get up and look directly at the camera. Mustafa has still not let go of my hand, which elicits a range of raised eyebrows. I just wish he would let go – my hand's gotten clammy and I'm nervous of all the attention on us. By their razor-sharp looks, all the ladies are gossiping about us and judging the bride; all the men (related or not), young or old and even those with wives, are gazing at me under the guise of admiration for the 'couple'. The photographer has been spewing instructions since the last one minute but I cannot seem to hear him. I feel wooden and on the verge of tears. This was not how I dreamt it to be. Will my life be like this too?

The man wants us to gaze at each other for the next photo with my hand on Mustafa's chest. Very reluctantly, I do as I'm told and the lights begin to flash incessantly. I can feel some other cameras focusing too but I can't prevent any of them.

For another picture, he tells us to hold each other, Mustafa by the shoulder and me by the waist and touch our foreheads as we look into each other's eyes...and that's when I've had enough! I shall not be making a fool of myself any further becoming a source of entertainment for these people who've nothing to do with my life. I see some of them snickering and my blood boils.

Mustafa hesitates at such an openly intimate display of affection in front of our elders. Taking that as an opportunity, I pull my hand away from his hold, nearly running towards the stairs and down the stage without even once looking back to see everyone's reaction. Tears are blurring my vision and, afraid of tripping on my gharara, I drop down on to the nearest chair, quite uncaring of my surroundings.

I cover my face with both my hands, now openly crying for everyone to see. This feeling of humiliation is so profound that I'm not able to go into the consequences of my actions; of open disregard of Mustafa's feelings and his social standing, of my in-laws' anger, of my parents' delicate position and the crowd's whispered gossiping.

'Nadia, what's the *matter* with you!? Everyone's watching and making up all sorts of things. Get up!' I hear my mum fiercely whisper into my ear. Someone else comes to see what the matter is, too.

'It's nothing, bhabhi. She's just shy and overwhelmed,' Mum tells my mother in-law in an appeasing tone. I'm getting hysterical by the minute and all my mum thinks I am is overwhelmed...? Yeah, belittle my feelings all you want, mama.

'If she behaves in this manner on every little matter, it won't do,' my mother in-law's riled voice reaches me. She can say what she likes but I won't get up from here until that dastardly photographer gets out of here with his bloody paraphernalia! And I say so in so many words – without the cursing, of course.

In the next ten minutes, the man has gone and the people have stopped whispering since I've come back to my rightful place. But Mustafa is not in the mood for sitting together anymore. Lines are marring his forehead and his jaws are clenched.

'You could've told me you didn't want your pictures taken, Nadia,' he says in a low voice, putting slight pressure on my hand he's taken into his own once again. 'Walking off like that wasn't a good move.'

Guilt fills me at his soft yet stern tone and I'm not able to look up at him. 'See, you gave them a reason to talk behind your back,' he indicates the gathered crowd with his head. 'And I didn't want just that!'

'I'm sorry,' I manage to say in a tearful voice. 'But, what else could I do? I couldn't stand that man and you weren't taking any notice of my discomfort.' I quietly pull my hand from his grip once again. This time, he knows I'm unhappy with him without me stalking off in a show of rebellion. He says nothing, however.

Soon, Mustafa tells his parents we're tired and want to take leave of my family now. I'm drained of emotions so I simply hug my parents and my two sisters and we're off to my in-laws' place.

That night, when my face is scrubbed clean and I'm free of all my fineries, I lie on the bed mulling over the day's events and my husband's reactions to me. I can't help thinking how contrasting our lifestyles are. I'm sceptical of our relationship working smoothly but I want to give it all I've got, give him a chance. Mustafa isn't half bad, I can feel it. He understands but he makes too much of people's opinions. And he reacts late.

I want to make him understand my feelings. I want to let him know what I think but my courage is failing me to talk to him after that stunt I pulled at the end. Mustafa is still in the bathroom. And so, taking the opportunity, I find a pen and a piece of paper and start to write him a little something he can easily find before he goes to sleep.

My love for you has only taken seed, presently
It lies nascent, inching towards promise silently.
It requires your time, your care and attention
It cannot just break into bloom, might I mention.
This marriage of ours — it brought us together

It didn't prophesy instant love, or sunny weather.
If you subject it to a glare, can it endure?
Or pull it out of the shell that keeps it secure?
How do you expect it to spread out, strengthen its roots?
When you expose it to be trampled under careless boots.
If not given time, it shall stifle, wither and die
Love requires patience, it will flower by and by.
Showcasing it to the world won't make it anymore real
Handled with discretion, its true colours will unveil.
Lovers and love don't need any polaroid token,
A gentle word, a caress and the sentiment's awoken.
You force it to wilt with a touch for pretence's sake,
Don't let a rickety base break the home you make.
Love shall give you all, my dear heart, in good time,
And you'll be a rich, envied man, even with no dime.

When I'm done, I quietly place it underneath his phone on the bedside table and slip back into the covers.

Tiredness makes me fall into a light sleep by the time he comes back. I begin to wake up to the rustle of the paper. So, he's read it. Good. I smile slightly and let out a long breath I didn't know I was holding till now.

A while later, I jerk awake only to distantly feel a hand hovering above my arm, touching the fabric of my sleeve, but it's removed before it can touch me. I freeze for a second but then minutely decrease the distance between us, hopefully undetected by Mustafa. I'm sorry for making him feel guilty but he needs to learn…to know that our love for each other can't bloom in a day. He needs to know that what's on show isn't necessarily real, and that which is real doesn't necessarily have to be on show.

LOVE, MONEY, TRUTH

Alev Adil

The Photograph

The photograph has faded, its original Kodachrome brightness bleached and gilded by time. M thrusts it in my hand in a frame set with *nazar* beads, for you to remember, she says. Thank you. So much. I don't add, I didn't need reminding. I hadn't forgotten. Three girls, the one in the middle has her chin up, a confident smile, her arm around a skinny angular creature whose face is partially shadowed by her dark hair and her hand around the waist of a third, looking distractedly to the left of the camera, a slight smile on her face. I take off my sunglasses and look into her eyes. I try to recognise her, the girl who was my most trusted friend, to bring something back from the past. I've spent my life learning to forget and move on. I hadn't forgotten, but what I remember and what she might want to commemorate and bond over, they are unlikely to be the same things. I say nothing. We both look at the photograph. She sighs, a soft luxuriant sigh. Time flies and goes away. Time loves to fly, she says.

Why Time Flies

The perception of time is mathematical. Thus, as we age time accelerates on a logarithmic scale. The physics of time acceleration measures time through the brain's ability to process information, and the amount of information it has to process. Time speeds up. The first year of my friendship with M and D was a fifth of our lives, a sixtieth now. The perception of duration is mathematical and it is also psychological. The silence stretches out between us. Time melts and oozes, the afternoon feels endless. Perhaps this visit was a mistake. Outside the patio doors a swallow is swooping down to drink water from the pool. I spot a lizard darting through the bougainvillea. It's very peaceful here in M's mansion in the mountains.

My condolences, I say. My deepest condolences.

Yes, thank you. Have some more, she passes the plate of pastries towards me. The sprinkler on the lawn, the sun beating down on the empty tennis court, the crickets outside, the silence between us.

What happened? I ask her. Do you want to tell me about it? You don't have to.

It happened so suddenly, she said. We had been to dinner with friends, he was tired when we came back. We went to bed. He had indigestion and couldn't sleep and got up after a short while. I drifted off and then I heard a strange cry. When I went down to the living room I found him lying on the floor in the dark, he'd vomited and couldn't breathe. I called for an ambulance, but we are so far away from the hospital up here in the mountains, and there is a militia checkpoint to cross too. It took hours to arrive. He was dead by then. He died in my arms. I don't know how long it took. Did he die quickly or slowly? I don't know. The ambulance took an eternity, that's all I remember really clearly. And holding him, I felt it was my duty to hold him, he was dying. But I didn't want to, not at all. And it haunts me that he knew that. Do you think he knew that? I can't bear his absence. I miss him so much but you know... Even though it's all so far in the past, I'm haunted by those events again. We made three beautiful children, a successful business and he built this perfect home for me. But, was I the one he truly loved? I know it was so long ago but... We both look at the photograph.

You had a good marriage, I tell her, which is true and also a platitude. I don't want to risk a truth that is not a platitude, at such a time. That would be an invitation to intimacy. But she is hungry for intimacy and takes it as such.

I'm so glad you came back. All these years. I missed you a lot. I always wondered, did you blame me for what happened then?

The clink of the little silver cake forks on porcelain. I eat so I don't have to speak, to tell stories I have tried to evade by a lifetime of remaining silent.

The Doctors

The doctors' daughters they called us. It was a kind of joke in my case, my father was a doctor of philosophy, not medicine. M loved to boast about being a doctor's daughter, nothing held more social cachet in her mind than being a doctor's daughter. The old order was over. The important families were tainted by their Ottoman roots. The power now lay with the new professional classes, especially those educated in America, though many still preferred a French or British education. A western education was expensive, either you had to be old aristocracy and sell all your land to fund your children's education or you might, if you had the right attitude and connections, get a US scholarship.

D, the girl in the middle of the faded photograph, was the expansive confident one. She wanted to be an actress. M was the sensible one and I was the bookish one. D was always performing, always the center of attention. I would be a writer and write films for her to star in. Everyone would love her. The whole world would adore her. That was the plan. Although of course her parents would never have countenanced that. We were expected to be high achievers academically and to become professionals, but louche and insecure careers in the arts weren't really an option. Medicine or law and a good marriage, those were our parents' ambitions for us. We three were inseparable, from primary school right through to lycée. M didn't want to be a star or a writer. M didn't want to be anything in particular, she wanted to have: beautiful things, a beautiful home, a beautiful life.

When I told my father that her father had told M he wasn't a real doctor he laughed uproariously, his performative laugh, the one that cloaked resentment or anger. No, I'm not a bloody butcher, he said. He funds the armed militias and then sews up the young idiots who fall for their patriotism, your friend's hero father. National hero, he's a CIA shill. Physician heal thyself. Knowledge is power, my rose, knowledge is power. There is no shame in being a doctor of philosophy.

And a lot to be said for keeping your mouth shut, my mother said. Maybe if you just kept to knowing and not telling. My mother didn't approve of the books he wrote. Political philosophy and political reality don't mix she told him. And they don't pay the bills. My father railed against the old feudal class but we mainly lived off the sale of the land my mother had brought to their marriage as her dowry.

Knowledge might be power, but it isn't a worldly power. We lived in a crumbling Ottoman mansion with an outside toilet and an old hamam whilst M's family had a brand-new villa designed on the American model. Neither the American dream nor the doctor's dream villa survived the war in the late 1970s. After the war M's father built a block of flats on the site of the ruined villa, more money to be made that way, and then when, in the 1980s, it ended up too near the new Green Line and sniper fire, they sold it to the government for a fat sum. M's father was a good businessman as well as a doctor. D's father kept out of politics. He was the first heart surgeon in the country. Her mother was a gynaecologist. It was rumoured, no it was known, that she secretly performed abortions and virginity refreshments for girls in trouble. She saved as many lives as her husband at a time when honour killings were rife in the villages. Whilst girls of our class wouldn't be murdered for these crimes, such dishonour would ruin their reputations and prospects, a social death if not a physical one.

New Boy in Town

Q's arrival at school caused quite a stir. He was three years ahead of us, in the final year of lycée so we didn't get to mix with him socially. He looked American, not just the clothes, the Levi's, Converse Hi Tops, Hanes T shirts and Golden Bear Varsity jacket. He had a center parting, floppy highlighted hair that fell in two inverted commas framing his face. He was glamorous and he wafted past us in the school corridor in an air of mystery and Paco Rabanne scent. Outside school his eyes were usually hidden by mirror aviator shades. Sometimes after school, when we were eating muhallebi on the terrace of the patisserie on the corniche we'd see him drive by in his daddy's baby blue Mercedes with the windows down, the Eagles and Santana drifting out seductively at full volume. He is just the coolest boy I've ever seen, sighed M. Those glasses, his jacket, that car...

But it was D who was most totally smitten, those eyes, those lips, oh those eyes, Ma Shaa Allahhh. She exhaled the longest, softest, most sibilant most drawn out maaa shaaa Allahhh ever. She reached across the table and gripped my hand tight, oh Z I swear I'm totally in love.

We weren't the only ones buzzing about the new arrival. All the grown ups were too. Why had they returned so suddenly, my mother wondered out loud. The boy has missed his final year and SATs preparation, wasn't he supposed to go to university in the US? The father had such a good position in Washington, why are they back?

It's not good news, my father replied. They are getting ready. They must have plans. The arrests at the student protests, rampant inflation, the parliament in disarray... a good time to engineer a coup? And there he is, their man in place, a new President in waiting.

The Americans might bring stability, my mother suggested.

Stability? My father laughed his darkest, bitterest laugh. When do the Americans bring anything other than ruin?

Terribly Complicated

I was recently at a dinner party in north London, a substantial Victorian villa, a Nigella Lawson recipe for roast chicken with peppers, olives and potatoes accompanied by a generous array of Ottolenghi vegetable side dishes that the hosts had bought from Upper Street on their way home from their respective jobs at a nearby university and a newspaper. They are of a certain age, and cushioned by the accumulated certainties that prosperity and good health confer. It would be ungenerous to call them smug, they are anxious people. They care about the environment, about growing inequality and extremism at home and also passionately about the problems of the global south, especially the plight of women in Muslim countries. She teaches world literature, campaigns for the PEN Writers in Prison committee and wrote a well-received book about gender, cultural hybridity, cosmopolitan identity and Islam analyzing the works of Azar Nafisi, Elif Shafak and Kamila Shamsie. They collect Islamic art, both classical and contemporary.

We were an eclectic bunch at dinner. *The Spectator* would characterise us all as middle class bleeding heart liberals but middle class covers a lot of ground, from those who might more accurately be called minor aristocracy to those for whom grammar school had been a route out of the working class. There were freelancers who lived in buttock clenching precarity, in unheated mold furred rented flats, who haunted the yellow sticker aisle of their local supermarket around 4pm and those who owned a lot of rental property, spent their summers in their Tuscan villas and bought their biscuits from Fortnum's. And as for our bleeding hearts, they do all bleed, but I'm increasingly certain they don't bleed for the same reasons. We avoided sensitive topics, especially world politics, given the current situation in the Middle East. Terribly complicated, the situation in the Middle East... Tragic. Our poor hostess, if we did discuss it where would it end? Someone might utter the G word, A might demand that I denounce Hamas. B might start on about charred babies. All that would put us right off our kunaffa. I'd brought the kunaffa, not homemade but I'd gone far out of my way to find it, from a highly recommended Iraqi place in Green Lanes.

Conspiracy Theories

The safe topic we finally alighted upon was conspiracy theories and theorists. One of the dinner guests had a yoga teacher who, since the pandemic had become increasingly unhinged. She'd always been kind of a health nut, worried about MMR vaccines and G5 masts but since lockdown she'd become even more eccentric and gave her class impromptu health lectures before and during the class. She claimed the Corona virus was a hoax, the vaccine not only a scam but a ruse to gain mind control through nanoparticles that changed one's DNA. Sunscreen was another conspiracy, sunscreen also altered your DNA, and prematurely aged your skin rather than protecting it. In fact, the latest cure all was perineum sunning. Direct sunlight to your perineum everyday would mainline vitamin D into your system in minutes, help regulate your hormones, relieve stress and enable you to sleep better. Arseholes in the sun. This made us all laugh.

We discussed the worrying growth of conspiracy theories, how they were triggered by anxiety, how the alienated, undereducated and powerless were more vulnerable to them. A psychologist at the table told us that those prone to conspiratorial ideation correlated with certain personality traits: paranoia, neurosis, narcissistic tendencies and a lack of self-esteem. They wanted to form a reliable view of the world – that nothing happened without a reason; they wanted to feel in control – if we unmask the villain, we can stop them; and they wanted to shore up a superior image of themselves as having greater access to the truth than their peers.

But I wondered, not out loud of course, what of the personality profile of those who always refuse to countenance or evaluate the evidence of conspiracies? Who insist when terrible things happen, against compelling evidence, that the powerful, governments, big corporations never knowingly kill or torture, at home or abroad. It's always a mistake, a bad apple or a lone wolf, whatever grainy evidence whistle-blowers like Kelly, Snowden, Manning and Wikileaks revealed to the contrary. There's also a certain personality type who always looks away and insists that there are never conspiracies at work, who subscribes wholeheartedly to the cock up theory of history: the type who is socially connected rather than alienated, well-educated and powerful.

The Plan

Where I come from everyone believes in conspiracy theories, however highly educated, socially connected and politically powerful they are, everyone. They live in the rubble of conspiracy theories, factional fighting, civil wars and the violence inflicted by US and her allies. It's a small society, you personally know the actors on the political stage or you're distantly related to them. We are always talking about who pays who, who calls the tune, who provides the weapons. Conspiracies are just the facts on the ground, though there are plenty of cock ups too. Where I come from, its like the psychologist said, most people are pretty neurotic and paranoid. As for narcissistic tendencies and low self esteem, we bring up the boys with lots of the former and girls with the latter. Levantine conspiracy theories are different from the Occidental variety in one crucial aspect – no one believes that if we unmask the villain we can stop them.

But that summer, the summer of 1978, the conspiracy that was foremost in our minds was how to conspire a meeting between D and Q that would kickstart their great romance. I was her sounding board and co-conspirator, M was far less keen. She was more worried about propriety, about doing anything that might sully her reputation. Every morning and at the close of day D and I hung around the school magazine notice board, giggling and waiting, because it was close to his locker. K, who was in Q's class came up in the second week and asked, was I a writer like my father? Would I like to write a story for the school magazine? Was that why I was so interested in the notice board? He was the editor and took his job very seriously.

I don't know what made me so brazen, the lark of it, the adventure of D's pursuit of love I suppose. Yes, I'm writing a story, well I'm researching it, perhaps it will be an article. Is a love story like Leila and Mejnun possible in the modern age?

That sounds very interesting. You don't have to check the board for the information. After classes on Tuesdays and Thursdays I am at the back of the library. The librarian lets me hold meetings there, quietly. I can advise on length, help with the edit. We don't have enough girls writing for the magazine. You are very welcome.

Afterwards in the patisserie D collapsed in giggles as she narrated the encounter for M. Is a love story like Leila and Mejnun possible in the modern age? This girl thinks on her feet but that K he is so, so serious, you are very welcome. She imitated his deep quiet voice.

He is a nobody, M said sternly, practically a peasant, a nobody scholarship boy.

He has a big nose and his Adam's apple bobs up and down when he gets excited in debating society, D added.

Actually, he is dangerous M said. I don't know why they let him edit the school magazine. You know I heard he has posters of Shay Guava, Qaddafi and Nelson Mandela on his walls at home, and... I cut her off, how had K become roadkill in this conversation? True he had a lop sided almost afro haircut and he was very shy and serious, but he was clever and unlike most of the top scholars generous with his time with the less gifted. He taught the juniors at chess club and tutored poor kids who wanted to take the scholarship exam to our school.

Che Guevara, I corrected M. Not Shay Guava.

Stalking Q's locker and waiting for him to drive by the patisserie terrace had yielded no positive results. We had still not managed to engineer a meeting between the potential lovers. We needed a proper plan. When I saw his Slazenger sports bag one morning inspiration struck.

Tennis lessons, I announced to the two girls, we're taking up tennis.

God Had Other Plans

I hadn't thought about K in years when I saw him, unexpectedly. I was at a small film festival in Belgium, I was on the jury for the documentary shorts. It was a low budget British documentary about a young Somalian rapper in Bradford. The director's approach was very poetic and verité at the same time. Sound and image were not synchronised. We heard the young rapper's verse, an Imam's call to prayer, his mother recounting the recipe of his favourite meal while we watched the young man walking through a run-down housing estate, across fields, abstract shots and colours too. In the voiceover the rapper told us his story, what had inspired him to become a rapper. Then it cut to interviews with those who had been key to his creative development. One of them was his Imam. This Imam was known for running a cultural centre and inspiring the youth. I always believed in him, the Imam said, he shone with the spark of inspiration. I, myself had wanted to be a poet, in my youth. But God had other plans. That deep, slow, serious voice. It was K. I recognised the voice at once, though it took a while to recognise the face, he had a beard, his face had become gaunt, haunted. Who knows how, or why, but K had ended up as an Imam in Bradford. I really thought that he would become a writer and a revolutionary. It's strange I don't remember giving it much explicit thought but somehow I had been certain that K would become a leader of some sort. Perhaps he had. I heard he had eventually gone to university in Egypt. He didn't have the money or contacts to go to Europe. The winds of war and the whims of our desires scattered us in the most unexpected ways, or perhaps not. Perhaps it's all our fate.

Love-Fifteen

I had weak wrists. I was awful at tennis. And I felt guilty because I knew that the lessons were more than my parents could afford but they hadn't demurred at all. I felt a fraud. D was not weighed down by any such guilt. She was driven by her desire, determined to impress and to win love. The coach was impressed by her serve. We whiled away the twilight hours in long gentle pointless parries, lobbing the ball backwards and forwards and then drinking sodas afterwards outside the clubhouse, waiting to see Q. And we did see him, regularly. Tennis was Q's favourite pastime.

What's that? D asked him one day as we took our places at the table next to him. She pointed at his white tennis shirt with thin green stripes. Is that a marijuana leaf on your top? How come you don't wear Lacoste?

It's Boast, he smiled. It's cool, it's a maple leaf.

Cool, D agreed. Cool. She sounded like a cooing dove. I love America. Tell me about it.

What do you like? What do you want to know about America?

Charlie's Angels, David Cassidy. They say I look like Brooke Shields, do you think so?

I was the prim silent chaperone. Sometimes M would join us. She didn't approve of D's behaviour but she liked the atmosphere at the tennis club. It was her kind of milieu, although she never played at all. She just sat on the club house patio sipping sodas in her tennis whites.

Love's Unkind

The next week when we all turned up for our afternoon practice the club house had been closed off for a private party, older boys and girls. Q was there. He beckoned us over, you can come. You don't mind if they come? He asked a girl with silver eyeliner and laced up roman sandals to match. This is Brooke, he winked at D, and her dark angel friends, what shall we call you? Kelly and Sabrina? There was music, and dancing. Love's unkind, what a fool believes, baby come back. By she's gone I was feeling woozy. Q had sneaked vodka into our sodas with a wink. I'd never had vodka before. I felt sick and slipped away to the rose garden behind the courts. I threw up in some bushes and lay on the grass, the ground beneath me seemed to be swaying like a boat.

Well, well, what's happening here? Q was standing over me. Then he was lying on top of me. When he started kissing me my first sensation was shame, that my mouth tasted of vomit, then asphyxiation, I couldn't breathe and then revulsion, his tongue, the taste and smell of him. He was sweating profusely, an onion and decaying meat smell. I tried to get up, but he had me in a steely grip, I couldn't seem to move at all. There was pain but I don't remember that clearly. I remember that there was pain, but it is only a memory. The revulsion though, that stench, is still fresh. I get involuntary flashbacks. His sweat and saliva, the strange spasm on his face. Then M was there.

Where did you get to Z? They've cut the cake? What? What are you guys doing in the bushes?

Q leapt to his feet, adjusting his clothes and pulling me up with him. The button on my skirt was torn, my panties around my ankle. Some weird alien slime was oozing down my thigh.

Your friend was not feeling well. I was helping her, the poor girl has been sick. He winked at M. She needs to go home now. And he was gone. It was over. I threw up in the bushes again.

Oh my god Z, that is disgusting. And I saw you guys making out, what will D say? Did you just steal her boyfriend?

I ran. I left. I couldn't go home and face my mother like this. I had to clean up first. I felt like I stank of shit, dead meat and alien pus. I ran back to school. I washed up as best I could. Thankfully I had a spare gym kit in my locker so I could change out of my rank, defiled clothes. The library was empty. I would rest there, get my breath back, find a way back to normality. Would I ever feel normal again? This panic of revulsion, how could I subdue it? First though, how to hide it?

Hello Z? It was K, calm and studious. Are you here to discuss your story? I shook my head. Leila and Mejnun in the modern age? How are they?

I decided against that story, I told him. Actually, I'm not feeling so well. Would it be OK, could you walk me home?

Expulsion

I don't remember that evening, how I evaded my parents, how quickly I managed to retreat to my room. Whether I slept at all, or whether I really did keep retching and vomiting through the night. But the nightmare wasn't over. School the next day was not a return to normality. At morning break D made a huge point of blanking me, she and M sat huddled across the yard, deep in conversation. D was crying and kept glaring at me. There was worse to come. I was summoned to the headmaster's office at lunchtime. K had been summoned too.

You were seen leaving school together yesterday, arm in arm. The headmaster said.

Not arm in arm, she was unwell, she merely leant against me.

Shut up you dog. You were seen, the caretaker saw you. You are animals, filthy animals. The headmaster was shaking as he put my gym bag on the table, the dirty tennis clothes I had hidden in my locker spilling out.

Your parents have been summoned, he told me. And you, thank God your father is dead and did not live to see how you dishonour your family. You, clear your desk and locker and get out. You will not graduate from this school.

Winds of Change

What have you done? My mother kept up a sotto voice wailing, like a mantra. What have you done? What have you done? What have you done? My father said nothing. He was in his study, making endless phone calls and packing a selection of his books. I was taken to D's mother's clinic to be examined. What happened? Will you let me look? Her voice was gentle but I shook my head. She lead me to a high medical bed and put me in stirrups. I'll just give you a couple of injections to make sure everything will be alright. Do you want me to make you fresh? You will be a virgin again, in just a minute.

No, nothing happened, no I don't want that.

But before I leave I tell her. It was Q. Don't let him anywhere near your daughter. She likes him, but don't.

First, we went to Istanbul, and a year after that my father found a job at a university in a small provincial town in England. I thought we were fleeing my dishonour but the winds of change were hot on our heels anyway. The university back home went up in flames. They shot the student demonstrators, then there was civil war. Or war, it depends on your politics. Q's father became Prime Minister.

The Wedding of the Year

They married eleven years later on a cliff side in Malibu. M got what she always wanted, the rich husband, the lavish, picture-perfect wedding.

There were security concerns about a wedding at home, they had a small official ceremony in the Presidential Palace. The main celebration was the Malibu bonanza. M wore an exuberant explosion of seed pearl embroidered organza and raw silk. Q was stouter and his hair shorter, other than that he looked the same, coarsened by time but largely unchanged. Hello did an eleven-page spread, that's how I knew about it. My mother bought a copy.

I had cut off my personal ties with the old country. Professionally everyone presumed that it was political. Perhaps it was, the personal is always political. Earlier in my career as a writer, editors would commission me for the anti-Islamic woman's point of view articles. I was never comfortable with their liberal certainties, their frankly racist and Islamophobic brand of feminism. I never even thought of myself as a Muslim, my father had raised me as an Enlightenment atheist, but the condescension and Islamophobia of these people taught me who I was, irrespective of what I believed. I gave up writing about anything outside the field of film a long time ago. They weren't interested in my thoughts on the so-called rules-based order anyway, they just wanted pieces on crying women victims of Muslim brutes and autocrats, woman's rights in the axis of upheaval. That's what they call them now, places where the Americans don't control everyone and own everything. My country is caught somewhere between the two, in the upheaval wreaked by the rules-based order. Q's family are still rich and powerful. Somehow some people know how to surf the waves.

You are a contrarian like your father was, my mother said, you are always rubbing people up the wrong way. She was right. But I know how to keep my mouth shut too, like my mother.

The Girl in the Middle

My mother kept in touch with D's mother, they were close friends. They used to write to each other regularly. D's mother and mine had grown up in the same small town, more of a village really. They were second cousins or something. Their family left a couple of years after us. They lived in Montevideo for a long time. Then they left Uruguay for America. I found a stack of letters when my mother died, recipes, reminiscences about their childhoods and their elders, updates on their and their spouses' health, their children's lives. My mother would ask her for an opinion on my father's broken heart, it seems he had had a stent put in. That must have been when I was living in Paris. Neither of my parents told me. I didn't know my father's heart was broken before he died. I should have guessed. D's heart was broken too. Her hunger for love was never fulfilled. She married and divorced three times. Her mother didn't seem to approve of any of the candidates. She was disappointed that D never had a career and wrote that she was impressed by mine. My mother must surely have exaggerated my achievements for that to be the case. She seems to have sent some newspaper cuttings of my articles. I looked D up on social media. There weren't many traces, just a largely inactive account. A group of middle-aged women were raising a glass by the sea somewhere #thegals #livingmybestlife. I wouldn't have recognised her if I hadn't known it was her. She was smiling brightly, the same smile, but her face was fat and her eyes very sad. The light had left them. She never leaves the house, her mother had written to mine. She eats American junk food and watches TV all day. All the money we spent on her education was wasted.

Desire

I'm so glad you came back. All these years. I missed you a lot. I always wondered, did you blame me for what happened then?

The clink of the little silver cake forks on porcelain. I eat so I don't have to speak, to tell stories I have tried to evade by a lifetime of remaining silent. And then I stop eating. It's time to speak, after nearly half a century of silence.

I came back to sort some things out. After my mother's death, our house.

Yes, your lawyer reached out to me. I had our people look into it. Actually I think it was vakf owned you know, not your family's.

There was a vakf, yes. But the vakf was put in place by my great grandfather, it was put in trust for my mother and her descendants, that's what I understand? What is this organisation that has taken it over? You are on the board of governors, perhaps you can help?

I don't understand vakf law darling Z. Yes, I try to do my bit for society. I'm on the board. It's a charity that provides citizenship and leadership training for underprivileged children.

They wouldn't even let me in the door.

No, well. Half a century as you say. It's been a long time. Things change. She gestures at the photograph and changes the subject. We were both heartbroken when you left so suddenly. And, of course D was very angry with you, for what happened with Q. I thought it was just a childhood crush, but she became quite ill. She would eat and eat and eat and then throw up. And she kept following him around, stalking him, waiting by his car after school, shamelessly. He had to tell her to leave him alone. It was embarrassing. My parents made me drop her. I had my reputation to think about.

I'm so sorry to hear that, I say. I watch her, there's something she wants to tell me. She's squirming in her chair. When she gave me photograph, I thought she might be preparing to deliver an apology. And I was preparing myself to accept it, there was nothing to be gained by refusing it. I would say it was a long time ago, we've all changed so much, which would be true. It would also be a lie. M was still driven by the desire to be rich, richer still. D was still hungry for love. I still wanted the space to tell my truth. We had changed, we had stayed the same. But when she finally speaks, it's not the apology I expected.

My marriage to Q, our romance began after we had both graduated. Our families introduced us, and you know I never really spoke to him at school, not like you and D. It was arranged between us, but I thought we both wanted it very much, that it was love. It was love. But, it had been difficult between us these last few years. I found out six months ago. He was forced to tell me. The business is bankrupt, all this, my beautiful home, it's going. He mortgaged, he borrowed against it. Nothing, there's nothing left, not a penny. But that last night, we argued about something else. He didn't want to make love to me anymore. I was angry, I demanded to know, what did he really want? I had never really been the object of his desire, had I? No, he told me, he had only lived one perfect moment of desire in his life, and that had been with you. The night he died, before we went to bed, that's what he told me.

TWO POEMS

Allama Muhammad Iqbal

I Desire

I want to have the extremes of your Love,
See, how silly am I, wishing for the unachievable.

I don't care if you maltreat me or promise to unveil your beauty,
I just want something unbearable to test my fortitude

Let the God fearing people dwell in paradise,
For, instead I want to be face to face with you.
(I don't want to go to paradise but want to observe the Divine Beauty)

O fellows, I am here for a few moments, as a gust,
Like the morning star I will fade and vanish in a few moments.

I disclosed the secret in public,
I need to be punished for being so rude.

Candle and the Moth

O Candle! Why does the moth love you?
Why is this restless soul devoted to you?

Your charm keeps it restless like mercury
Did you teach it the etiquette of love?

It circumambulates the site of your manifestation
Is it inspired by the fire of your light?

Do the woes of death give it the peace of life?
Does your flame possess the quality of eternal life?

If you do not brighten this sorrowful world
This burning heart's tree of longing may not turn green

Falling before you is the prayer of this little heart
This little heart knows the taste of impassioned love

It was some zeal of the Primeval beauty's Lover
You are a small Tur, it is a small Kalim

The moth and the taste of the Sight of the Light!
The small insect and the Longing for the Light!

Sir Muhammad Iqbal (1877–1938), philosopher and poet, is a great of twentieth-century Indian poetry. Described as 'The Poet of the East', he wrote in Urdu and Persian, and produced a string of masterpieces – including *Javed Nama* (Book of Javed), *Bal-e-Jibril* (Wings of Jibril), *The Secrets of the Self*, *The Secrets of Selflessness*, *The Call of the Marching Bells*, and *Complaint and Answer*. Iqbal's thought was firmly focused on reforming Islam. The allusion to the Mount of Tur is a reference to the story of Prophet Moses and the burning bush.

THREE POEMS

Kabir

I

I feel like laughing
When I hear that the fish in the water is thirsty.

In shallow seas and ocean depths, he searches.
He wanders with sadness in his heart.

One goes to the Ka'ba, another to Kashi.
Without knowledge of the soul, man aimlessly roams.

Kabir says: 'Listen, o brotherly saint,
It is the innate spirit that will meet the imperishable Lord.'

II

What is to be done tomorrow, do it today; what is to be done today, do it
                                                                    now.
If the moment is met with destruction, then when will it happen?

To ask is akin to dying, do not ask or beg from others.
It is better to die than to ask, this is the teaching of the True Guide.

Where there is the ego, there is adversity.
Where there is doubt, there is insalubrity.
So says Kabir:
        How can the four illnesses be removed, save though patience?

III

O mind! Have love for the Master.
When His refuge arrives, each one is saved:
     such are the ways of the Lord.

Witnessing the body's beauty, do not be forgetful of the Lord,
     no different is it to the dew on the grass.
The physical form is raw—and in the end, it rests fallen,
     like the sand of a torn-down wall.

Do not allow birth to cycle the wheels repeatedly:
     caste, life—all will pass.
Kabir says thus, climbing upon the fort of the body,
     and drumming a victory drum.

Kabir (1398–1518) was an Indian mystical poet celebrated by Sikhs, Hindus and Muslims alike. He suggested that truth is located within the person who walks the path of righteousness and regards every living and non-living thing as divine. The emphasis of his philosophy was on dissolving the ego. Kabir has large groups of followers in India who function much like *tariqas* in Sufism. The poems are translated by I. A. Visram, a doctoral candidate in the study of religion at the University of Oxford.

REVIEWS

DISCOURS D'AFRIQUE

Abdullah Geelah

In 2007, French President Nicolas Sarkozy delivered an address before an assembly of carefully selected academics at Cheikh Anta Diop University in the Senegalese capital. The speech was a diplomatic attempt to stitch the frayed seams of the relationship between France and Africa. Sarkozy's infamous *Discours de Dakar* invited Africans to engage in self-critique, acknowledging both the crimes of the transatlantic slave trade and European colonisation while simultaneously suggesting that Africa had somehow been complicit in its own tribulations. 'The tragedy of Africa,' Sarkozy declared, 'is that the African has not fully entered into history [...] they have never really launched themselves into the future'. His view of African progress was typically colonial and condescending. An all-too-familiar perception which has been propagated by a litany of western narratives that have, over decades, oscillated between depicting Africa as a land ensnared in perpetual conflict and as a continent on the precipice of a renaissance. The response from Africans to such perception has always been, and continues to be, instant, incisive, and inexorable. Sarkozy's suggestion, however, that Africa 'has not fully entered into history' was particularly incendiary. This was not borne out of harmless ignorance of African history and civilisations (*les obélisques de Louxor* are a constant reminder of such history even if a trip to the Louvre were too prohibitive for *Monsieur le Président*). It was representative of a deep-rooted and lingering bias that has long viewed African history through the lens of racism, reductionism, and repudiation. And so brazen to see this preposterously displayed within an institution that has the distinction of being named after a figure who is widely regarded as the preeminent African historian of the last century: Cheikh Anta Diop (1923 – 1986). 'Imperialism, like the prehistoric hunter', Diop wrote in his groundbreaking *Civilisation ou barbarie: anthropologie sans complaisance* (1981), 'first killed the being spiritually and culturally, before trying to eliminate it physically'.

Sarkozy's address reflected standard polemics about Africa in the European academe. Consider, for example, Hugh Trevor-Roper (1914 – 2003), erstwhile Regis Professor of Modern History at Oxford, who stated in his book *The Rise of Christian Europe* (1963) that 'Africa had no history prior to European exploration and colonisation, that there is only the history of Europeans in Africa. The rest is darkness'. Her past, 'the unedifying gyrations of barbarous tribes in picturesque but irrelevant corners of the globe'. Such views, derived from the European (mis) conception of world history, presented Africa as a historical vacuum. The absence of written records in many ancient African societies was mistakenly interpreted as a lack of history. For Europeans, only certain sources were worthy for historical documentation. Oral and other intangible cultural traditions were therefore ahistorical and unhistorical. African history, framed by a European paradigm and predominantly penned through an exogenous perspective reliant on non-indigenous sources, entrenched such misconceptions. A narrative continuum extending from antiquity's Herodotus.

Zeinab Badawi's *An African History of Africa: From the Dawn of Humanity to Independence* (2024) is neither another rejoinder to European prejudice towards African history nor an apologia for African historiography. It is a serious attempt at synthesising African history for popular consumption and reaffirms African historical realities and agency without the domineering presence of the European gaze. From the very first page, the reader is immediately struck by Badawi's opening salvo: 'everyone is originally from Africa, and this book is therefore for everyone'. This lays the groundwork for the inaugural story about one of our earliest human forebears – Dinkenesh. Her name means 'you are marvellous' in the Amharic of her latter-day progeny, a far cry from the 'Lucy' moniker inspired by the Beatles song coincidentally playing on the radio during the discovery of her fossilised remains. Dinkenesh's story, and those of our other hominid ancestors whom we meet in the first chapter, show that Africa is anything but a historical void.

The book demonstrates a remarkable breadth of African history. It commences with the advent of *homo sapiens* in East Africa and concludes with the African peoples' struggle against, and eventual freedom from, European colonisation. Each chapter is broadly framed by a socio-political and historical outline of the African civilisation and/or period in question. It is then peppered with the author's own visits to archaeological and/or cultural sites and interviews with leading African scholars *in situ*. The scope is ambitious in its overview of key epochs and themes: the ancient Egyptian and Sudanese civilisations, the ascension of Christian Axum, the Amazigh and Islamic dynasties of North Africa, Mansa Musa and the West African kingdoms, Great Zimbabwe, the Kongo Kingdom, and the flourishing of the Asante, Edo, Ndebele, and Zulu cultures. The book further delves into two of the most substantial and far-reaching episodes of human trafficking in global history: the transatlantic slave trade and its more enduring Indian Ocean counterpart. (And whilst Badawi is mindful to avoid making this challenging aspect of African history the book's main focus, slavery features as a constant and inevitable motif.) She also presents the spread (and indigenisation) of the Abrahamic religions into Africa and highlights often misunderstood traditional African spirituality. She ends with a hope for a new Africa – an appeal to the continent's youth and her future leaders. The book interrogates essentialised portrayals of African history and makes room for marginalised stories, contributing to a more representative and inclusive historiography. In particular, Badawi pays assiduous attention to the impact of African women in shaping their socio-political landscapes. For instance, Badawi scrutinises the reign of Queen Njinga (1583 – 1663) of the Ndongo and Matamba Kingdoms, located broadly in what is now Angola and the Congo. Queen Njinga adeptly managed political turmoil and staunchly opposed Portuguese colonial ambitions in south-west Africa. Rather than romanticising female leaders, Badawi recognises their complex legacy. While acknowledging Queen Njinga's astute intellect, diplomatic acumen and strategic military prowess – which left an indelible mark on Angola and beyond – Badawi notes Queen Njinga's own admission that she

Zeinab Badawi, *An African History of Africa: From the Dawn of Humanity to Independence*, WH Allen, London, 2024.

had given 'many enslaved people to various governors and representatives' including the Portuguese.

Born in Khartoum, Sudan on 3 October 1959 to the late BBC Arabic journalist Mohammed-Khair El-Badawi and educator Asia Mohammed Malik, Badawi's background is deeply intertwined with her homeland's past. Her antecedents, of Nubian (and part Ethiopian) heritage, preserved age-old traditions that had inspired her curiosity as a young girl on family trips to Sudan (the family having settled in London in 1962 following her father's work for the BBC Arabic service). Her great-grandfather, Sheikh Babiker Badri (1860 – 1954), was a soldier in the Mahdist army against Lord Kitchener's British forces at the Battle of Omdurman in 1898 (and whose memoirs serve as a primary source for the book's section on the Mahdi's resistance movement). He was also a Muslim social reformer. He championed women's education and founded the first private school for girls in Africa in 1907. Badawi *père*, a committed pan-Africanist, newspaper editor, and notable anti-colonial activist, was incarcerated by British colonial authorities. He contributed to the establishment of a pre-independence political party (the Socialist Republican Party) and formed the first labour union in what is now South Sudan – demonstrating his unwavering commitment to social justice and national unity as an Arabic-speaking northerner in the Nilotic south. Another relative played a significant role in Malcolm X's spiritual growth during his 1950s Sudanese sojourn – a connection which further underscores the influence Badawi's family has had on shaping African and diasporic historical narratives. For those who are familiar with Badawi's life, this makes *An African History of Africa* particularly poignant. Indeed, her excitement and profound interest (notwithstanding her understandable tilt towards Sudan and Abyssinia) in each subject matter of the book are palpable. She is often awed or struck by the sites, artefacts, fossils or cultures she encounters as part of her fieldwork in the numerous African countries she visits. This adds a human touch to the book and shows the author's authenticity in being an interlocutor of African history. Similarly, her anecdotes (such as her father being sprinkled with water from the Nile as an infant 'in a custom that is an echo of Christian [Nubian] baptism' or how his memories 'as a little boy growing up in the far north of Sudan ... of people leaving pots and pans in the graves of newly deceased relatives' reflect ancient Kushite funerary rites) provide a living and personal link with our African past.

Given her extensive background as a seasoned journalist and broadcaster, Badawi appears uniquely qualified to interlace this intricate narrative of African history into a captivating chronicle. She became arguably the first Sudanese woman to graduate from Oxford in 1981, having read philosophy, politics, and economics at St. Hilda's College. She followed up with a postgraduate history and anthropology degree at the School of Oriental and African Studies (SOAS), University of London, where she is now its President. Her four decades of experience in the media has made her an effective communicator and global networker – grilling some of the world's most important personalities on programmes such as *HARDtalk* and *Global Questions* and serving on the boards of a number of African organisations and international bodies. It was an encounter with Getachew Engida, the former Ethiopian Deputy Director of UNESCO, which inspired her own work in this area. On Engida's bookshelf she noticed, and was impressed by, the tomes of African history under the title *The General History of Africa* (GHA). Launched by UNESCO in 1964, the GHA was conceived by post-independence African leaders out of the necessity to reclaim Africa's cultural identity, rectify the widespread ignorance surrounding the continent's history and dispel the discriminatory prejudices that have long plagued it. The original eight volumes (which are still being updated and expanded) are scholarly, having been developed by over 350, mostly African, experts. Despite the shortcomings with their comprehensive coverage and reader accessibility, the books complicate our understanding of African history and integrate it into the broader narrative of humanity by emphasising its relations with other continents and the contributions of African cultures to the overall progress of humankind. In 2017, Badawi turned the tomes into a twenty-part series *The History of Africa with Zeinab Badawi* on BBC World to 'bring the volumes back to life'. While *An African History of Africa* might seem derivative of the documentary series, it is a complementary effort in bringing the GHA to a wider audience. This book-documentary model of African history was more recently attempted by Guy Casely-Hayford in his 2012 BBC television series and corresponding publication *The Lost Kingdoms of Africa*. Casely-Hayford, a cultural historian and scion of a prominent Anglo-Ghanaian family, shares similar credentials with Badawi as a credible and reliable conduit to African history. Nevertheless, *The Lost Kingdoms of Africa* offers a light examination of just eight African kingdoms, presenting an almost cursory exploration of the continent's multifaceted and multipolar history even within a narrower scope. The selection of these particular kingdoms arguably warrants a more profound introspection and analysis, yet the excessive reliance on polished prose and slick videography in both the book and the series indicates a lack of any earnest challenge at a detailed investigation of the chosen civilisations. This raises questions about whether the content was conditioned by the author's (or some other third party's) specific interests, and the ensuing Eurocentricism (to whom, indeed, are these kingdoms 'lost'?) is conspicuous. This juxtaposes with Badawi's explicit objective of foregrounding the African historian in her book and documentary series, precluding any inclination towards the western paradigm.

Badawi's methodology reflects the approach of the GHA in integrating various disciplines (sociology, anthropology, palaeontology, oral, and other cultural traditions) which serves as a corrective to narratives imposed on Africa by others, particularly those dominated by western perspectives. In particular, Badawi uses contemporary ethnographic observations (for example, the Hadzabe tribe in Tanzania's Rift Valley) to expound the nature of prehistoric society. Prohibitive though this may be in scientific terms, it is interesting to the lay reader. Moreover, we are shown how 'oral tradition in Africa gives rise to interpretations that can run counter to the biases of written accounts'. For example, in the historical account of Sonni Ali of the Songhay Empire. Sahelian oral history views him as a 'strong and effective ruler' vis-à-vis his negative portrayal by Arab historians in written records owing to his 'lapsed Muslim ways'. With the GHA as a constant reference point and interviews with African scholars, engaged citizens, and cultural figures, these reinforce the centrality of African voices in their own history. The reader is therefore provided with a contextual understanding of specific events or periods, recognising the wider forces and influences at play. This differs from John Reader's *Africa: A Biography of the Continent* (1997), an equally bold attempt at a comprehensive (albeit geographically limited) study of the African continent, which mainly uses European sources and thus excludes African and diasporic voices from their own history. Badawi's book could similarly be compared with J.D. Fage and Roland Oliver's seminal work *A Short History of Africa* (1962) in terms of its breadth and handling of the content. *A Short History of Africa* stands out for its well-structured and reader-friendly presentation, blending storytelling, critical analysis and interpretation effortlessly. The text has remained a favourite among readers, evidenced by its numerous reprints and updates since its debut. Whilst the authors are European scholars of African studies, they use a vast array of African literature – alongside archaeological findings, oral histories, linguistic ties, and social frameworks. However, their work falls short by not adequately incorporating a broader range of interdisciplinary methods (such as, anthropology and linguistics) which could have deepened the history and proffered richer outlooks on the cultures and societies explored.

Writing a comprehensive survey of a continent's history (especially one which is conterminous with humankind's) poses two fundamental limitations: the risk of superficiality and narrative coherence. Covering wide-ranging themes might lead to insufficient depth in individual topics and, at times, Badawi's accounts of certain personalities are either condensed or fleeting. The one-and-a-half pages dedicated to Sayyid Mohammed Abdullah Hassan (c. 1856 – 1920), for example, is noteworthy for emphasising his religious zeal, military dexterity against three imperial powers, and literary contributions. This could have been further enhanced with some critical commentary on the Sayyid's involvement in the large-scale killings of his compatriots (a complex legacy as documented in the oral poetry of Somali clans who refused to join the Dervishes in their *jihad* against imperial forces). These fundamental limitations are self-evident, particularly when one acknowledges the formidable undertaking of encapsulating the multifarious histories of African societies and cultures within a single volume (something which Badawi concedes in the introductory pages). While these constraints may sporadically disrupt the flow of the narrative, Badawi's lucid writing style, underpinned by insightful research, sustains the prose satisfactorily to its end. A potential way to address this rub is for the reader to engage with the book as a foundational resource for understanding African history – a tool for further research, reflection, and reference – and to listen to the audiobook as well. Badawi's mellifluous and authoritative voice animates and beguiles the printed text and, accordingly, the history is 'seared into the imagination'.

An African History of Africa is not a reductive retelling of Africa's story. It is our shared African story as told by African storytellers. It will no doubt play a pivotal role in advancing African historiography and shedding light on the rich tapestry of African history, cultures, and civilisations from a truly African perspective. 'The negation of the history and intellectual accomplishments of Black Africans was cultural, mental murder,' Diop continued to say in his *Civilisation ou barbarie* 'which preceded and paved the way for their genocide here and there in the world'. Badawi's book, and encouragement of young Africans like me to 'invent the present and future for the continent', indicate a spiritual continuation of Diop's philosophy. She enjoins us to do so with 'heads held high' and 'hearts full of pride' in our 'magnificent past'. And thus we rededicate ourselves anew to this eternal *Discours d'Afrique*.

CAUCASUS INSIGHTS

Anna Gunin

'Home, grief, deracination' – here is the trio of themes running through journalist Tom Parfitt's debut book *High Caucasus*. Just as Geoffrey Chaucer described a walking pilgrimage to Canterbury, this memoir-cum-travelogue charts Parfitt's voyage by foot in search of healing for the vicarious trauma he experienced while reporting from scenes of sheer horror. It is a work steeped in empathy. Through it, Parfitt, who has worked as a foreign correspondent for *The Guardian*, *The Daily Telegraph*, and *The Times*, provides a brilliant introduction for Westerners keen to understand the territory and the peoples of the North Caucasus, as well as the complex relationship that exists between the Caucasus and Russia.

Tom Parfitt's story begins in Beslan. He is sent by his newspaper to report on the school siege that took place there in 2004. 'Some gunmen have stormed a school in southern Russian…Chechens, I guess,' an editor in London tells him. The setting is the Second Chechen War, which was launched in 1999 by the newly appointed Prime Minister of the Russian Federation Vladimir Putin. It is the job of a professional journalist to report on violent incidents with the cool detachment and forensic analysis of a surgeon. And yet the act of witnessing atrocities takes its toll on even the most proficient of reporters. In Beslan, Parfitt witnesses' scenes of devastating trauma. One moment in particular is to etch itself into his mind:

> Her left hand grasps at the air.
> She is groaning like a wounded animal.
> She has just learned that her child was killed in the school.
> The grief has entered her body fast and deep, and she is crumpling to the ground.

Back in Moscow, Parfitt continues to be haunted by the nightmare vision of this bereft mother. He finds himself unable to blot out the terrible scenes that were unfolding around him in Beslan. And so he resolves to embark on an epic walk across the Caucasus mountain range, all the way from Abkhazia and the shores of the Black Sea to Dagestan's Caspian coast. In this way, he hopes to trudge the trauma out of his system, while also learning about the entire region.

Tom Parfitt, *High Caucasus*, Headline, London, 2023.

There is a popular legend that when God was populating the Earth's lands with various peoples, he emptied out all those ethnicities remaining in his pot on to the mountains of the Caucasus. It would be hard to find a spot on the planet richer with ethnographic variety. As Parfitt hikes through the slopes and forests of the region, he recounts tales and legends from the history of each locality. He also fills the reader in on the contemporary issues relating to the area. Journalism clearly courses through his veins, and so despite the aim of the journey being to take a much-needed break from reporting, Parfitt is constantly questioning the people he encounters, probing to understand their perspective of the world, reflecting on what they tell him.

The one republic in the North Caucasus that has captured headlines around the world for the past few decades is of course Chechnya. Ever since Dzhokhar Dudayev declared independence in the early 1990s and Boris Yeltsin sent in the tanks to crush the separatist forces in December of 1994, the Chechens have been demonised by Russian state propaganda as terrorists, while conversely being hailed in the West as heroes attempting to break free from the yoke of the Russian empire. Throughout *High Caucasus*, Parfitt remains a profoundly humane and open-minded narrator. He neither romanticises the people he encounters on his journey nor diminishes them to any sort of stereotype. He continually challenges the tropes that endure among the Russians and in the Russian media: 'The idea that a North Caucasian is simultaneously ignorant, cruel, and double-dealing persists in Russia today. What I discovered in Chechnya and the neighbouring republics made me think just the opposite. ... I found, time and again, that people in the Caucasus behaved with a dignity that transcended their circumstances; a dignity that I doubted I could match if I had suffered a similar fate.'

High Caucasus is engaging and compelling from the first page. Parfitt paints a personal and emotional world before the reader's eyes, rather than offering a dry analysis or recounting events aloofly. He sets out to explore trauma in all its aspects: how it affects the people whose stories he has reported on; the corrosive effects it has on his own mental health while he's reporting; the abiding marks and psychological scars that episodes of historic trauma have left on entire peoples. His own recurring nightmare of the woman whose child was killed in Beslan is evocatively conveyed in Parfitt's supple and melodic prose: 'every now and then, there she was, the mother of the dead child: tumbling, grappling, falling through my dreams in muffled horror.'

It is a well-known maxim that travel broadens the mind. By encountering people from backgrounds essentially alien to our own, we become exposed to mores, philosophies and ways of thinking that are new and exotic. On occasions, these outlooks may be puzzling, perhaps even striking us as offensive. With an arresting frankness, Parfitt examines his own meek response when confronted with Cossacks complaining about 'the Jews and the magnates' who are accused of ruining Russia. The cast in *High Caucasus* is exceptionally colourful, coming from such a diverse sweep of ethnic groups, each with their own distinct identity, language, and history. The Russian mentality too is represented: we see glimpses of the capricious aggression and paranoia that are a common feature of a certain strand of Russian jingoist.

This is a deeply personal work, as much about the beasts that lurk in the forest as about the fear of monsters that fills our minds. One incident captures this beautifully: 'at dusk, I spotted several bears. On close scrutiny through my monocular, they turned out to be a tree stump, a boulder and – distantly – a lump of horseshit.'

A substory running through the book is the interest shown by the Russian secret services in Parfitt's adventures. His encounters with police, border guards and army servicemen, with the dark shadow of the FSB – successor to the notorious KGB – always in the background, fill the narrative with a crackly tension. Crossing border posts by foot armed with detailed maps and being a foreign journalist make Parfitt a prime suspect for the crime of nefarious intelligence gathering. 'Brushes with the security services', he writes, 'are part of the territory of being a Western reporter in the former Soviet Union'. He describes the interrogations he is subjected to, conveying his anxieties as things hot up at various points in his journey. For he is crossing through a country that functions as a police state, where citizens and travellers are not accorded the rights and freedoms to which we've grown accustomed in the West. This is a land where men in uniforms wield the authority to detain you arbitrarily, they can confiscate your property at whim, and there is a continual atmosphere of lawlessness and impunity.

Another theme that is ever present is that of the relationship between the dominant Russian culture and the local traditions of the mountains and valleys Parfitt traverses. Politically and militarily, these lands are the site of separatist movements. There are discussions of the profoundly painful legacy of the horrendous atrocities and waves of ethnic cleansing that took place both in Soviet times and earlier, under the Russian tsars. Entire peoples were forcibly removed from their lands to free up the territory for Russian colonisation. Parfitt is a narrator of extraordinary empathy, and he tackles this subject with great sensitivity, as well as exploring the enduring effects of these traumatic episodes. 'After the demise of the Soviet Union, things had begun to fall apart...Suddenly, the North Caucasus was convulsed by nationalism.'

The tone of *High Caucasus* is often leavened with some levity. Parfitt's journey involves not only the fauna one might expect in this region of forested mountains, such as eagles, wolves, and bears; there are also surreal surprises occasionally sprung on the reader. 'The next day, ambling down a track where clouds of white butterflies sucked at my boots, I was amazed to see a Bactrian camel standing beside a cottage. It looked happy, if somewhat perplexed, in this alpine setting. The owner told me he had brought the creature from Astrakhan, the dry steppe country by the mouth of the Volga. "Just for the beauty of it," he said.'

For centuries, Russia's southern borderlands and the mountains of the Caucasus have figured prominently in the Russian imagination. The Caucasus has represented a place of wild freedom, of liberation from the autocratic control of the tsarist empire, a land of peril, adventure and exile. The writings of Lev Tolstoy, Alexander Pushkin, and Mikhail Lermontov include works such as *Hadji Murat*, *The Prisoner of the Caucasus*, and *A Hero of our Time* respectively, all set in the region. A classic film from the Soviet cinematic canon is the 1967 comedy *Kidnapping, Caucasian Style*, which, as Parfitt says, 'was another iteration of the captivity trope'. It depicts the adventures of a young and guileless Russian student who sets out on an ethnographic field trip to the Caucasus. Parfitt is told in jest by his Moscow friends that he is following in the footsteps of that film's hero. One Russian whom Parfitt encounters in his travels is Dima, an ascetic who has sought refuge from the modern world in the remote highlands. We later discover that Dima is on the run from an important bureaucrat bent on punishing him. 'The Caucasus', Parfitt observes, 'has long been a place of exile; a halfway house on the road to redemption. ... Pushkin was sent to the south as censure for his subversive poems, but felt liberated from the philistine society of St Petersburg'.

As well as describing newcomers to these lands, Parfitt also examines the deep bond forged between the many indigenous peoples and the soil they have lived on for centuries. The Caucasus has the remarkable diversity of a melting pot, and yet rather than forming a homogenous fusion culture, each people preserves their traditions with a fierce pride and passion. Often we have a sense of stepping back in time, as we witness shepherds with crooks living a truly simple life unchanged since ancient times, frying pastries in remote huts, oblivious to modern civilisation. This stripped-back living surely has therapeutic properties for the travellers and newcomers who take refuge in it.

As Parfitt faces the daily challenges of his journey – the weather, the hostile terrain, the beasts in the forests and the locals who may or may not help him – his obsessive reliving of the traumas he witnessed as a reporter begins to abate. We sense the effect that hiking through nature is having on his mind and body. Not all of it being recuperative: 'my right knee had begun to produce an unpleasant grinding noise when it was put under pressure'. And yet trauma is always lurking in the shadows. The cast of local characters encountered on his journey often have tales of terrible suffering to share. 'It was very hard...There were many of us Karachays living in squalor. In the beginning, six or seven people died every day, from hunger, from disease.' Many of the sites Parfitt treks through are filled with the ghosts of the past – 'haunted ground,' as he writes. 'Seypul's story of the deportation got me thinking about what it would really be like to be pulled from your home – from your homeland – and transplanted to another, unfamiliar place, unsure if you could ever return.' The compulsive acts of empathy that clearly form an essential part of Parfitt's makeup are what imbue him with the gift of fine journalism. It is a quality that the current world sorely needs more of. As we read of these many individual stories, through Parfitt's guidance they come alive in our imagination. Rather than depicting the superficial shape of events, he makes us keenly sensitive to the experiences the characters have undergone.

The book's narrative is interwoven with reflections from Parfitt's childhood in Norfolk. This too is part of an attempt to connect an exotic world with a world that is familiar. The approach knits the two worlds together empathetically. Parfitt also digresses with descriptions from travel writers of bygone days, which offers fascinating insights into the way the Caucasus was seen through the eyes of earlier Western explorers. As we are told, travellers to the Caucasus 'found a sublime beauty that struck them as both pure and poignant; a vestige of a disappearing world and a place of solace in the face of relentless Progress.'

One work that is evoked by reading *High Caucasus* is Alexander Radishchev's *A Journey from St. Petersburg to Moscow*. Published in 1790, Radishchev surveyed the provincial world of ordinary Russians, detailing their hardships with a compassionate eye. Radishchev's underlying motive was to inform the Empress Catherine the Great of the harsh conditions that abounded in the empire she ruled over. Radishchev was arrested and sentenced to death. Parfitt writes of his travels as an Englishman protected by his British citizenship, hopefully safe from the capricious arms of the Russian state. Nevertheless, when the full-scale invasion of Ukraine is launched in 2022, Parfitt suddenly has to abandon Moscow, his home for two decades, with his Russian wife and child: 'it was a nasty blow for me and my family'. Many Western correspondents left, while others decided to remain in Moscow – Evan Gershkovich being one of them. He was arrested in 2023 on charges of espionage, and after sixteen months behind bars was finally freed in a prisoner exchange.

Parfitt's trek took place in 2008, when 'the mass arrest of conservative Muslims' in the region was still occurring and arbitrary extrajudicial killings were rife. Dead bodies of young practising Muslims would turn up in the forests with signs of torture. Keen to learn what was prompting the locals to join the 'rebel underground', Parfitt is met with an understandable reticence on the part of the people he encounters. An imam in a mosque he visits is 'pale and morose and guarded'. Occasionally, people open up. 'Tembulat said it was police persecution of conservative Muslims that had motivated many of the 2005 attackers. "They beat people, they shaved crosses in their hair, they forced them to drink vodka."' A man named Arsen offers Parfitt the following explanation:

> In Islam, there are three steps one must take in the event of persecution. ... The first step, if you live in a Christian state, is to apply to the authorities and request protection from harassment. Which they did: they wrote one hundred and sixty- two official complaints, all with no result.

> The second step is to ask to be resettled to a place where you can fulfil your religious obligations. Four hundred and eighty Muslims from here wrote an appeal to the federal authorities asking assistance to move to another land. The powers refused to help'.

> Arsen paused for a moment to sip his tea. I noticed he smelled faintly and sweetly of incense. 'And the third step?', I asked.

> 'The third step comes if all efforts are exhausted and the persecution continues,' he said, pushing away his cup. 'That is when you no longer have the right to sit at home, when you must come out and defend your religion.' Arsen lowered his voice and leaned forward.

> 'The third step,' he said, 'is jihad.'

High Caucasus opens with a dedication to the '*memorialtsy*' – the people who work at Memorial. Parfitt credits them with planting the seed of his fascination for the Caucasus, 'why had the Caucasus got under my skin? One reason was that I had come to love and respect a group of activists working for the Russian human rights group Memorial in Ingushetia, the Muslim republic next to Chechnya'. One of the key people working in Memorial was Natalya Estemirova, who was half Chechen and half Russian. Parfitt was friends with Estemirova and writes about her lifelong mission to fight for the rights of her compatriots. In the epilogue comes the devastating news of her assassination, which took place in 2009. He meets with her daughter, who now lives in London.

For centuries, blood feuds have featured strongly in the cultures of the Caucasus. Parfitt's memoir conveys many tales of violence upon violence. He is clearly appalled at how entire communities can so easily become locked in a cycle of killing, retribution, and hatred. And yet healing relief comes in the form of the 'wellsprings of goodness' he encounters on his long journey through the region. His peregrination also takes him through scenes of wondrous beauty that help to displace the darkness of the grief he has witnessed.

> Each detail seemed cut in glass. I wanted to stamp the scene in my mind. Would I see something so magnificent ever again? Was this Herzog's glimpse of the sublime, a moment that made all those before and after fade? I could do with such a paling of the past if the nightmare of the falling woman was to retreat altogether.

The stories Parfitt relays of the mass killings and forced expulsions of entire ethnicities from their ancestral land are still horrifyingly pertinent so many decades and centuries later. As the Western powers that in normal times loudly champion the rules-based order quietly suspend their values to support Israel's slaughter in Gaza, the themes of *High Caucasus* are more searingly relevant than ever. Humanity faces a choice: to bear witness to the unbearable trauma of another people or to turn a blind eye. The act of witnessing is profoundly terrible and harrowing. Parfitt's memoir about coping with the ensuing distress provides a roadmap for how to heal the soul in the aftermath of catastrophic events. A book for our times.

LONGTERMISM

Christopher Jones

We are at a civilisational turning point. This is the message in a literary celebration of longtermism by one of its most visible advocates. William MacAskill's *What We Owe the Future* begins by asking us to engage in a thought experiment. We are asked to first imagine living all the lives of all humans who have existed before in history and prehistory for the past 300,000 years. Then, considering the average life expectancy of mammals and other animals on the planet (700,000–1 million years), we are asked to imagine living the lives of hundreds of thousands of generations and trillions of people in the future. The thought experiment is our introduction to a moral philosophy that privileges humans, past, present, and future. We are also asked to imagine that on balance these are happy lives and that there are potentially humans filling vast spaces on earth and in space for millennia and more. The thought experiment asks us to expand our imaginations to the possibility of vast human happiness on future worlds, far into the future.

William MacAskill, *What We Owe the Future*, OneWorld, Oxford, 2022.

The publication of the book came out with a lot of fanfare and excitement in Silicon Valley and elsewhere with its roots in the effective altruism movement and transhumanism circles. Longtermism is associated with MacAskill and his friend Toby Ord based on ideas of Nick Bostrom and others. The basic premise is that we should not discount the future, but rather take moral responsibility for the happiness of future generations — for the good of the species. MacAskill is a moral philosopher and Research Fellow in Philosophy at Oxford, so be warned that there are a few deep, but navigable chapters that dive into moral change, value lock-in, and the metrics of happiness. Some of it is likely to be over the head of readers without philosophy backgrounds; I did not find all of it entirely persuasive, but it is logically presented. There are fifty pages of footnotes – generally worth exploring – the bibliography is not included but can be found on the book's website.

Overall, I found the book worth the time to read with some caveats. I do not trust many of his conclusions or arguments but found the text both informative and provocative. On balance, there is much more that I like about the book than I dislike. First and foremost, as a futurist, I celebrate the long view, the long-term perspective offered by this moral philosophy. One of the challenges of the times is a short-term perspective, particularly noticeable in large governmental and corporate organisations. Longtermism theory requires a commitment to consider distant futures -centuries, millennia, and even further into the timestream. It also assumes we are a migratory species that will eventually expand into outer space. Those are domains of the foresight enterprise. The concepts of utopia, eutopia, and dystopia get some attention – we should probably expect a eutopian future—unfortunately the narrative or bibliography does not connect with the rich literature and history related to those concepts. That was a disappointment. Similarly, there seems to be no awareness in the text of existing futures studies and foresight literature on long-term futures.

Longtermism's firm embrace of heroic anthropomorphism brought out my inner misanthrope. To his credit, as a vegetarian, MacAskill attempts to draw attention to the suffering of animals, particularly industrial meat production. He attempts to quantify the happiness of animals, including wild animals, which seems to me an unfortunate approach – using human values to make such an assessment. However, on balance, his advocacy for growth and scale of human activities does not acknowledge what deep ecologist would argue is the 'intrinsic value' of animals, rocks, mountains, and trees. Those are perilously threatened by human activities, particularly population growth and economic development. At his core, MacAskill preaches the importance of economic development and growth. And BIG human aspiration. Big growth!

From an alternative futures perspective, his interest in counterfactuals, eutopias, and the alternative futures of growth, stagnation, and varieties of collapse can be applauded. His argument about value lock-in are compelling and likely accurate. A good portion of the text explores the extent to which the slavery abolition movement, particularly in the UK, represents the kind of values shift that could well be lost if we enter periods of civilisational stagnation, decline, and collapse. MacAskill acknowledges the threat to several civilisational values (for example, scientism and capitalism) posed by drivers of change, such as artificial intelligence and climate change. He gives some slight attention to what he calls periods of plasticity — sounding much like postnormal times: 'different moral worldviews are competing, and no single worldview has yet won out'. We are between epistemes.

This arguemnt is clearly most evident in several chapters devoted to civilisational stagnation and collapse. Much of the text directly or indirectly addresses existential risk. He offers his forecast probabilities of four scenarios for 2100: Stagnation, 35 percent; Exponential+ Growth, 30 percent; Continued+ Growth, 25 percent; and Collapse, 10 percent, although he notes that all scenarios have a 10–50 percent probability of occurring. As noted, there is no discussion or any reference to the large literature on alternative futures. Given his forecast, the stagnation is the most likely future, with collapse a strong possibility, his concern is for the continuation of civilisation, or the revival of industrial civilisation. His advocacy for artificial general intelligence (AGI) is, at least in part, driven by his belief that AGI will stimulate hyper-exponential economic growth by the end of the century. He sees this driver as the force that raises all boats, that allows for the decarbonisation of the economy and emergence of solar energy economics. If we stagnate, he advocates leaving as much fossil fuel resources in the ground as possible for the reemergence, the re-start, of industrial civilisation in future centuries or millennia ahead. He seems locked-in to the growth and industrial paradigm.

Other strengths of the book are his advocacy for political experimentation, innovative 'charter cities,' and connections to his earlier work on effective altruism. Lastly, he deserves credit for bringing attention to existential risk throughout the text, although his soft peddling of the risk and potential recovery from World War III was troubling. MacAskill feels the risk of all-out war is possible, even likely, but questions the assumptions about 'nuclear winter', and posits that the Southern

Hemisphere is also likely to bounce back from such a catastrophe. He appears truly worried about global pandemics and the dark side of AGI.

Sadly, there seems to be very little reflexivity or self awareness of the irony of advocacy for western civilisation from an Oxford scholar. I also cringe at the celebration of the rise of the global middle-class, reduction in poverty, overall, and other hopeful statistics, given the misery of the bottom billion — never mind the mind games of statistics about relative happiness. Americans remain at the top of the global heap, in terms of being parts of the hegemony, but mostly seem miserable. Relative deprivation after watching the finale season of *Succession*? It is hard to be a booster for longtermism when the greatest beneficiaries of the future are still the elites.

My futures-oriented values seem to have been baked in during my graduate studies: a Gaian perspective, informed by deep ecology, post-normal science, and feminism. I am with Gandhi, thinking that western civilisation *would* be a good idea. In practice, I'm not so sure it's worth saving! Longtermism, as expressed by MacAskill, is an arrogant anthropogenic dream that is a nightmare for much of the rest of the planet. Growth is malignant, not progress. His text drips with assumptions tied to what Canadian futurist Ruben Nelson calls the Modern Techno-Industrial (MTI) paradigm. Economic growth is good! Techno-fixes are the solution! Big is better!

If anything, MacAskill adds fuel to the postnormal times condition, with ample contradictions, chaos, complexity, uncertainty, and ignorance. He is either ignorant of, or chooses to ignore, the message and analysis of the MIT study, *Limits to Growth*. He alludes to, but never addresses the growing concern about the growth paradigm, anti-growth social movements, such as the slow growth and no growth movements, and fractures in the global economic system revealed by the coronavirus pandemic. No mention of the promise or perils of an emergent 'circular economy.' Perhaps that is a weak signal for him of coming stagnation?

MacAskill invokes the 'seventh generation' principle as articulated by the oral constitution of the Iroquois confederacy. While the concept is worth honoring, and while we admittedly have some responsibility for future generations, the context of the idea matters. In the context of horticultural or pastoral societies it had a different meaning. I am not sure Iroquois grandmothers would embrace the civilisation that he advocates. For our possible gene-splicing, spacefaring ancestors in the twenty-second century, 'seventh generation' will have a far different meaning. While 'seventh generation' has been a successful marketing strategy, there is little evidence it is being used as anticipatory corporate or national government policy. Bolivia and Bhutan may be the exceptions. Longtermism is wrong to colonise a concept that might be viewed as antithetical to growth as it is articulated by this movement.

His longtermism moral philosophy fancies that the level of the development of our species as adolescent compared to the average lifespan of mammalian species. We are young and rash and yet too immature according to the life-cycle analogy. There is no way to know whether we are a typical mammal species/representative of other species measured. There is obviously a range, an average of one million years or so, but perhaps we are unique. Even if we have been a distinct species for the last 300,000 years, perhaps we have already peaked. Moreover, we are the obvious cause of the current mass extinction event, as so clearly demonstrated by Elizabeth Kolbert's *The Sixth Extinction*. Perhaps we have passed our useful planetary shelf life? Perhaps we are spawning our silicon digital offspring or cyborg descendants and its time to leave the cosmic stage? If we can't get it right in the next century or so, perhaps we are simply an evolutionary cul-de-sac?

There are any number of variables including cosmic and terrestrial existential threats, from cosmic gamma ray bursts, to nearby novas or supernovas, coronal mass ejections, super volcanoes, and runaway greenhouse events that could be the end of our species. The point is that McCaskill's estimates may not reflect the realities of coming AI or climate catastrophes or other threats that we have dodged. Furthermore, in his analysis of stagnation and collapse there is no recognition of the work of Joseph Tainter and others who are more concerned about bureaucratic complexity as the main driving force of potential collapse. McCaskill's call for more growth, greater complexity, more people, and more development would seem to feed the prospects for MTI civilisation's collapse. Rather than contributing to the solution (vegetarianism and solar conversion notwithstanding!), he appears to add to the postnormal times condition by advocating for the acceleration of the speed, scope, scale, and simultaneity of technology, innovation, and development that bring us even more complexity, chaos, and contradiction, that is swirling around us. It seems to me that robotics, AGI, quantum computing, genetic manipulation, molecular engineering, and other high technologies, for all their promise, have dark sides that are likely disruptive at a minimum and potentially existential threats not only to civilisation but the entire *Homo sapiens* species.

QUILL, BIRD AND WORLD

Naomi Foyle

Vellum Publishing is a new independent publisher based in Manchester, currently launching an intriguing list of poetry and non-fiction with a focus on internationalist and Muslim voices. Vellum's first three poetry titles are *Dismantling Mountains*, a collection of meditations on social justice from American poet Samantha Terrell; *Seven Men I Know: a pile of poems and short stories*, an anthology of Turkish writers translated and edited by Mevlut Ceylan; and *Only Words*, an unofficial 'New and Selected Poems' of the British-Canadian Sufi poet Paul Sutherland, which includes his compelling narrative sequence *Poems on the Life of the Prophet Muhammad: Peace Be Upon Him*. The books reveal Vellum's intent to become a significant new publisher in the British poetry landscape. Paul Sutherland's work will be given a full review in a future issue of *Critical Muslim*.

Samantha Terrill, *Dismantling Mountains*, Vellum Publishing, Manchester, 2023.

Mevlut Ceylan (ed.), *Seven Men I Know,* Vellum Publishing, Manchester, 2024.

In *Dismantling Mountains,* Samantha Terrell takes an often-aphoristic approach to the moral questions broached by everyday life. Short reflections on human frailty, social inequality and life's vicissitudes, written with a light touch and pleasing musicality, at their best Terrell's poems offer readers a delicate yet potent blend of spiritual poetry and social critique. Well-aware of her position of privilege, she never takes it for granted. The 'embarrassed' parent in 'Poverty' comments:

Your child
Has no bath

While I scold mine

For too much splashing on the floor.
So much excess,
What's it all for?

Far from handwringing rhetoric, however, this question stems from
Terrell's deep commitment to global justice. The simple and memorable
'World Peace' concludes:

I wish the world for my child.
And what I wish for my child,
I wish for the world.

Elsewhere, she astutely narrows her aim. In 'Of Peace and Pocketbooks',
she's a suburban spoken word poet, deploying a sharp use of slant rhyme
from behind her white picket fence to take shots at media complicity in
America's military industrial complex:

... And I'm not the first
to say it,
But I hope I'm not the last:

That the business of war
Is the biggest
Perpetrator
Of all and, lest

We somehow
Forget it,
Our regular news
Retains the rights to its sponsorship.

She also clear-sightedly turns her targets on herself and her community.
'Life-Preservers Fail Us' concludes:

There's a striking
Lack of diversity
In your group
Discussing cultural sensitivity

But everyone's giving accolades
For your platitudes.
I guess these are
Our life-preservers.

When reality's too painful,
We see what we want to see —
Allowing the truth to
Give way to mediocrity.

Aware, however, that possessing a political consciousness can dampen one's love of life, Terrell also celebrates creativity and joy as sources of self-empowerment. The carefully balanced 'Accommodating Enthusiasm', deserves to be quoted in full:

Nerves and bird songs intertwine,
Giving voice to inner-feelings —
Previously stored up
Songs locked in lungs

I make manic notes
In the margins of my mind,
Already rationalizing
Why I had resented the birds,
Why I had denied them my song.

The tension between singer and monkish annotator plays out in throughout the collection, in poems that often comment wryly on history and theology, though at times can be a little too much 'on the nose'. In its laudable attempt to distill our similarities to each other, 'Equality', for example, smooths over vital questions of human difference. More subtly observed is 'Shark Bait', which sees through distracting attempts to divide us into 'sharks and minnows', ultimately warning:

Beware instead, of
Quiet, still seas
Since the absence of conflict
Does not equate to the presence of peace.

Not a new insight – the final quote is credited to Nelson Mandela among others – but a well-placed allusion that develops the collection's reflections on peace as an active choice always in need of renewal. The majority of Terrell's poems are well-worth returning too, for their uplifting reminders that, while the path through life is a rocky one, as the opening mythological poem 'To Rise' concludes, long ago:

> ...   humankind   discovered
> A task for which they were uniquely suited –
> Picking themselves up again, since picking things up works best with opposable
> Thumbs and a yearning soul.

Seven Men I Know is a beautifully crafted tribute to seven contemporary Turkish writers, offering short selections of their work skilfully translated by Mevlut Ceylan, each prefaced by a short biography and an intriguing illustration by Hasan Ayın. The introduction by Rogan Wolf thoughtfully sets the cultural context for this labour of love by Ceylan, himself a poet of note living in self-imposed exile in London, who in his long commitment to translation and small press publishing 'has made much good of his otherness, his emissary role'. On this occasion, Ceylan has gathered seven late writers, showcasing their considerable talents and whetting the reader's appetite for more. One hopes that interest in this volume might lead to a fuller anthology, including the voices of women and younger poets. But as a personal homage to writers one assumes were Ceylan's friends and colleagues, *Seven Men I Know* gives a tantalising introduction to a generation of Turkish poets, essayists and fictioneers concerned with Islam and modernity, East and West, and, like creative writers everywhere, the tragedies and tensions of everyday life.

Nuri Pakdil (1934–2019) was a versatile writer, a playwright and poet best known for his highly accomplished essays. In Ceylan's lean translations, his aphoristic couplets demonstrate a keen, roving intellect, and a careful, catlike tread. In a few short words, 'Pure' bodies forth the gravitas of prayer:

> The deep voice descends
> in the form of silence.

The theme of religion develops with reflections on Mecca and eternity, while elsewhere 'Flames' is a witty title to conjure with:

> He says that there is his fancy,
> as he comes closer she hurries away.

Sezai Karakoç (1933–2021) was a 'pioneer of Turkish literature' who founded his own publishing house and drew on classical Islamic poetry to explore contemporary tensions. His long narrative poem 'Of the Father and His Seven Sons', a title that resonates with the structure of the anthology, has an enduring appeal of a lyrical folktale. One by one, the father's sons leave for 'the West'. Seduced by fame, unrequited love, money and power, education, wine they are murdered, lost, forgotten, even including the poet:

> Reciting his poems in deserts
> he was dissolved as grains of sand on the roads

Only the seventh son, travelling after his father's death, resolves to redeem this tragic situation. His actions bring into focus a sharp contrast between the restless change of 'the West' and the spiritual steadfastness of 'the East' — an opposition one might consider geopolitically reductive, but as a metaphor for faith, retains relevance and power.

Erdem Bayazıt (1939–2008) was a poet, editor, academic and member of parliament. His poetry, though, floats miles away from political rhetoric. Here is work that draws from the well of faith to water human frailties. There is a gnomic quality and disarming vulnerability to his brief lyric poems that draw the reader back to ponder their imagery. In 'Farewell' the speaker laments:

> People are as alien to me as hearts of stone
> Trees lining the street will be sentenced without me
> How can I hear a lute
> describing the loneliness
> of my window

Bayazıt's long work 'The Book of Poems (Fragments)' contemplates death with equanimity, however. The speaker, strengthened by the 'peace of prayer', seeks:

... like gushing water,
the earth and heavens,
this side of the world and the other,
night and day,
The Book that has been read,
The Book that our heart desires to read.

Akif İnan (1940–2000) was a lecturer, social activist and much awarded
poet, regarded as a leading voice of his generation. From the evidence
here, his mercurial lyricism certainly sets him apart. The ghazal is a difficult
form to translate, given its intricate structure, and while I can't vouch for
the fidelity here (not knowing Turkish or even being able to see the
original), Ceylan's version of 'Ghazal (2)' suggests an innovative freedom
with the form

Before your eyes touched my heart,
O İstanbul, where were those birds?

Sea is my tongue's lexicon;
songs, my brother, where were they?

In the ghazals and elsewhere, İnan also had the gift of expressing the
intense intimacy of faith. At least it is hard to imagine a human lover with
the power of 'You':

Your eyes are everywhere day and night,

you are every climate and each word is yours,
your devoted hands are in my palm,
your scent would fill my lungs.

Only to be with you, to be with you,
I believe is the finest thing of life.

Alâeddin Özdenören (1940–2003) worked with other poets in the
anthology as an editor and publisher, and won the 1996 Writers Union of
Turkey Poetry Award. He was especially known for his poems in memory
of his son, Kerem, who was killed in an accident. 'Mountain', 'Unaware'
and 'Kerem's Satchel' all lightly lift an unbearable load:

in the depth of your satchel

little birds have made their nests

your satchel was very heavy my son
but what a lovely weight that must have been
no sadness in you when you carried it

Longevity is sadly not a hallmark of these seven writers, four of whom died under the age of seventy. The loss of Cahit Zarifoğlu (1940-1987) was surely deeply felt, but in a short life he covered much ground, working as a translator, teacher, and journalist, founding a publishing house and literary review, and latterly working on children's literature. While 'This Era had no Tail or Head / It was Simply a Blur in the Mud' exhibits a disturbing eroticism, other poems read – in a sophisticated twist – as work written by children for adults. In the clever 'Daughter and Father' the daughter very much gets the last word:

just be quiet will you
here is another balloon
don't burst it
OK?

daddy
don't tell me that
tell it to the balloon
just say
don't burst
OK?

Rounding off the anthology are flash fictions by Rasim Özdenören (1940–2022), Alâeddin Özdenören's twin, a much-awarded novelist, essayist and one of Turkey's most prominent short story writers, translated here by David Boxen and Mevlut Ceylan. With its insomniac stream of consciousness, the first of the stories, 'The Pussycat', could qualify as a prose-poem. A slice from the middle give a flavour of this brief, beguiling piece:

One begins to hear silent voices, unknown melodies. You can compare every sound to the sound of anything. That hour of the night anything is possible. Old man Faulkner thought of Berlioz's music which he heard in Jardin du

Luxembourg as Tchaikovsky spread on a slice of stale bread. This means that
the time the master enjoyed most was during a breakfast unwillingly eaten.

The other, slightly longer tales, have an elusive, parable-like quality that
chimes softly with the spiritual themes of the poetry in the book. Though
it is the troubled thoughts of 'The Patient' that conclude the book, one
imagines Ceylan, the loving ambassador, nearing the completion of *Seven
Men I Know*, and lingering on the ending of 'Between Two Stations':

> Ah, I have come to the crux of the matter.
>
>   I was here. We were together. We used to board the train together. But
> two people boarding a train do not always take the same route from then on.
> This was something like that. We made the journey together, but our routes
> thereafter diverged.

At times in the short biographies of these creative men, tense shifts from
past to present. This does not feel like an error. Writers become their
writing; and in that sense are always with us. Their work is a mesh of past,
present and future, drawing people together across languages, continents
and years. Art too is such a dissolver of time. Special mention must be
made of the line drawings by Hasan Ayın, which playfully, in fascinating
detail and Escher-like repetition, interweave the motifs of nib, quill and
bird throughout the pages of the anthology: enduring emblems of the
writing life etching tribute to men whose souls have now flown.

ET CETERA

ON MY ROOTS

Hassan Mahamdallie

The sun was setting fast as I gazed out over Sum Sum Hill. As night descended the treeline on the horizon increasingly came into focus, and the lights picking out the small dwellings scattered across the rolling landscape began to glow orange.

It was the end of a long hot day driving round Trinidad, the Caribbean island situated hard off the coast of Venezuela, in my latest effort to fill in the vast blank that signifies my father's family tree. This time around my niece Nadie had kindly volunteered to help me seek out various members of one branch of my Trinidad family to which she belongs – the Mohammeds.

Muslims are a small minority in Trinidad and Tobago – around five percent. The majority are of Indian descent, although there is a growing number of Muslims hailing from the African population. When I am in Trinidad I always stay by my cousin Darling's house in a suburb of the capital, Port of Spain. Now Darling's name is not really Darling – that is the name she goes by. Her actual name is Mayroon – but everyone calls her Darling. It suits her. Just about everyone in my Trinidad family has at least one other name that they go by. This confuses me. Nadie's dad (the son of one of my father's sisters) is known to everyone as 'Popsie', but his actual name is Nazir. One of Nadie's brothers is known as Dave – but his actual name is Shezad. And then there is Damien, Annie, Jenny, Sledge, Baby, Nylon, Shirley, Barbie, Sailor, Lina, Nelle, Tasha, Kimmy, Kevin, Diamond, Boysie, and Race (more of whom later). I have even met one relative named after Stalin, but I believe that is his actual given name.

At the break of dawn Nadie arrived to pick me up from Darling's house. I squeezed into the front seat of her small family car, with her three young but miraculously uncomplaining daughters jammed in the back. As we drove south Nadie explained to me that there are four branches to our common bloodline – the Mohammeds (hers), the Khans, the Alis, and the Mahamdallies (mine). The Mahamdallies are the scarcest and most difficult to track down. On this particular trip we would concentrate on the Mohammeds.

The whole day long, until the sun began to set on Sum Sum Hill, we criss-crossed the former sugar belt that makes up the south of the island in search of various Mohammeds and memories of long dead people, by which I might continue to piece together my Indo-Caribbean diasporic identity. However, the day's exploration started not with a familial visit, but with a refreshing paddle in the grey roiling waves of the Atlantic Ocean at Manzanilla Point on Trinidad's east coast. This served as a symbolic beginning to our day's quest – Manzanilla being the area of settlement of one of the first of Trinidad's Muslim communities.

The original inhabitants of Manzanilla, from which many of the present-day locals are descended, were disbanded soldiers from the British Third West Indian Regiment. The West Indian colonial regiments were originally composed of former African slaves and freed Blacks conscripted by the British to serve as infantrymen (cannon fodder) and deployed in various spheres of conflict in defence of the empire – one of which was the 1812 War, known in the USA as the second war of independence. After seeing active service in battles against American military forces in the southern states, veterans of the Third Regiment were discharged by the British and taken to Trinidad, and settled as free men at Manzanilla Point, at a location furthest away from nearby slave plantations. The British planters in the vicinity were fearful that if their enslaved Africans got to know of the free black colony of former fighting men, it would encourage an insurrection.

The proud and hardworking Manzanillans were each granted sixteen acres of land. They were eventually joined by womenfolk, and thereafter eked out a living on their army pension and by growing rice. In 1841, a Christian missionary's report to the then British colonial governor noted with dismay that 'Many of them are nominally Mohammedans and are under the guidance of five so-called Mandingo priests'. So Manzanilla was a fitting jumping off point in our effort to connect with as many members of the Mohammeds as could be crammed into one day.

Nadie's daughters on the beach at Manzanilla.

I always knew my father by the name I thought everyone else knew him by – Oscar. He was Oscar to me, Oscar to my mother, Oscar to his workmates and to his friends. Growing up, I never thought anything much about it. In those days Oscar was not an uncommon name – perhaps Oscar Mahamdallie was a slightly jarring combination, but then all of us had clunky hybrid names – my mother was Yvonne Mahamdallie, I was Hassan Nigel Mahamdallie, my elder brother was Karim Mark, my younger sister was Zelica Yvonne Mariam, and so on.

It wasn't until as an adolescent that I chanced upon the old passport my father had travelled on to get into Britain back in 1955, that I realised the name I knew him by was an anglicisation and diminution of his birth name – Asgarali. Asgar/Oscar. Oscar/Asgar. Suddenly there was a connection to something real – but it was obscure and out of reach to me at that time, and would remain so for many years until my first visit to Trinidad in my early thirties. Later on I would find out his complete full name was in fact Salim Asgarali Mahamdallie.

Towards the end of his life, I interviewed my father about his beginnings and immediate family, but unfortunately, I was too late – by the time I got to talk with him he was in the grip of Parkinsons and could remember very little. All I could really glean from him was that he was born into a large family of sugar-cane cutters, descended from Indians imported by the British during the second half of the nineteenth century to serve as an indentured plantation workers.

His father, my grandfather, had been the village imam, and my father's remaining early memory was being sent by his mother to deliver to his father his daily chillum pipe of marijuana. My father said all his siblings were involved in sugar cultivation. He was the exception, being the youngest child and the apple of his mother's eye. She sent him to school to learn how to read and write and do math. (In the ship's record of his subsequent passage to England his occupation is listed as 'clerk'.)

Growing up I had only ever met one of his siblings 'Gina', a sister who had escaped her allotted fate by migrating to the Dutch colony of Curaçao, where she met a naval officer Hans who married her and took her back to live with him in the port of Den Helder in the north of Holland. When I was a young teenager in the 1970s, I was sent twice, or maybe three times, over to Holland to spend the summer holidays at Auntie Gina's. She was a tiny but formidable woman who had the habit of attracting foundlings who she would then raise as her own. On these vacations I would be send down to Amsterdam for a few days at a time to stay with Gina's adult son and daughter and get a taste of city life. They both lived in the Javastraat area of the capital, at that time principally the home of immigrants from the former Dutch East Indies, and regarded, rightly or wrongly, as a hotbed of criminality. I would stay by Gina's adoptive son Farley, who I was in awe of due to his 70s Shaft-styled Afro haircut and three-quarter length brown leather coat. Tragically, Farley was to meet an early death. (Am I dreaming when I recall he had a handgun which he used to take out and place on the smoked glass coffee-table top in his living room?)

I would also stay with Gina's daughter, who I will call Nancy for present purposes. She was an attractive resourceful woman who ran a small but lively bar and had married an older man, a pineapple-faced Columbian, Pepe, who was rumoured to be involved in cocaine importation. I do recall on one visit calling in at the bar, only to find it almost deserted. I was curious as to why the joint was so quiet. I was told that a few days earlier a client had been shot dead as he drank at the bar counter, an incident that proved to be bad for business. I don't think the establishment ever really recovered and eventually went bust. Nancy later served some prison time, but thereafter turned her life around, and still lives in Amsterdam today. We have lost touch I regret to say.

This then was the extent of my connection with my father's side of the family as I was growing up. I don't remember him saying anything at all about his homeland – not that we children ever had a meaningful conversation with him. He worked seven days a week. He had a fulltime job with the Greater London Council (GLC), and at weekends would do casual work at the bookies and as a football pools-checker on Saturday nights.

There was so much we didn't know about him. We weren't the only ones – neither did my mother. When they first met in the mid-1950s he told her he was an Indian student. God knows why. Maybe it was a status thing, concocted to impress. I'm sure my mother, being exceptionally sharp of mind, quickly saw through that particular counterfeit identity.

After he retired from the GLC Oscar moved back to Trinidad, hoping to get a nice sales job with an old childhood friend who had built a successful soft-drinks business in Port of Spain. He sent for my mother who I think he hoped would join him to live out there. Disastrously, during the visit she found out that her husband had been married before he migrated to Britain. He had hidden this inconvenient wife from my mother for over thirty years. His marriage to my mother had quite possibly been a bigamous act, and the foundational deceit upon which their whole life together had been built. My mother returned home to London and instigated divorce proceedings. I do not know the whole truth of this. My mother did tell me something very very dark and tragic that she had heard about his first wife, but I cannot substantiate it, so I cannot repeat it here.

It is curious that my father was twenty-nine years old when he left Trinidad for the UK, unusually mature for that Windrush generation, who were typically in their late teens or early twenties when they boarded the boat to 'the mother country'. So what had his adult life been up to that point and what had prompted him to leave the island for a completely new existence as Oscar? What else about his past had he kept from my mother? I am reluctant to probe too deeply.

All I can say is that on one of my visits to Trinidad, while being driven through the neighbourhood by one of my cousins, he pointed out a middle-aged man ambling down the street. 'That's your older brother that your father had by his first wife. Do you want to meet him?' Shocked, I froze, and for a few seconds contemplated the bizarre and consequential collision of worlds such an encounter would provoke.

'No. No. it's OK. What would I say to him? Best to leave things be'.

'OK' said my cousin, and we drove on by.

Thankfully no such disturbing revelations confront me this time round. The first leg of the journey proper was to strike out from Manzanilla, driving inland and south to the crossroads town of Rio Claro.

We were looking for Shireen, one of Nadie's aunts. The only directions we had was that Shireen lived at the end of a trace opposite an old abandoned factory somewhere on the outskirts of the town. We drove up and down for about half an hour before a local pointed us in the right direction. Shireen and her husband did indeed live at the end of a trace, in a typical south Trinidad dwelling – a wooden house raised on stilts (to keep floodwater and wild creatures at bay), with stairs leading up to the living quarters and a clothes line and hammock slung underneath.

Shireen was surprised to see this tall indeterminate-shaded stranger fetch up on her doorstep claiming to be a blood relation, but like all the others I visited that day, she took the encounter in her stride in a typically welcoming Trinidadian way.

Next we drove out into the forested interior, bumping along narrower and increasingly broken down roads to call in on Annie – another of Nadie's relatives. Annie's wooden and corrugated iron bungalow was small but neat and tidy. It was overrun by her grandchildren and some puppies. We left with a bag full of fresh mangos and other fruit from the tress that grew in wild abundance around her dwelling.

Toward's the end of the day, and many visits later, we pointed the car in the direction of the place from where all the families - the Khans, the

Mohammeds, the Alis and the Mahamdallies – spring, the town of Claxton Bay and its environ, Sum Sum Hill.

At some point in the latter half of the nineteenth century the god-like hand of the British Empire had reached out and plucked our foundational ancestor out from his Mother India and without much thought dropped him into the cane fields of Claxton Bay. I do not know his name, so I will call him The Indian. He is for me a representative of the 143,939 men and women that between 1845 and 1917 were shipped out of ports such as Calcutta and taken half way around the world and transplanted in a small damp tropical island off the South American land mass. The Indian 'coolies' were 'fresh labour', there to replace the African slaves, who after emancipation had deserted the sugar plantations *en masse*, refusing to work under their former masters and overseers.

I do know that The Indian, after completing his five year's compulsory indenture out in the fields, returning each night to the miserable barracks that the slaves had previously been housed in, was presented with the choice of a 'free' passage back home or, if he so wished, a five acre plot of Trinidad land and £5 in cash. This incentive was enough to convince him to stay put, and after a few years The Indian had somehow accumulated the wherewithal to buy up parcels of surrounding land in the Sum Sum Hill area of Claxton Bay, thereby incrementally transforming himself into a Trinidadian with a stake in the future.

The settlement of Claxton Bay can be traced back to the early nineteenth century, and the development of a large sugar plantation owned by Bristol merchant and slave owner William Claxton. In time a steam tramline was built to link the cane fields directly to a specially constructed iron jetty on the Claxton Bay shoreline. From here the barrels of raw sugar were loaded onto ships bound for London, to be refined and sold as a preferred sweetener to the English cup of tea or exported abroad.

Then in the early twentieth century extensive deposits of crude oil were discovered in the interior of Trinidad by a geologist in the employ of British industrialist, Alexander Duckham. Duckham bought up the rights to extract this valuable commodity and commissioned the building of a twenty-mile pipeline (an unrivalled engineering feat for its time) that ran across forest, swamp and flatland, pumping the oil all the way west to the coast at Claxton Bay, where it was stored in huge terminals. Utilising the iron jetty originally built to ship sugar, the oil was then pumped into tankers destined for Duckham's London refinery, where it was turned into superior grade motor lubricant for the combustion engine – the world famous Duckham's motor oil. (The company still bears the name of its founder – Alexander Duckham & Co Ltd.)

My father was (as far as I know) born in 1925, and so his early life would have straddled the colonial era of sugar and the modern era of oil for which Claxton Bay is known today. As a child I am told his family would call him Mahmood (the one worthy of praise). Yet another name to add to my list. On our way to Claxton Bay Nadie took a spin through some of the highlights of our family history. The figure of Osman (John) Mohammed, the husband of my father's sister Khatoon, and the root of the Mohammed branch of the family, loomed particularly large. John Mohammed was widely feared. He was a cattle trader who would walk his goods all the way from his village in the south, northwards to the livestock market in Port of Spain, no small journey in those days.

According to family folk law one day a passerby in the village street accidently bumped into John Mohammed, walking off without apologising. Something like that. The man probably thought nothing of it. This proved to be a grave mistake on his part. The next day John Mohammed lay in wait at the same spot, armed with a razor sharp machete used to cut down cane. At some point the man who he regarded as having given him a public slight the previous day walked by. John Mohammed attacked him with the machete, chopping off the man's hand at the wrist. John walked away but was later arrested, charged, brought before the magistrate and jailed. Such was his reputation that in prison no one, warders nor inmates, would go near him, and after he got out, even members of his own family tended to give him a wide berth. Is this story true? Did Osman (John) Mohammed really have such a violent and menacing temper? I can't say for sure, but there is something about the tale. For me it symbolises the rough, tough and brutal hardscrabble lives of Trinidad's early Indian community, elements of which I came to recognise were embedded in my father's personality, to such an extent that even his Oscar persona could not always successfully keep them submerged.

It was late afternoon when Nadie's car rolled to a stop outside a set of gates on Sum Sum Hill. We were here to meet Race, one of John

Mohammed and Khatoon's sons, and thus my first cousin. I can't tell you Race's proper name, or how he came to be known as such. I found him sitting outside a small shack on the family property. Inside the shack I discerned a small black and white TV, on which I think he was watching video tapes of old Hindi films. A heat-exhausted dog lay prone at his feet. He was, I guessed, somewhere in his late seventies or even eighties.

Race

Race's face was framed by a shock of white hair and a white beard. He was shirtless, and his wiry spare body was clad in shorts and flipflops. His left breast sported a faded tattoo of a heart and a cross pierced by a dagger.

Race was hard of hearing, and what with my London accent, communication between us was difficult. Fortunately for us, one of his son's was on hand to mediate. The following conversation took place.

Race: *(standing up and shaking my hand vigorously)* What's your name?
Me: Hassan.
Race: *(not understanding looks at his son)*.
Race's son: *(loudly in his ear)* Hass – An. Hass – An.
Race: Hassan?
Me: Yes.
Race: Hassan. Oh! Glad to meet you *bhai*. *(Urdu word for brother)*
How much bredren that you have?
Me: Twelve.
Race: Twelve in all?
Me: Yes. Six brothers and six sisters.
Race: *(pumping my hand)* I'm glad to hear that man! *(pause)* Salim, is he living or is he dead?
Me: Dead.
Race: Oh, sorry to hear that. His name was *Salim Asgarali*.
Me: That's correct.
Race: When I was small, at my mother's knee, he did want to come into England. His mother said he is the best son she have *(wagging his finger to indicate she had not wanted him to leave)*. Half the day he would work, and half day he was a teacher at Mt Pleasant Government School *(he indicates down the road)*. And he save his money and he go to England.
Hassan shows Race a photo on his mobile phone of Salim Asgarali, taken when he was a young man in the 1950s).
Race: That's Salim, a handsome fella bhai. Real handsome.
Hassan shows Race an old black and white photo of his mother.
Hassan: That's my mother.
Race: *(Surprised)* A white woman?
Nadie: Can you remember the names of Uncle Salim's brothers and sisters?

Race: Raheem is one. And Subhan is another one. *(He laughs in a bitter way)*. Subhan robbed them all of their land and gardens. *(He makes a movement with his hands)*. Robbed them all and he scatter them.

Scattered, we certainly were.

After watching the sun set over Sum Sum Hill, as she drove me back to Port of Spain, Nadie tells me of her father's memories of growing up. The family was so poor that the children would be fed sugar and water at night to stave off the pangs of hunger and help them sleep. In the morning they would be given a piece of plain roti dipped in oil and a fried egg, and the family meal would often times consist of small crayfish from the stream that ran at the back of the house or whatever they could forage from the surrounding bush.

Each little bit of information, a name, a story, a history, a myth, even a lie, is a piece of the puzzle. But I cannot pretend that the more I discover, the stronger my connection to my Trinidadian ancestors becomes. The gulf between me and them is just too wide and too deep and too separated by the ebbs and flows of time.

Nonetheless, I feel privileged to encounter, however fleetingly, all of these interesting, kind and unique people, as I pursue my ultimately pointless goal to fully know myself.

AFTER HURRICANE BERYL

Amandla Thomas-Johnson

Day 1

At midday, after a two-hour wait for crates of bottled water and vats of petrol to load, the horn blows and the ferry slowly chugs away from the port at Kingstown, the capital of St Vincent and the Grenadines. We are headed to the storm-hit islands of the Grenadines. Passengers, returning to what remains of their homes, huddle to the back of the deck to avoid the rain, as the vessel tumbles in the bitter grey sea.

The Grenadines is a chain of pristine islands that runs southward from the island of St Vincent and continue as part of the country of Grenada, in the Southern Caribbean, about 200km from the South American mainland. Among them is the private island of Mustique, a favourite holiday spot of the British royal family. Prime Minister Boris Johnson controversially spent Christmas on the island in 2019, at the invitation of the Von Bismark family, descendants of the first chancellor of the German Empire. Further south lies Canouan which once hosted a golf course owned by Donald Trump. Unlike the visitors who sun themselves in neighbouring St Lucia and Barbados, the Grenadines attract an exclusive set for which a yacht is a basic prerequisite.

But on the last weekend of June 2024, the harbours of the Grenadines were emptied of their yachts. A Category 5 hurricane was approaching. Dubbed Beryl, it was one of the strongest hurricanes of recent years, breaking many meteorological records for its fury and intensity. In late June and early July, it devastated part of the Caribbean. So, before the arrival of

Beryl, the rich yachties had sailed south, seeking shelter in Trinidad and Tobago, outside the hurricane belt. According to that country's government, by Sunday 30 June, around a hundred yachts had arrived or were on their way. Locals on the Grenadines, mostly the descendants of enslaved Africans, were left to the mercy of a mighty tempest. How they fared unfolds as we head south, toward the southern Grenadines, where Hurricane Beryl made landfall on the morning of 1 July.

On Canouan, the trees have been stripped bare and the hills run with mud. Wilted coconut palms bow low over a beach dirtied with silt and scattered with wooden pirogues. The heavy rains and the runoff from the hills have turned the water a greyish blue and in it is visible the upturned side of a half-sunken white speedboat. Despite the devastation, the great homes on the hill overlooking the harbour have kept their roofs. But now a desperate queue of cars and people form on the quay to offload the bottled water and fuel that will be a lifeline.

Mayreau, home to less than three hundred, is the next stop. Roofs are shredded and water tanks and metal debris litter the beach. Two young women point to the remains of a home up on the hill and giggle. Having spent a few days of respite on the mainland, buying food and enjoying the odd cocktail, they are returning to dilapidated homes on one of the islands. According to them, the owner boasted of owning a huge mansion with fourteen ensuite bedrooms. The joke was that he had partitioned it into fourteen mostly windowless tiny cells furnished with only a wash basin and a single bed. Humour is not the only way the islanders come to terms with the catastrophe. By the bar, one man with a powerful jaw and a bright orange tie-die T-shirt declares that there are no poor people in the Grenadines. Never mind that Beryl has just rendered thousands homeless. Another in a beret and with the air of a poet is affronted, calls him ignorant and receives an insult to his mother. In another part of the ship, a woman still struggling to come to terms with the new reality of condensed living, shouts that she simply cannot share a bedroom with anyone else.

Another island comes into view. A deep valley cuts into it, almost splitting it in half, as two vertiginous peaks rise above. This is Union Island, dubbed the Tahiti of the Caribbean for its volcanic silhouette. My family has lived on Union Island for centuries. It is now five o'clock as the ship enters the harbor and despite the fading light, the coral-laden waters emit a turquoise glow. But the island is now unrecognisable. The hills are blackened and the homes and hotels along the waterfront are smashed to pieces. The scene on the way to the family village is like a zombie apocalypse film set. Homes are reduced to piles of rubble. A toppled telephone antenna has smashed through a secondary school. A car rolls through the village without a windscreen, its lights blown out, and a piece of waterproof sheeting affixed to the roof to protect it from the rain. 'Beryl is a whore!', my cousin shouts out from the back seat.

Beryl has wiped out or badly damaged most of my family's homes. For this trip, I will stay with Masani, a cousin, who is returning to the island after a few months in the US. Her home withstood the winds, except for a small prising away of the rafters that allowed a colony of bats to take up residency. Luckily, my 104-year-old great-grand aunt took shelter here during the hurricane. A boat sits in her old bedroom.

Seven of us sleep in the house. A homeless family, a young couple and two children, occupy the bottom floor. After the hurricane, they emerged from a kitchen cupboard to find their home had taken off. Upstairs, Masani shares a bed with another woman and I have one to myself. As night falls it becomes clear that this is no ordinary place. Fat flies swarm and hit us in the face. The mosquitoes whine incessantly, instilling fear, even if they do not bite. The smell of burning plastic and rotten meat fills the valley.

With no electricity or phone network there is no access to the world beyond these shores. We sit and talk in the dark, our silhouettes framed by the flicker of candlelight.

Camillo Adams, aged sixty-nine, says: 'I didn't take it seriously. The last major storm to hit Union was Hurricane Janet in 1955. I was two months old. I grew up thinking that storms were something you got excited about. It was a good thing my son was taking it seriously.

'I was checking my phone for the wind speed. It was at 26 kilometres then it jumped to 34. Then 41. After that, 76. Of course, once it gets to a certain speed you know it's serious. The last time I checked it was 96. It took off my roof. We couldn't secure our belongings as we had to protect my two grandchildren. My ten-year-old grandson asked, "Pups, what's making that sound?" I told him it was the wind howling. Then the rain started. When we tasted it we realised it was salt water. It wasn't rain, it was the wind pushing the sea into the air.

'There's not much I can do now, I'm sixty-nine and a retired senior citizen. My son is dealing with everything. We will rebuild but it will take a while. If there is a lesson to be learned it's that we need to build better structures. We need to have a new consensus about how we build houses.'

Day 2

The aftermath of a hurricane hampers daily life at every turn.

Nature's revenge includes a strain of brownish-green algae growing in the water tank. At just three-square miles in size, Union cannot sustain rivers, so people store rainwater in tanks. I am informed by the man staying downstairs that while it is safe to bathe in the water I will itch after the second go. I draw the water from the tank and pour it into a bucket. Disgusted by its sickly hue, Masani reaches for a bottle of Clorox and bleaches it. It starts to turn white. Can one perform ritual abolitions in this? I do not have a choice. And I don't get the itch, thank God.

The hurricane poses spiritual problems for others, too. It has disabled the island's fourteen houses of worship. There is a Muslim community on the island but no mosque. It is Sunday morning and the Rockaway Seventh Day Adventist Church, would usually be full to the rafters. Today it is empty, the hurricane having blown away the rafters leaving a gaping hole in the roof. Unlike most Christians, the Adventists follow the Old Testament and observe the Sabbath on a Saturday. The service is held at a large white house by the main village junction, one of the few to have its roof intact. Locals and white missionaries sing effusively from a porch. Their voices rise to an impassioned harmony as they thank God for saving this single roof. Their church and homes in ruins they still find reason to be grateful.

With the power grid down and the phone network knocked out, contacting the outside world is a chore. Two weeks after the hurricane some survivors have yet to talk to their families. One large house hosts a Wi-Fi spot connected to the Starlink satellite system. It opens for a few hours in the morning. You might just get there provided you can bathe, find something to eat, and if required, worship in time. It opens for a few hours in the evening but the network gets jammed by the numbers wanting to use socials, download movies, or, in my case, check what is happening at the Euros. This is provided you have found a way to charge your phone.

Janti Rammage, who lives across the road from the Wi-Fi house has a solution. After the hurricane, he installed two solar panels and hooked them up to a charging station for public use. When I arrive just after midday myriad phones are plugged into a messy web of extension chords and sockets. There is a shortage of available sockets but after some rearranging, I plug in two phones and a massive charging bank Masani uses to power her fan. Now you must sit and wait for hours.

Rammage is a maverick businessman. He constructed Happy Island, a man-made islet for rum lovers and fine dining made from conch shells. He wears a black Rasta cap over a thick column of dreadlocks, green camouflage shorts a black vest and a chain with a steel skull, medal and a couple of rings. His face is lined and he has a mischievous grin. In 1979, Rammage was part of an attempted rebellion on Union Island. The island felt neglected by the St Vincent mainland and tried to secede. Earlier that year, Grenada, the country immediately to the South, had undergone a socialist revolution. The rebels wanted to join in. St Vincent didn't have an army and asked Barbados for troops. When the St Vincent police force was sent to quell the rebellion, the Bajan troops replaced them on the mainland. The nineteen insurgents, including Rammage were captured and imprisoned.

Crumbling some marijuana into a calabash, Rammage sets out his vision for Union's future. Because the island still suffers from neglect it must form a village council. He blames mainland Vincentians for the island's social ills and says they should be issued permits before they visit or settle on the island. Union must form an economic union with Canouan and Cariaccou (a neighbouring island that forms part of Grenada) to ensure tourism profits are not siphoned away to the mainland islands. He sees Union reinventing itself as an island open for mass tourism and where local businesses are geared toward attracting large cruise ships. The hurricane, he says, 'is the resurrection of the souls of our ancestors, a wake-up call for us to act.'

Masani has now joined us. And screams what she desires utmost: 'Independence!'. At the same time, younger islanders need to rebuild society rather than leave to find work abroad. As eligible Commonwealth citizens, a favoured destination for Unionites has been the British armed forces. Masani's own son joined the US Navy without telling her. 'Our children are aspiring to be slaves!' she yells. 'They're not using their brains! No plumber, no technician, roof man is pure garbage!'

What Masani means by independence remains unclear. Does it mean complete secession or greater autonomy within St Vincent and the Grenadines? I suspect the latter. An independent Union Island would probably rank along the Vatican as the smallest country by population in the world but without the treasures of the Sistine Chapel *et alia*.

Stemming the brain drain seems like a good start to get the island up and running again. A Pan-Africanist who had gone to university in New York and lived London, Masani understands the wiles of imperialism from up close. For her, the haemorrhaging of a tiny local population to the armed forces of former colonial overlords was deeply insulting (I personally know Vincentians who fought in Iraq and Afghanistan). And for every Unionite lost, empire makes a gain, the sort of population arithmetic the Guyanese historian Walter Rodney says allowed Europe to underdevelop Africa. Only now youngsters — descendants of those Africans whose capture made this transfer of wealth possible — were voluntarily rushing to the other side.

Rammage's solution reflects his position as restaurateur and private-island owner already benefitting from prosperous yachties. Turning Union into a tourism destination might create jobs but with it new hierarchies of wealth and power with a pool of underpaid cleaners and waiters toiling at the bottom. This is the tourism trap Derek Walcott, the St Lucian poet and Nobel Laureate, spoke of.

> But in our tourist brochures the Caribbean is a blue pool into which the republic dangles the extended foot of Florida as inflated rubber islands bob and drinks with umbrellas float towards her on a raft. This is how the islands from the shame of necessity sell themselves; this is the seasonal erosion of their identity, that high-pitched repetition of the same images of service that cannot distinguish one island from the other, with a future of polluted marinas, land deals negotiated by ministers, and all of this conducted to the music of Happy Hour and the rictus of a smile.

Rammage had come a long way since the rebellion.

Dana Joseph, a teacher, says: 'I thought I would only lose my roof. But when I saw my aunt's roof blow off next door and hit the front of my house taking off all the wooden boards, I realised my home would not survive. We tried to shove the bed in the gap to minimise the blowing and then ran to the kitchen to attempt to escape outside and to the apartment downstairs. The problem was the door was sealed and would not open. Suddenly the house just lifted off. We came out where the kitchen door was and the house was gone. We ran out and managed to get to the apartment downstairs but I got an injury to my leg. We were there for four hours. The hurricane would not stop. The windows were breaking and we could see things flying around outside.

'It was terrifying. My children were crying. It will be etched in my mind forever. I lost everything. I bought a new fridge almost a year ago but it landed at a neighbour's house. The only thing we did save were some documents I put in a vacuum-sealed bag. But I'm happy that I have life and am here to talk about it. Anything that was lost can be rebuilt.'

Day 3

I visit my late grandparents' home to look at the damage. Videos had circulated online but I wanted to see it, to feel it for myself. The front metal gate is flung wide open. I walk up the steep concrete steps into the yard. The water tank and the ancient stone oven are still there. But the crops she used to grow, the peas and the corn, are no more. Goats roam freely, eating as they please. By the porch, guano seeps down a wall. With the roof gone and the windows blown out, the inside is now on the outside. A TV and wooden cabinet are still there but the photos have blown off the wall. The record of our memories has gone.

As the only grandchild born in Britain, the 1940s cream-coloured concrete house perched on a hill above the little cemetery and the sparking blue sea beyond was a veritable symbol of my heritage. It was where I would watch my grandmother stir the *wangu pois,* the local dish made of cornmeal and peas, as she taught me the family's lineage and local culture; play with my cousins; be given my first traditional bush bath; and catch my first chicken.

It was a home away from home.

That night, I walk to the waterfront with Masani. We had discovered that if you walked to the part of the island closest to Grenada you could pick up a data connection. She was bored and wanted to download a film. She was now into Turkish films and had watched nearly all the episodes of *Resurrection: Ertugrul*, the hit Turkish television series. Tonight, she hoped to find one about African kings and queens.

On the shore was a jumble of fishing boats. As we tried to connect to the network, I looked across the dark water at the flickering lights on Petit Martinique and Cariaccou, the Grenadian islands smashed by hurricane Beryl. A police car patrolled on a road above, its light scanning the shore and up the hill, to deter looters.

Failing to get a strong enough connection, we head home and meet at the crossroads a group of young men hanging out and drinking — or *liming* - on some steps. They are the modest men who will — not always out of choice — most likely spend the rest of their lives on the island. They do odds jobs, fishing and conch diving. And they live day to day. I see them every time I come to Union. This corner, where the words 'Gaza Strip' were scrawled many years ago, is their *liming* spot, most nights. Masani seizes the moment to incite them to independence.

Mainlanders abuse women and wield cutlasses 'chopping hand and foot', she says. The discussion gets heated and the smell of Hennessy fills the air. One man, lithe and dark, accuses her of ignorance and she savagely attacks him. 'You are the only one for them,' she charges. 'All of us are for independence,' she says, overstating her support. An awkward silence descends.

Masani speaks. 'Well, I came out in this hot night wearing thick tights and two pairs of panties, and look — she points to me — I have my bodyguard with me.' She has everyone in stitches.

As the laughter dies down, one man is moved. 'All those who couldn't live without internet have fled to St Vincent and left we here,' he says in the dark. 'Now we have to lime together. It's how it used to be. United.'

Gary Wilson, shop owner, aged fifty-one, says: 'The night before the hurricane we were down on the waterfront liming. It was calm and cool. By the time morning reached, the wind had started to change. We thought it would be an ordinary storm. The problem is that many of us took it for granted. If enough of us were on the phone watching to see how dangerous it was, people might have moved earlier on. That was a problem.

'When the wind started I was already home and saw real crazy stuff. Galvanised roofs ripped off, poles flying, water drums gone, black tanks flying. Up and down, up and down. Sea water came right underneath me and walked away with the gate and fence. Bottom road was full of seawater. The wind sounded like a screeching violin. I don't want to go through that again. We took it for granted. We weren't expecting it like that.

'Right now we're cleaning up the place. They're paying us to clean up so we can eat. Not everything the aid workers bring we eat, we like to cook. We've been working for two weeks.

I give thanks that my little business survived. When I came back, I said: "the market stand up, oui!" I thought it was gone. That storm tried its best but it couldn't move it. It tried, it tried, it tried. But it just couldn't move it.'

Day 4

Hurricane Beryl has also left me jobless. I had planned to come to Union to volunteer at an annual summer school my mother founded on the island almost fifteen years ago. Now I am unsure why I am here. Before I left St Vincent, I bought a bunch of pens thinking I might teach in the homeless shelter. A sense of familial solidarity also drives me to go as does a desire to witness and collect testimonies of what has happened. But what good is any of this when people do not have food to eat or roofs over their heads? This question constantly gnaws at me. I feel guilty whenever I take a picture or ask someone for an interview. I can only bring myself to interview one person at the homeless shelter. And I sense that others feel I am not doing enough. But what can I do? I'm a journalist and an English instructor. I write and I teach. I do not fix or build.

Tabiah Regis, a local photographer friend, suggests we climb one of the main peaks to document the destruction. I am conflicted but I give in. On the way to meet her at the Adventist church, I run into a teacher I know. He says he has fifteen guests coming the next day and needs help fixing the roof. I cannot bring myself to decline.

Dr Tony Stewart lives in a high-ceiling home with his family set on the side of a valley overlooking the village of Ashton. I fear heights and have never been on, let alone fixed a roof. This is the worst place to start. I carefully climb the ladder then ease myself onto the metal galvanised roof. I crawl forward on my hands and knees, unsure if it can hold my weight. Then, with the unsteadiness of a young toddler, I slowly clamber to my feet. Because rainwater is seeping into the house, our task is to relay the waterproof tarpaulin, nailing it into the plywood sheathing beneath.

We have been up there for nearly four hours when night falls. I cannot see well and the hammer falls askew. I look up at Dr Stewart. Surely, we have to stop now. He signals that we must press on. I remove the bent nails and start again. The sound of the hammer blows bounces off the other side of the valley like the call and response of the local drums. I look up to see seven fires raging around the valley, as dead leaves, furniture, and waterlogged electronic equipment go up in smoke.

It is now nine o'clock and I am performing the most daring feat yet. I am on my stomach, faced forward hammering on the edge of the roof, a deadly drop in the dark before me.

Surely, Dr Stewart, a writer and teacher, knows something about health and safety. Perhaps, but the work needs to be done. Writer or teacher. It must be done.

Kay Stewart, aged sixty-nine, says: 'that morning I got up and made breakfast. The day before, I had filled up all the water bottles because I was getting ready for my aunt to come and stay with me. I had to make sure I had water and I had food. I was ready! The only thing I didn't do was board up the windows like I did when Hurricane Ivan was passing.

'You see we didn't expect Beryl would come. We thought it would pass us straight. But after nine o'clock the wind starts to blow. And I ask myself, what kind of wind is this? When I look outside it is strange, the sky is strange. Then the wind starts to build up. I'm hearing, crick, crack, crick, crack. I say, what? Then I see the neighbour's mango tree break and fly toward me. I think it is coming for me so I duck. But it drops between the houses and smashes our downstairs windows.

'I tell my aunt to go inside a side room and stay there. I pray, Jesus Christ, this thing is trouble! God, don't make this door open, seal this door. And it never opened again.

'Wind and rain, wind and rain. I am mopping because the windows are broken and the water is coming in. Mop then throw the water outside, mop again, throw out the water. Wind and rain, wind and rain.

'There is a bright light. Then it goes back dark again — rain like crazy! The wind is bashing on the door like somebody is trying to get in and they can't. So, I run upstairs, but the windows are going booshoo! Booshoo! So, then I run back down. When I look outside, I see a vehicle lift up and then drop back down. Out of nowhere, a galvanised roof flies into the vehicle.

'It was a horrible time. I don't pray for that for no country. If it came in the night, it would have wiped out the island because people would have run out of their homes and got killed. But God sent it in the day for a purpose.'

TEN UNDESIRABLES

One of the greatest ironies that has come out of our contemporary existence is how we have managed to make an infinitely interconnected, globalised world filled with unimaginably closeminded individuals and communities. While it is clear that desire should more frequently reoccur as a topic in both our introspections and public discourses, perhaps desire itself is not the place to begin. Often the best way to figure out what it is a person, a community, or an organisation wants is to ask what it is that they most fear. So, while synthesising our greatest desires may feel the best nightcap to this issue, what might be more fruitful is a foray into the undesired.

1. Erasure

Erasure has become the undesirable zeitgeist of our time. We are determined to erase everything – from flora and fauna, to artic ice, to cultures and languages, as well as communities and societies. Countless languages, cultures, and peoples with their own history stand before the razor's edge. Modernity took a hammer to tradition. The Postmodern condition was never about knowledge – as suggested by French philosophers – but amnesia and erasure of grand narratives, including history and tradition. The latest erasure, proceeding in front of our eyes, is that of Palestine and its people. In ten years, Palestine and its people may no longer exist, erased by western imperialism like indigenous Americans and so many peoples before. But we must not abide the most undesirable loss of a people, their culture, their history, their light. Evidently, the United Nations, the Declaration of Human Rights, the International Courts are all for naught. The whole world is on one side and the West on the other. The only argument that seems to matter is might is right. The only hope for Palestine is that our capacity for memory does not go the way of our attention spans. The bare minimum is ending the present brutality in Palestine. Systematic extermination is intolerable, but beyond that it might be worth aiming to find a deeper compacity to appreciate the differences between us and balance traditions so that as we enter a deepening in the complex fabric of humanity; and we do not forget where we came from.

2. Some Being More Equal Than Others

Once we managed to outwit the last apex predator above us on the food chain, to maintain our place on the top, our desire to remain so targeted the only one who could threaten that position – ourselves. Although George Orwell might have thought it a clever way to depict the road from revolution to totalitarianism in 1945's *Animal Farm*, the penning of 'some pigs are more equal than others' also represents one of our greatest undesirables – especially from those who already hold themselves as more equal than others. Yet, perhaps Orwell's words are merely a statement of reality. Nothing can really be equal, right. But even if we accept this, then there is a whole other discourse to be had on equity. If we cannot be equal, as things stand at the present, because of our history or the institutions that maintain this society of ours, then perhaps through exploring that history in order to understand what happened and seeking reforms in our institutions, we can – maybe – make certain things better. And over time, as long as we do not allow the affirmative actions taken to become new chains of dependence, we might find ourselves more and more equal with each passing generation, equipped with an awareness that prevents the repetition of history. We could begin by trying to respect what differences exist in our world and at least attempting to treat each other with equal respect and dignity. And let us not forget, *Animal Farm* ended with the pigs losing their pig-manity as they slowly became that which they had originally rose upon against – humans.

3. Loss of Our Humanity

When we are not trying to kill and eradicate one another, we seem rather set on trying to perfect ourselves. In an ultimate twist of fate, in our attempts to perfect ourselves we have fallen for a trick where we unintentionally are abandoning our humanity. Efficiency began quietly but grew as it launched the Industrial Revolution. Asking what the easiest way is to make money quickly became how do I put the least possible money into making more money and the forging of wealth. It seemed harmless and maybe a bit clever to use cheaper products, even when manufactured obsolescence was introduced. If the thing broke or stopped working, then they would have to buy a new one, look at how we cheated the market saturation problem. But then automation rolled along, hitting hard as people started losing jobs. Efficiency reached the heights of its cruelty when it was imbibed by society. Why go through the trouble of writing and mailing a letter when I can just type out a quick email or send a quick text? What's the point of math when I have a calculator? There's no time for anything in our fast-paced lives. Isn't there an app for that? Why interact with the real world when everything is online and seems easier. When we started letting AI do our thinking for us, that was the point of no return. The Post-humanists will disagree that this is an undesirable, they say full steam ahead! But do we desire those images of automatons, creepy hive-minds, and boring homogenous post-human apes pushing buttons? To be human is to be imperfect, to fear death, and ultimately to die. You might learn this from those who came before us if you picked up a book. But the most creative output we see in the post-human future is prompting AI to generate the next image you need (so you don't have to pay an artist) but it never does quite get past the uncanny valley, does it? If that isn't the final nail in the coffin of hope for the future in which we have completely shed our humanity, we don't know what is.

4. Abandonment of Creativity and the Liberal Arts

Education has pivoted from forming well rounded, learned humans towards making efficient, job-ready and employable people – even when there is no guarantee that the careers they prepared for would be around by the time they finished their degree. The challenges we face in postnormal times are unprecedented and require serious creativity and imagination in order for us to navigate them. Meanwhile, universities close departments in the liberal arts and we wonder why people are incapable of thinking. Beyond being able to think, heaven forbid it be in a critical way, we need to be able to work with very little to find new solutions. Who would desire a world where children are not read to, do not read, and do not continue reading into adulthood? Young people should learn multiple languages, explore new cultures, experiment, and wonder. How desirable is a world where the first, and perhaps only, problem solving technique is to check the internet, consult social media, google it, or ask ChatGPT. Creativity is wasted on disgruntled artists who are ignored for AI generated art which requires no intellectual property negotiations and no royalties. And the cherry on top for this is that all along we are being colonised. In fact, it is the ultimate colonisation as we willingly submit with open, yet ignorant hearts, to the bias of others who care nothing for our own true desires, but see to their desires through the AI and the algorithms they have created. They control wants, they hold all the power, they control knowledge. They even control what is truth.

5. The Death of Truth

'Truth isn't truth' gaffed the former Mayor of New York turned lawyer for Donald Trump, Rudolph Guiliani, summing up the *espiritu del tiempo* of the Post-Truth Age. Our hypersensitive age of political correctness took on the relativism of postmodernism like millennials to ketamine. Relativism makes for some thought provoking 'films' and does well for everyone's sentiments, but it is the death of morality. When everyone becomes their own moral agent, lawless anarchy is the logical conclusion. What those beholden to such misinterpreted philosophies fail to see is that a robust notion of morality is a requisite, to be instilled as a child or in the formation of a society's adults. But if all is relative, where do we even begin? Maybe in some utopian, drug-induced comma, a world could exist where we do not need rights and wrongs, but the reality is that we are faced with a great many wrongs and even more disagreements on what is right that needs greater discussion and polylogue to sort out. Our contemporary world is too complex, too chaotic, and filled beyond the brim with contradictions. Cop-outs to true thought, like relativism, undermine the great intellectual human project of finding a way to know and live with one another. Those who knowingly feed the machines of fake news and deception, commit a dastardly crime in order to hide from the fact that something truly wrong, and often horrible, has taken place. Extreme cultural relativism is not just dangerous ignorance, it is contra to any desire towards a better human future. Add to this the miscarriages of truth created and promulgated by the AI we allow to infect our modes of communication and information gathering. We need to speak power to truth. This begins with resisting the tempting alure of the post-truth malaise and instead challenging ourselves to contribute towards the larger discourse aimed at seeking truth and ultimately justice.

6. Rule by the Extreme

Lost and aimless in a post-truth world, we have little to desire beyond the comfort of an extreme position to clear up the messiness of relativity and opinions. For many of our deepest desires to be realised a certain level of openness to other ideas and opinions as well as insights and frames of reference is not just helpful, it is essential. As ideologies become more extreme and fundamentalist, choice and freedom become the first victim. Perhaps it is a worthy sacrifice to be living the 'truth', but little by little you are suddenly living by the interpretation of others, that by this point if you attempt to criticise, you will become that which is against them, since you are not blindly, strictly for them. Before you know it, you are living in someone else's interpretation and seeing out the desires of others. And in order to lose out on the protection and purpose given by the extremist rulers, you carry out the increasingly singular, simple, and ad hoc orders, that are progressively more violent, of those who desire to be right and potentially to wield godlike powers. Moderation increasingly marginalised, democracies radically jump from one extreme to the next with each election cycle as more authoritarian regimes double down on whatever oppression is necessary to keep their will supreme. Extremist tendencies to further the extreme creates greater instability as truth evaporates under the heat of suspicion and paranoia. These violent delights indeed, have violent ends.

7. Peace Falling to Pieces

Many argue that we are living in the most peaceful times in history. But the indicators being used to make such claims, when critically evaluated, do not amount to much. It is hard to say there isn't a country on earth right now that doesn't have its own civil strife, and quite regularly journeys to the brink of civil war. Additionally, since the pandemic, whenever a conflict does break out, careful steps are taken to appease both sides so as not to create dramatic economics consequences. Other wars are merely forgotten about or contained. We seem to have developed a thick tolerance for conflict and war in our contemporary world that is incredibly worrying. States are allowed to operate anywhere, anytime with impunity and due to the complexity of global trade networks, everyone is too afraid to speak out for fear of backlash in the form of sanctions or international isolation. Human rights violations are no longer deal-breakers. In relation to the breaking of international law, everyone is living in glass houses and why would you want to start throwing rocks about. A weird neo-nationalist survivalism has taken over, where governments and denizens are happy when their currencies are going up, regardless of the costs to their souls or morality. The United Nations, along with various other intergovernmental organisations have failed to establish an order or to demonstrate any agency as wars spring up left, right, and centre without anyone batting an eye. The desire of diplomacy seems no longer to be peace, but to be whatever makes the markets happy, the people, their lives, and their dignity be damned if it must come to that.

8. Harm Coming to the Children (Or Other Loved Ones)

As creatures who desire, long, and hope for something better, if this desire for the better cannot be in sync with those of our children and loved ones and extended for them into the future, then the whole exercise is rather futile. But we cannot forget that hubris can be rather intoxicating. While it is natural to project our hopes and desires onto others, we must not assume that the next generation will desire and hope for the same things we hoped. Things change, so too does context, and if they didn't our desires and hopes would hold no weight. What we think is important, they may find fickle and rather silly, as we often find the concerns of our parents and grandparents. And what we waste little time and energy on may, in fact, be crucial for them. And for those things that really matter, like traditions and cultures, that we want to carry on beyond us, it is essential that we respect and dignify the next generation so that they will carry on the important stuff. Often the future is held in this contradictory dichotomy: at one moment, we coddle our children and wall them off from the world, and at the next moment we use our children as a human body shield to deflect that which we are afraid of, do not understand, or do not wish to get into. Neither extreme does any good for that future or for those we love. At the heart of desire is choice and choice must be made free. With efforts focussed on educating and leaving behind a world not on the brink of utter collapse, we can have confidence that the choices they make will arc towards the good, the true, and the just.

9. Ugliness

Beauty may indeed only be skin deep, but ugly, that goes right to the soul! And a general state of ugliness is a pretty undesirable thing indeed. While beauty may not always be attained, it is rarely not the aim. And there is no fault in trying. The whole aim of art, from the visual to music to performance and film, is for beauty, the good, to win out over ugly, the evil. Billions are readily spent on the cosmetic and fashion industries alone in order to avoid the most undesirable end that is ugliness. Curated skin-care routines, exploitatively marked up fabrics, and 'corrective' measures, ranging from over-the-counter hair colouring to surgical skin bleaching, see us on the road towards aesthetic, age-defying, life-defying idealism. But do our inward thoughts, motivations, actions, and pursuits look as beautiful as the coordinated patterns on the runways at the next major fashion week? Is a pig in lipstick as transcendent as we think? We are pattern recognising creatures and certain things go together to create an aesthetic pleasure, of course we are all different and the spectrum may flow one way or another, but how could great art museums and exhibitions exist if we didn't agree on at least the ground level. And of course, ugliness has its utility and can easily be weaponised (and for good cause too) but it is never the aim for ugliness, but instead to challenge notions of beauty

that might have overspent their time in the zone of fame or that have found
themselves otherwise problematic. For beauty to live and shine in our
contemporary, like all good things, it must change with the times. Context
matters and need not be a linear path. Indeed, it may all be in the eye of
the beholder as we may agree or disagree on what is more or less beautiful,
but it is essential that the aim for beauty remains a worthwhile pursuit in
all facets of life, the vein and the noble. The weeds of this just becomes a
matter of taste.

10. The Numbing of Taste

A great battle rages on for the futures of taste. On one side is a nigh futile
attempt to undo the results of our last century's attempts to make what we
consume last forever, and more deviously, get us addicted to the
consumables that give us the greatest access to inexhaustible capital. On
another front, there is a major push to make food organic again (at no
spared expense!) while also experimenting with taste enhancing
techniques that prevent the act of 'having lunch' from seeming an act of
self-flagellation. And those trials of taste have played no small role in the
first side of the battle, flavour enhancers themselves doing far worse things
to the human body than destroying our ability to regulate blood sugar! A
third front has also called its banners to war through looking for more
sustainable futures approaches to mealtime. One way this front has fought
is to find food production methods that work with and even counter
climate change. Another way, should climate change make the old way
completely untenable, is to find new things to eat, but what disbalances
will this create in the further future? Lab-grown meat or insects, anyone?
Meanwhile, floating around the periphery of this culinary battle is fad
culture, from fad diets to food as fashion. Likewise, a more socially
informed and concerned consumption lurks. Is the food we eat actively
promoting genocide? Quite likely! Yet, when push comes to shove, it's the
burden on the wallet that cast the winning ballot for what taste good to
many – an entirely different, yet not unrelated, problem in much need of
address! How much longer will this debate remain palatable! In ten years,
many of our favourite meals may no longer be available on the menu.

The point of framing this list on the undesirables was not so that we can place a quick, yet unsustainable plaster on the problem, but so that we can illuminate our true, deeper desires. And desire should be something we take a lifetime of reflection and critical thought to craft, not to fall from one desire to the next and then ask how it all went wrong. Desires can and should take us towards something better, but that only happens in the light of day. Do not fear your desires. Desire more and let us pursue those desires together for a better future.

CITATIONS

Introduction: Orbits of Desire by Ziauddin Sardar

Ibn Arabi's *The Translator of Desires* is beautifully translated by Michael Sells (Princeton University Press, 2021). The 'comfort for the eye' quote is from pxxiii. The Book of Song quote is from George Dimitri Sawa, *Erotica, Love and Humor in Arabia: Spicy Stories from the Book of Songs of al-Isfahani* (McFarland and Co, Jefferson, 2016), p38; and Umar ibn Abi Rabiah poem is from Roger Allen, *An Introduction to Arabic Literature* (Cambridge University Press, 2000) p104.

All the poems by Allamah Muhammad Iqbal mentioned in the essay can be found on-line. But I have used *Bang-i-Dara: Call of the Marching Bell*, translated with commentary by M A K Khalil (Lahore, 1997), *The Mysteries of Selflessness*, translated by A J Arberry (John Murray, London, 1953) pxi; and *The Secrets of the Self,* translated by R A Nicholson (Macmillan, London, 1920), pxvi.

The quote from Tamara Tenenbaum is from *The End of Love: Sex and Desire in the Twenty-First Century* (Europa Edition, London, 2019) p100; and from Rene Girard is from *All Desire is A Desire for Being* (Penguin, 2023) p263. 'Make the world us. Only ours to shape' is from Episode 8, of *Fallout* (Amazon Prime); and the words of the Native Indian female lawyer to Chief Thomas Rainwater are taken from *Yellowstone*, Season 5, Episode 8 (Paramount).

Desires by Holly J Gill and Nikki Blaise, self-published, and available, for those who desire such things, at Amazon.

See also: Mustansir Mir, *Iqbal* (Iqbal Academy Pakistan, Lahore, 2006); Muhammad Munawwar, *Iqbal: Poet Philosopher of Islam* ((Iqbal Academy Pakistan, Lahore, 1985); and Muhammad Iqbal, *Tulip in the Desert*, translated and edited by Mustansir Mir (Hurst, London, 1990).

A Stick with Two Ends by Jeremy Henzell-Thomas

I have referred to the following sources:
Muhammad Asad, *The Message of the Qur'an* (Dar al-Andalus, Gibraltar, 1980, reprinted by the Book Foundation in 2003 with a complete romanised transliteration of the Arabic text). John Ayto, *Dictionary of Word Origins* (Bloomsbury Publishing, London, 1990). Al-Ghazali, *Ihya 'ulum al-din* (Revival of the Religious Sciences), Books XXII and XXIII (Kitab Riyadat al-nafs *On Disciplining the Soul* and Kitab Kasr al-shahwatayn *On Breaking the Two Desires*, translated by Tim Winter (Islamic Texts Society, Cambridge, 1995). Alan Tao, *Tao: The Watercourse Way* (Souvenir Press, London, 2011), 96.

John W. Ritenbaugh, 'What the Bible says about Desire' (Bible Tools, Topical Studies) at https://www.bibletools.org/index.cfm/fuseaction/topical.show/RTD/cgg/ID/134/Desire.htm. St. Paul, 1st Epistle to the Corinthians, 12:31 (New International Version of the Bible, Biblica, 1984). Rabbi Avi Weinstein, *Jewish Concepts: Desire*. Jewish Virtual Library at https://www.jewishvirtuallibrary.org/desire. David Webster, *The Philosophy of Desire in the Buddhist Pali Canon* (Routledge, London, 2005). Deepak Chopra, *The Way of the Wizard: 20 Lessons for Living a Magical Life* (Harmony Books, 1996). Ana Waller, 'The Four Stages of Desire: From Everything to One Thing', *The Minds Journal*, 14/9/2019. https://goodmenproject.com/featured-content/the-four-stages-of-desire-from-everything-to-one-thing/. Virginia Woolf, George Eliot. (The Common Reader, Harcourt, Brace, and World, New York, 1925); *Moments of Being: A Collection of Autobiographical Writing* (Pimlico, 2002). Mevlana Jalaluddin Rumi, Mathnawi 1, 1747, Mathnawi III, 1616-1620, 4414-4417, in *The Pocket Rumi Reader*, edited by Kabir Helminski (Shambhala, Boston, 2001), 89, 136, 165; Mathnawi VI, 377, in *Jewels of Remembrance: A Daybook of Spiritual Guidance From the Wisdom of Rumi*, selected and translated by Camille and Kabir Helminski (Threshold Books, Putney, Vermont, 1996), 134; *Magnificent One: Selected new verses from Divan-I Kebir*, translated by Nevit Oguz Ergin (Larson Publications, Burdett, NY, 1993), 90. C.G. Jung, *Collected Works* (Princeton University Press, Princeton, NJ, 1957), Vol.4, 567, Vol. 5, 194; *The Red Book, Liber novus*, edited by Sonu

Shamdasani (W.W. Norton, 2009). Darcy Lyon, *The Wisdom of Desire* (iUniverse, 2010). James Hillman, *The Soul's Code: In Search of Character and Calling* (Bantam, London, 1997). Susan Sontag, 'Wagner's Fluids'. *London Review of Books*, Vol.9, No.22, 10 December 1987. https://www.lrb.co. uk/the-paper/v09/n22/susan-sontag/wagner-s-fluids. Gary S. Comer, *Soul Whisperer: Why the Church must Change the Way it Views Evangelism* (Resource Publications, Eugene, Oregon, 2013). *The Drop that Became the Sea: Lyric Poems of Yunus Emre*, translated from the Turkish by Kabir Helminski and Refik Algan (Threshold Books, Putney, Vermont, 1989), 29, 39, 44, 53. William Blake, *The Marriage of Heaven and Hell*, edited by Will Jonson (CreateSpace Independent Publishing Platform, 2014). Muhy'iddin Ibn 'Arabi, *Tarjuman Al-Ashwaq: A Collection of Mystical Odes* translated by Reynold A. Nicholson (Theosophical Publishing House Ltd., London, 1978); Muhyiddin Ibn 'Arabi, *The Wisdom of the Prophets (Fusus al-Hikam)*, translated from the Arabic to French by Titus Burkhardt and from French to English by Angela Culme-Seymour (Beshara Publications, Aldsworth, 1975), 8. Jane Clark, 'Introduction to Tarjuman al-ashwaq', 11/11/2012 at https://open.conted.ox.ac.uk/sites/open.conted.ox.ac.uk/files/ resources/PDF%20introduction%20to%20Ibn%20 %CA%BFArabi%27s%20%27Tarjuman%20al-ashwaq%27_0.pdf. Michael A. Sells, *Stations of Desire: Love Elegies from Ibn 'Arabi and New Poems* (Ibis Editions, Jerusalem, 2000), 67. Moeen Afnani, 'Unraveling the Mystery of the Hidden Treasure; The Origin and Development of a Hadith Qudsi and its Application in Sufi Doctrine'. PhD dissertation, Near Eastern Studies, University of California, Berkeley, 2011, 129.

'Is the hadith where Allah refers to himself as a hidden treasure who wanted to be known considered authentic?' ('Ask a Question', Al-Islam). https://www.al-islam.org/ask/is-the-hadith-qudsi-where-allah-swt -refers-to-himself-as-a-hidden-treasure-who-wanted-to-be-known- considered-authentic.

The Book of Hadith: Sayings of the Prophet Muhammad from the Mishkat al-Masabih selected by Charles le Gai Eaton, edited by Kabir Helminski and Jeremy Henzell-Thomas, with an Introduction by Jeremy Henzell-Thomas (The Book Foundation, Bristol, 2008). *Ghazals of Ghalib*, edited by Aijaz Ahmad (Columbia University Press, 1971).

Balancing the Ego by Luke Wilkinson

My references are in order of appearance in the article:
Imam al-Ghazali, *Kitāb Sharḥ 'Ajā'Ib al-Qalb, The Marvels of the Heart, Book 21 of Ihyā 'ulūm al-dīn*, translated from the Arabic with an Introduction and Notes by Walter James Skellie; with a Foreword by T. J. Winter. 2010.

Winter, Timothy. *On Disciplining the Soul: Kitāb RiyāḌat al-Nafs, & On Breaking the Two Desires, Kitāb Kasr al-Shahwatayn : Books XXII and XXIII of The Revival of the Religious Sciences (IḥYā' 'Ulūm al-Dīn)*. 2016 Print.

https://www.childrenscommissioner.gov.uk/resource/pornography-and-harmful-sexual-behaviour/

John Maier, 'The Philosophy of Porn', https://www.prospectmagazine.co.uk/ideas/technology/37788/the-philosophy-of-porn

Ghamari-Tabrizi, Behrooz, *Foucault in Iran: Islamic Revolution after the Enlightenment*. (University of Minnesota Press, 2016).

Ghazzālī, Behari, and Behari, Bankey. *The Revival of Religious Sciences : A Translation of the Arabic Work Ihyā 'Ulūm al-Dīn*. Vrindaban: Mata Krishna Satsang, 1964. Print.

Watt K. Thomas Walker Arnold and the Re-Evaluation of Islam, 1864-1930. *Modern Asian Studies*. 2002;36(1):pp. 20.

Kierkegaard, Søren, and Alastair. Hannay. *Fear and Trembling / Kierkegaard ; Dialectical Lyric by Johannes de Silentio (Kierkegaard)*, translated with and Introduction by Alastair Hannay. Penguin, 1985. Penguin Classics.

Mulvey, Laura. Visual Pleasure and Narrative Cinema, Screen, Volume 16, Issue 3, Autumn 1975, pp. 6–18.

Sunan al-Tirmidhī 2777 (hadith on the second look).
Ṣaḥīḥ Muslim 2687 (hadith on drawing near to Allah).
Sahih Muslim 1006 (hadith on satisfaction of sexual desire).

Iqbal, Muhammad, *The Reconstruction of Religious Thought in Islam,* edited and Annotated by M. Saeed Sheikh ,*with a New Introduction by Javed Majeed.* 2013. Print. Encountering Traditions.

Lings, Martin. *Muhammad: His Life Based on the Earliest Sources.* 2nd. Cambridge: Islamic Texts Society, 1986.

Claude Addas, The Experience and Doctrine of Love in Ibn 'Arabī, Muḥyīddīn Ibn 'Arabī Society, 2002. https://ibnarabisociety.org/love-in-ibn-arabi-claude-addas/ .

Gibran, Kahlil. *The Prophet, with an Introduction by Robin Waterfield.* London: Penguin, 2002. Print. Penguin Classics.

Smith, Margaret. *Rābi'a the Mystic & Her Fellow-Saints in Islām : Being the Life and Teachings of Rābi'a al-'Adawiyya Al-Qaysīyya of Baṣra Together with Some Account of the Place of the Women Saints in Islam.* Lahore: Hijra International Publishers, 1983.

Helwa, A. *Secrets of Divine Love : A Spiritual Journey into the Heart of Islam.* First. 2020.

Reading and Reform by Peter Matthews Wright

I have mentioned the following works in this essay:

Al-Ghazali's Path to Sufism, tr. R. J. McCarthy S. J., Louisville, KY: Fons Vitae, 2000; Ryan P. Burge, *The Nones*, Minneapolis, MN: Fortress Press, 2021; William Blake, *The Complete Poetry and Prose of William Blake*, ed. David V. Erdman, Berkeley: University of California, 1982; Jacques Derrida, *Specters of Marx*, trans. Peggy Kamuf, London: Routledge, 1994; Ralph Waldo Emerson, *Complete Writings*, New York: Wm. H. Wise & Co. 1929; Carlos Fraenkel, *Philosophical Religions*, Cambridge University Press, 2014.

Ortega y Gasset, *History as a System*, tr. Helene Weyl, New York: W. W. Norton & Co., 1961; *The Gospel According to Luke*, 10:29-37; Antonio

Gramsci, *Selections from the Prison Notebooks*, tr. Quintin Hoare and Geoffrey Nowell Smith, New York: International Publishers, 1971; Marshall G. S. Hodgson, *The Venture of Islam,* vol. 1, Chicago: University of Chicago Press, 1974; Sir Muhammad Iqbal, *The Reconstruction of Religious Thought in Islam*, New Delhi: Kitab Bhavan, 1974; Charles Jencks, *Critical Modernism*, 5th edition, London: John Wiley & Sons, Inc., 2007; Alfred Kazin, *Writing Was Everything*, Cambridge, MA: Harvard University Press, 1991.

Thomas S. Kuhn, *The Structure of Scientific Revolutions*, 2nd edition, Chicago: University of Chicago Press, 1970; Aylmer Maude, *The Life of Tolstoy*, vol. 1, New York: Dodd, Mead and Company, 1910; *Merriam-Webster's Collegiate Dictionary*, 11th edition, Merriam-Webster, Inc., 2003; Ray Monk, *Ludwig Wittgenstein,* New York: The Free Press, 1990.;
Ebrahim Moosa, *Ghazali & the Poetics of Imagination*, Chapel Hill, NC: UNC Press, 2005;
Reinhold Niebuhr, *Man's Nature and His Communities*, New York: Charles Scribner's Sons, 1965; Richard Rorty, *Contingency, Irony, and Solidarity*, Cambridge University Press, 1989 and *Philosophy as Cultural Politics*, Cambridge University Press, 2007.

The Talmud: Selected Writings, tr. Ben Zion Bokser, New York: Paulist Pres, 1989; Leo Tolstoy, *Hadji Murat*, tr. W. G. Carey, New York: McGraw-Hill Book Company, 1965;
Gauri Viswanathan, *Outside the Fold*, Princeton, NJ: Princeton University Press, 1998;
Michael Walzer, *The Revolution of the Saints*, Cambridge, MA: Harvard University Press, 1965; David Sloan Wilson, *Darwin's Cathedral*, Chicago: The University of Chicago Press, 2002.

Ludwig Wittgenstein, *Philosophical Investigations*, 3rd ed. tr. G.E.M. Anscombe, New York: Macmillan Co., 1968 and Tractatus Logico-Philosophicus, trans. C. K. Ogden, London: Routledge, 1981; Peter Matthews Wright, 'Expanding the Circle: Emersonian Evasions, Islam, and Norman O. Brown,' *Soundings,* vol. 105, no. 4, (2022), 415-439; Benedetta Zavatta, *Individuality and Beyond: Nietzsche Reads Emerson*, Oxford University Press, 2021.

The ISIS Prisons Museum by Anonymous

For the connections between the Assad regime, Iraqi Baathists, and ISIS, see 'Secret Files Reveal the Structure of Islamic State', by Christoph Reuter, *Der Spiegel*, 18/04/2015.

Find the ISIS Prisons Museum online from October 2024.

After the Arab Spring by Mohammad El Sahily

Background information and material can be obtained from the following websites:

https://www.babnet.net/rttdetail-189886.asp

https://www.arab-reform.net/ar/publication

https://lb.boell.org/ar/2017/05/09/byn-lsdm-wlmqwm -lmshrk-lnswy-wmalt-lrby-lrby

https://carnegie-mec.org/sada/2014/12/sisis-moralism? lang=ar&center=middle-east

https://dawnmena.org/ar

https://lb.boell.org/en/2017/01/18/between -trauma-and-resistance-feminist-engagement-arab-spring

https://arabcenterdc.org/resource/womens-rights -and-state-feminism-in-the-arab-world/

https://www.opendemocracy.net/ar/---6/

https://www.newarab.com/features/unfinished -gender-equality-revolution-arab-spring

https://daraj.media/32906/

https://www.hrw.org/ar/news/2022/07/04/lebanon -unlawful-crackdown-lgbti-gatherings

https://www.hrw.org/ar/news/2020/05/07/375050

https://www.amnesty.org/ar/latest/news/2023/09/lebanon -attack-on-freedoms-targets-lgbti-people-repressive-legislation-unlawful-crackdown/

Disguises and Desires by Boyd Tonkin

Ali and Nino by "Kurban Said", translated by Jenia Graman with an introduction by Paul Theroux, was re-issued by Vintage in 2000. Tom Reiss's *The Orientalist: in search of a man caught between East and West* (Vintage, 2006) extends the research into Lev Nussimbaum originally undertaken for a *New Yorker* investigation in 1999. For an evocative memoir of the cosmopolitan Baku that both writers left, see *Days in the Caucasus* by the Azeri author – her name was Umm El-Banu Assadullayeva – who wrote as "Banine" (translated by Anna Thompson-Ahmadova; Pushkin Press, 2020). Melissa Katsoulis's *Telling Tales: a history of literary hoaxes* (Constable, 2009) gives a spirited overview of deception and disguise in the book world since the 18th century. More theoretical but still lively, Christopher L Miller's *Impostors: literary hoaxes and cultural authenticity* (University of Chicago Press, 2018) concentrates on the French tradition of cross-cultural authorial impersonation. Romain Gary/Émile Ajar's *La vie devant soi*, translated as *The Life Before Us*, was re-published by New Directions (2022) in Ralph Manheim's translation. Percival Everett's *Erasure* (2001) is published by Faber & Faber and Rebecca F Kuang's *Yellowface* (2023) by The Borough Press. Asif Kapadia's film of *Ali and Nino* is available on DVD and Blu-ray. Tamara Kvesitadze talked about the Batumi sculpture that became known as "Ali and Nino" for the BBC World Service programme *In the Studio* (23 April 2019).

The Other Spaces of Desire by Liam Mayo

Foucault, M. (1998) [original 1967] 'Different Spaces', in J. D. Faubion (ed.), *Aesthetics, Method, and Epistemology: Essential Works of Foucault*, Volume 2, Penguin, London, 175-185.

Complex Desires by C Scott Jordan

The following works were referenced throughout this article: Benedict Anderson's *Imagined Communities: Reflections on the Origin and Spread of Nationalism* (London, Verso, 2016); Asad Haider's *Mistaken Identity: Race and*

Class in the Age of Trump (London, Verso, 2918); and Judith Butler's *Who's Afraid of Gender* (New York, Farrar, Straus and Giroux, 2024).

The author feels that the subject of intersectionality has been a done a great disservice in terms of reference materials (and the same goes for Critical Race Theory, though this can also still be considered an emerging field, so hope remains) and it is hoped that a greater diversity of thinkers take on the concepts and build theories. Nevertheless, the foremothers of intersectionality, largely from the black feminist community, pull no punches in conveying their ideas. Among that group, Kimberlé Crenshaw's *On Intersectionality: Essential Writings* (New York, The New Press, 2015) and Angela Y. Davis's *Women, Race & Class* (London, Penguin, 2019) are a great place to start and guided much of the thought on intersectionality conveyed in this article.

For more on postnormal times theory, see *The Postnormal Times Reader*, edited by Ziauddin Sardar (London, CPPFS & IIIT, 2018) and *The Postnormal Times Reader* Volume 2, edited by Ziauddin Sardar, Shamim Miah, and C Scott Jordan (London, CPPFS & IIIT, 2024) as well as the website postnormatim.es

The poem mentioned is 'Kinder than Man' by Althea Davis and was self-published in a collection titled *Poems for the Weeping Kind* in 2023.

Exile is a Hard Job by Marjorie Allthorpe-Guyton

To read more on the history of the Venice Biennale see J.J. Charlsworth, 'The Biennale at the End of Globalization', *Art Review*, Features, 3 April 2024; on Eduoard Glissant, see Matt Reeck, 'An Eye to the Future; on Edouard Glissant's Sun of Consciousness', *Los Angeles Review of Books*, 2 February 2020; on Nil Yalter see her conversation with Lauren Cornell , *Mousse Magazine*, 15 April 2024; to read more on sonic materialism see Christopher Cox, *Sonic Flux: Sound, Art and Metaphysics*, University of Chicago Press, 2018; on the legacies of artists and pavilions from the African continent see Eric Otieno Sumba, 'Out of Venice', The Venice Issue, *Frieze* no 242, April 2024; to read more on indigeneity see Patrick

Wolfe et.al, 'The concept of Indigeneity', *Social Anthropology* 2006, 14, 1, 17-32 and the Indigenous Studies Group, TORCH, Oxford University https://www.torch.ox.ac.uk/critical-indigenous-studies-network

Ready or Not by Maya van Leemput

'Welcome to Postnormal Times', originally published in *Futures* 42 435-444 (2010), is included in *The Postnormal Times Reader*, edited by Ziauddin Sardar (CPPFS/IIIT, London and Kuala Lumpur, 2019). A great deal of postnormal literature can be found in *Postnormal Times Reader* volume 2, edited by Ziauddin Sardar, Shamim Miah and C Scott Jordan (CPPFS/IIIT, London and Kuala Lumpur, 2024). Both volumes, as well the exhibition catalogue, can be downloaded from postnormaltim.es

American Diary: After Hurricane Beryl by Amandla Thomas-Johnson

I have mentioned, Rodney, W., Davis, A. Y., Harding, V., Hill, R. A., Strickland, W., & Babu, A. R. M. (2018). *How Europe underdeveloped Africa*. (Verso, London, 2018); and Derek Walcott, 1992 Nobel Lecture — *The Antilles: Fragments of Epic Memory*. NobelPrize.org. https://www.nobelprize.org/prizes/literature/1992/walcott/lecture/
See also: Trinidad to provide space for boats sheltering from Hurricane Beryl. *Trinidad Guardian*. (2024, June 30). https://www.guardian.co.tt/news/trinidad-to-provide-space-for-boats-sheltering-from-hurricane-beryl-6.2.2040483.ab00e35116

CONTRIBUTORS

• **Alev Adil**, writer, artist and literary critic reviews for *The Times Literary Supplement* • **Marjorie Allthorpe-Guyton** is former President of the International Association of Art Critics (AICA), British Section • **Amenah Ashraf**, an alumnus of Aligarh Muslim University, India, likes to write and read romances with a message • **Anonymous** played their part in establishing the ISIS Prisons Museum • **Rachel Dwyer**, former Professor of Indian Cultures and Cinema at SOAS, University of London, has just published *Picture abhi baaki hai: Bollywood as a guide to modern India* • **Naomi Foyle**, poet and science fiction writer, is fiction and poetry editor of *Critical Muslim* • **Abdullah Geelah** works in a large City firm and is keen on mosque architecture • **Anna Gunin**, translator from Russian of literary fiction, memoire and poetry, is a winner of an English PEN award for writing in translation • **Allama Muhammad Iqbal**, poet and philosopher, was one of the major intellectuals of the twentieth century • **Jeremy Henzell-Thomas** is a regular contributor to *Critical Muslim* • **Christopher Jones** is Senior Fellow of the Centre for Postnormal Policy and Futures Studies • **C Scott Jordan**, Deputy Editor of *Critical Muslim*, is also Executive Assistant Director of Centre for Postnormal Policy and Futures Studies • **Kabir**, mystic poet and philosopher, thrived in the fifteenth century • Maya Van Leemput is the UNESCO Chairholder on Images of the Futures and Co-creation, a futures researcher, and a multimedia maker • **Hassan Mohamdallie**, Director of the Muslim Institute, is Artistic Director of Dervish Productions • **Liam Mayo** is a seasonal lecturer in social sciences and humanities at the University of the Sunshine Coast in Australia • **Mohammad Sahily** is a writer and political activist based in Beirut • **Amandla Thomas-Johnson**, a journalist working for Aljazeera and *Middle East Eye*, is travelling the Americas • **Boyd Tonkin** is a writer and literary critic • **Luke Wilkinson** is pursuing a PhD in Theology and Religious Studies at the University of Cambridge, working on the history of Muslim-Christian relations in Malta, where he grew up • **Peter Matthews Wright**, Associate Professor of Religion at Colorado College, is the author of several scholarly articles on the Qur'an and other classical Islamic literature.